PARTING THE WASHINGTON SEA

BY

Bruce, JAMES O'BRIEN

Finally a Non-biased book of "just the facts."

Chris

Copyright © 2021 James O'Brien

All rights reserved.

ISBN: 9798736148875

To All Freedom Fighters Past and Present.

Where We Go One, We Go All

CONTENTS

Introduction _____ 8

1. Patriots are in Control _____ 13
2. We are at Historical Crossroads _____ 20
3. Dark to Light _____ 30
4. Peace is the Prize _____ 37
5. A New Era Dawns _____ 42
6. Freedom from Mind Control _____ 48
7. Declaring a New Independence _____ 55
8. New Sheriff in Town _____ 61
9. Pioneers of Peace _____ 68
10. A More Perfect Union _____ 74
11. A Sacred Victory _____ 83
12. Parting the Washington Sea _____ 91
13. Divine Political Providence _____ 98
14. God Wins _____ 104
15. Winter White House Cleaning _____ 111
16. They Came, They Saw, They Co-opted __ 120
17. Treasures in Heaven _____ 128
18. There From Here _____ 136
19. Ship of Theseus _____ 148
20. Back to the Future _____ 161

Extended Epilogue: Captain's Log _____ 172
Chronicles of the 2016 Election

Coda _____ 260

ACKNOWLEDGMENTS

Cover photograph by Joshua Woroniecki.
Author photo by Linda Wake-Garza.

Captain's Log: Chronicles of the 2016 Election includes writing from over 50 'Anons' who contributed to the debates in this section, which first appeared in social media, and are now preserved for all eternity – and beyond that even.

For that I thank you all.

INTRODUCTION

If you are reading this book, you have likely already embarked on a journey beyond the shallow waters of the main stream. Or perhaps you are just dipping the first hesitant toe in the deep end to check the temperature. What is it that drew you to this work? Do you want a confirmation of what lies upon the distant shores at the other side of the Great Awakening? Do you possess the requisite curiosity to follow the rabbit all the way down the hole, not knowing where that journey might take you? Because, indeed, an essential part of going down that burrowing tunnel is the abandonment of the guaranteed certainty the conventional world offers as both its daily sustenance and its bread and circus. To journey into the unknown requires guts galore, a certain individualism not perturbed by the judgments of group dynamics, but most especially Faith with a capital F. True Faith comes from knowing that at your source is the Source of all things.

Of course, we are not things, we are people, however we have incarnated into a realm of "things" and the materializing influence is strong in this world. It brings with it a certain amnesia as to both where we are from and where we inevitably return at the close of our lives. Since we know that death is a certainty, perhaps the only true certainty in our lives, we can use our death as an advisor in these material realms. Our death can be asked for advice as to the importance of any given situation and help put things in their proper perspective. It can also contribute to the aforementioned guts galore, giving us the courage to make big bets at the table stakes of life, knowing there is a safety in our eternal nature beyond this world. People sell out for the most petty reasons, and we have seen this time and time again in the political world, most recently with the 2020 election steal. The fear of the unknown and the over-embrace of the material world has produced individuals in power in the Halls of Washington and other places who cling to their 30 pieces of silver, when they could have trusted God.

The aforementioned "materializing influence" is not necessarily a bad thing. It is what keeps energy bound in matter and allows us to have a physical world to begin with. It gives us an outfit for these bodies and a temporal backdrop with which to stage the dramas of our physical lives. However, when our lives are directed by this materializing influence instead of our eternal spirits, the influence becomes the "Satan" of our historical context.

The ego which most modern individuals identify with as their true selves was never meant to be the Captain of the ship of our experience, but rather a material plane counsel, an advisor which employs a sense of fear to protect the body from harm. The early incarnating spirits were so connected to their Unity in Source they sometimes forgot they were incarnated and accidentally harmed or terminated their physical vessels. The ego was assigned to the incarnating spirit as an able bodied seamen, so to speak, with the ear of the Captain, but not the source of navigation itself. Only the eternal spirit, with its understanding of its connection to the Unity at the Source of Life has the wisdom to direct the path of our journey. Its inherent trust in where it originated from and for what purpose it was created lends it the appropriate wisdom to be an infallible guide. That doesn't mean stumbles will not occur, but rather that there's always a Hand to lift us up and dust us off. One which will never fail us if we put our trust in it. After all, for those following the unfolding story of the United States of America, what is this country's national motto? In God We Trust. In his most famous address, President Lincoln spoke about the birth of this nation as "conceived in Liberty, and dedicated to the proposition that all men are created equal."

And today, we are likewise "engaged in a great civil war, testing whether that nation, or any nation so conceived and so dedicated, can long endure." On the pages of this book we are met on a great battlefield of that war. This war is as much for your mind as anything else. There are those who have dedicated themselves to the materializing influence, and who worship the false idols of control and power instead of the Living God. Yet, truly, each human being has the power within them to create their own lives, beyond the spell of whatever the default world might be promoting.

You who read these words come from the Source of Life. That Source created you out of the only material that exists: Itself. When you recognize and embrace your eternal nature, you can throw off the shackles that have bound you to the history of an old and dying system that no longer serves you or the populace at large.

This Old World Order, whose Cabal agents have metaphorically made deals with the Devil for temporal power, will do whatever it can to delay your awakening to the power you possess and the knowledge that you create your own reality. You project onto the screen of your life the world which you believe in. And then you make it "real" through your experience of it. The deeper reality is that none of it is real in the actual sense of the word. Because not only do you project your own body and senses, you project the entire backdrop canvas of the drama, and all of the characters included in it. The agents we refer to as the Cabal or the Luciferians, utilize their mind control techniques to get you to project the world they want, the one in which they are in control of everything, perched atop their occult-eyed pyramids. Is that who you want to be-- their unwitting subject?

Or do you desire to awaken and take back control of your own reality, in co-creation with the Source of existence itself? Do you not understand that a far greater world awaits than the dark ages you have heretofore known as your history? While we are not advising putting your head in the sand and ignoring the world of politics and the media, we are encouraging you to take a journey into understanding the truth which has existed behind the curtains of your current contemporary drama. When you pull back the curtain on the Wizard of OZ, you see him for what he is, a desperate technocrat with little to offer but a counterfeit reality of his own making, and a fearful projected visage to keep you at bay.

Do you want a wind-up heart or the real thing? Will a cheap medal as an emblem of your supposed courage suffice or do you want the real thing? One path offers you a paper degree to prove to your fellows you've attained wisdom, and the other path, the one with a beating heart, promises you the wisdom that comes from the Hero's Journey. On the other side of this journey is a treasure which will not fade with time. Its pearls of wisdom are no trinkets, but the only value you can take with you beyond this lifetime.

The Patriots we refer to in this text are not only those who have origins in the United States of America. The USA is an ideal, and currently the last beachhead being fought over in the battle between Good and Evil. It is the only Land consecrated to the Living God by its founding fathers, who took their direction from The Founding Father Himself. The documents with which they declared their Freedom, proclaimed these rights as having their origin with the Creator. This covenant was their cornerstone.

Though its path through time has been fraught with intrigue, and nearly conquered from within, the United States has not yet fallen from the Grace of God, not while there are yet those left who will stake "their Lives, their Fortunes and their sacred Honor" on its enlightened ideals. This great story is not over, in fact it is just now getting good.

While the life, death and resurrection of Jesus Christ is the Greatest Story Ever Told, the Washington DC drama, characterized by the political quest of Donald J. Trump and the Patriots of the Alliance, is the Greatest Political Story Ever Told. It will be studied for generations to come. The Trump presidency has elements of Washington, Lincoln and JFK within it. And the Alliance that supports him has the same goals as those Agents of Liberty. The monetary system and the preservation of the Constitution are among the key elements of what this legendary fight is all about.

Within these pages you will take an elliptical journey down the rabbit hole of the Trump presidency, which will concurrently take you into the past, present and future. Time travel will be involved, so to speak, which will then deposit you at a key square on the Dark to Light chessboard, the one which will encourage you to make the key move from pawn to Queen, the most powerful piece in play– and the defender of the King's Liberty.

Future Proves Past.

Thus, we are also providing a document of the past for future reference, because in the past you can always find the seeds of the present. After the main chapters of this book there is an extended Epilogue, which recounts the debates and conceptual battles which took place on social media with the author of this work. Though each of us creates our own reality, we also exist within a context of 'others' who do the same within a shared perspective. In this hall of mirrors, we always find our own reflection staring back at us, yet we also encounter other versions of ourselves in time.

In the end, there is only One of us here. That is the trip of all trips.

So, in a sense, we find ourselves working to convince other versions of ourselves to wake up within this game construct so that together we might create another, better world. The time is now to do such things. It is written, by the Author behind all authors. Others have prepared the ground before us, and none better than Jesus Christ. We walk in His footsteps.

Freedom awaits on the other side of this historical passage. It may seem that the agents of the Luciferian Order are in control. But their kingdom is rapidly turning to dust. When it blows away, you will still be here, with a dustpan and a plan from on high to create something far better, something beyond the confines of your current restricted imagination. In truth, this is what you incarnated for. Have you been so involved in the concerns of survival all this time that you forgot what you were surviving for?

You were made for these times. The Great Awakening. You are a key component of the transition from the Old World to the New. Those who wake up early and find their courage will be a clarion call for their brothers and sisters still slumbering within the historical prison. But the doors are open now, and a dawning sunrise awaits in the meadows beyond its gates.

We have long fought to reach this moment. The United States will be the first nation to throw off the shackles of its oppressors, and it will then be a brother and sister to the rest of the world, showing what is possible when you allow Divine Providence to guide your statecraft and not the monetary and sexual blackmail of the previous, darker order now fading away.

"It is for us the living, rather, to be dedicated here to the unfinished work which they who fought here have thus far so nobly advanced... That this nation, under God, shall have a new birth of freedom– and that government of the people, by the people, for the people, shall not perish from the earth."

In God We Trust.

Where We Go ONE, We Go All.

So, Let's Go...

1. PATRIOTS ARE IN CONTROL

On March 27, 2020, President Trump authorized the US Treasury to take control over the Federal Reserve. This is easily one of the biggest news stories in the last 100 years, yet many are completely unaware of it, because it was not reported in any real way on mainstream news outlets.

Many know that the Fed is not a government agency, but a privately owned banking cartel, which in 1913 instituted a monetary system in which their currency, unlinked to any hard assets like gold, was loaned into existence at interest to governments, and by extension their citizens. They came quietly in the night, and usurped the power of money away from We the People.

The first dollar was indeed loaned into existence, but more than a dollar required in return payment. Thus, by its very model, government debt could never be repaid, since not enough money exists to repay it. More money can only be borrowed into existence to service the interest payments on the existing debt, while creating more of said debt. The majority of funds collected by the IRS go to servicing the interest on debts to the Fed and not to any public utilities. In this respect, the Fed has more power than the US Government which it loans its money to. But not any more.

The Trump Alliance is far bigger than simply one US President, though Donald Trump is easily one of our greatest, on par with Washington and Lincoln. One day, he will be up on Mount Rushmore, and those who did not understand what he stood for while all this was actually happening can explain to the next generation the mind control aspects of popular media and how, unfortunately, it also worked on them. Because every day it gets more obvious, as people from all walks of life break through the noise of those who might rule us, and discover the story that is playing out on the world stage. The true definition of Apocalypse is not the destruction of the world, but an unveiling or unfolding of things not previously known and which could not be known apart from the unveiling.

We have entered the unveiling stage of world history. To those who wish to know, all information is available on virtually every subject right at your fingertips, if you can get past the entertainment media complex, which is owned by 6 corporations, the members of which all sit on each other's boards and the boards of the international banking conglomerate, upon which the Fed once sat like a crown jewel.

But crown jewels ain't what they used to be. And in this Apocalypse all historical Titans must fall. A new world will not be birthed via the control mechanisms of the old. That means the Medical Cartels & Big Pharma must fall. Illness-for-profit is the name of their game. Diseases can be, and sometimes are, created in labs and afterwards the non-cures promoted to the population. These non-cures keep the disease in a holding pattern long enough to extract maximum profit. After all, there is no profit in cheaply curing any disease.

In order for the people to know they must be shown, beyond any and all doubt. For most, telling alone will not be enough. I write these words chiefly for posterity. For those deeply ensconced in the anti-Trump world, no words will ever be enough. No article or news story will ever meet their standards of validity, and as long as they can still palm off everything they don't like or agree with as conspiracy, they will continue to do so. What is at stake are their well-cultivated illusions, upon which their cherished anti-Trump beliefs are cemented in media-justified intellectual certainty. Trump is an ignorant racist buffoon and his followers are morons. These truths must be self evident if Jimmy Kimmel & Bill Maher repeat them every night on TV. But the TV has rarely been a fountain of truth when real power is at stake. You can detonate buildings in front of some people and they will believe it when you tell them it was hijacked planes. Even the building that no planes hit, that was from hijacked planes, too. The laws of physics mean nothing when you have been brainwashed by the media and have Stockholm Syndrome for those who have historically led you around by the nose.

In a way, we are all still sitting inside the prison of an old history. The doors are open, however, and nothing stops us from leaving except our own hesitation regarding what might lay on the other side. True, there are yet some of the old guard left, wardens telling us we may not leave, that they are still in charge of us. But the sun is bright in the meadows outside the prison gates, the birds beckoning us forward with song. The prison might have fed us and housed us for longer than we care to remember, but we were never truly free while in its confines.

What awaits on the other side of this historical moment is true freedom. It is the promise at the end of history's story. 5,000+ energy patents have been shelved for 'national security reasons' over the last 70 years. Nikola Tesla was one of the great geniuses of history and yet the majority of his work was suppressed. Did you know Donald Trump's favorite uncle John Trump went to MIT with Tesla and they worked together, having a shared interest in particle acceleration? Did you know John Trump inherited the notes of Tesla upon his death? Those notes went into the right hands.

Energy is one big piece of the puzzle, but first we must start with banking. That's the golden rule. Those with the gold make the rules. Can you imagine what the world would be like if Good instead of Evil was in charge? If our best and brightest were empowered to improve this world?

The Federal Reserve will be forced to swallow its own debt and the US Treasury will institute a new gold backed currency from the ashes of the dying Fed. The first step has already been taken for this, with many other steps concurrently behind the scenes. When it is launched it will seem as if it happened overnight.

The old petrol-based energy technologies will then be replaced by a release of new energy tech that will make our current alternative energies look like children's toys. One of the (many) reasons Space Force was instituted was to mine products such as Helium 3 from the moon. It's an extraordinarily rare element on earth, but exists in far greater supply on the moon. A pound of it is worth over a billion dollars. The reason is that it can be utilized in nuclear fusion. We currently utilize nuclear fission, splitting uranium atoms to produce steam which powers turbines to create electricity. The problem is that the end product is very dangerous nuclear waste. With nuclear fusion via Helium 3, the end product is organic and harmless.

But you thought Trump was just a big goofball instituting Space Force, didn't you? Just another goofy moron who keeps outsmarting the most entrenched and powerful cartels the world has known at each and every turn. And yes, Covid19 was created and released to counter the freedom fighters of the Trump Alliance and to stop the inevitable awakening of humanity on Earth. The plan was discovered and largely mitigated, though there has been obvious fall out. And no, they don't get to lock down the world indefinitely and inject us all with their Gates vaccine. Their plans will be used against them. The whole world is watching and they will be unmasked for all to see. Many already do see, quite clearly, but there are just as many still entranced by the spell of Hollywood and the Media.

They thought we would all follow the stars. We may follow the north star, and light our way at night by the glimmer of constellations, but the bought-and-sold 'stars' of Hollywood have never had less value. Most of them report to those who gave them their stardom, their 'special job' of prominence, and as such, that is where their allegiances can be found, even when those allegiances run counter to the benefit of humanity. Define sell-out. Define rationalization. There are notable exceptions, of course, and you can't knock someone for wanting to work in a creative field like the arts. However, there is no excuse for steering the public wrong at such a critical juncture. And those that do are the chaff and not the wheat of this harvest. They should change their tunes while they still have the chance.

An Anon once said in regard to what Trump faces: "What's the most difficult thing in your life? Multiply that times a billion. Now try to fix that problem on a public stage with thousands of brilliant psychopathic adversaries working against you."

Eventually, all will come to realize that a Divine Providence has guided the Trump Alliance quest to rid the world of the death cult control of the old guard and free humanity. Trump is a true hero of the American People, and by extension, the entire World. Some see it now. Some will see it later. But ultimately it will be an established permanent truth.

You can tell the difference by what they promote. Trump has promoted Hydroxychloroquine. It is a generic drug that costs 63 cents. He has no stake in it, beyond the fact that it works, and for much more than just Covid. His opponents promote a thousand dollar pill that they own. And they promote a vaccine with medical chip tracking. These are the same people that believe there are too many humans on Earth and we need to reduce the numbers. They're so in-your-face obvious about their plans at this point they might as well be wearing Dr. Evil costumes. This is what I mean when I say that people cannot be told, they must be shown. If you haven't figured out at this point that they put things in vaccines that are not radiant products of health-promoting vitality, then you are simply not paying attention. And this is a bad time to be not paying attention. Therefore, the stage play will get more and more obvious until all but the most blind can see it.

Right now, we still have a great many well-meaning people advocating for their oppressors and battling against the Trump Alliance—that very Alliance which is opening the gates of our metaphoric jails and smashing down the prison walls. But you can't be forced out of your individual cell. Freewill is still paramount. While it is true that the Titans are going down whether they like it or not (and they most certainly do not like it) each individual must decide for themselves how to interpret events and proceed forward on their own two feet.

What awaits us? Trump himself told us in his inaugural address.

"The time for empty talk is over. Now arrives the hour of action...

We stand at the birth of a new millennium, ready to unlock the mysteries of space, to free the Earth from the miseries of disease, and to harness the energies, industries and technologies of tomorrow."

In order to unlock these technologies and free the Earth from disease, those who controlled the technologies and hid the cures from us must be comprehensively defeated. And make no mistake, we are here to defeat them, absolutely and at every level. And when we are done there will be nothing left of their 'new world order' power structure. It was never the new world order anyway, it was the old, and it has no chance of maintaining its structure in the reality of the increasing light upon the planet.

The Aboriginals, the Natives, the great seers from the past, they knew this time was coming. And none of us are here today by accident. At one level or another, you signed up for this time, and chose to be here now. It's a heck of a wave to surf, but it will take us to a far better shore, one we can only imagine from our current vantage point. It's promise is worth whatever it takes to get there. In the end, it is only the ghosts of the past we leave behind.

As light increases, frequencies change. As light increases, what was once hidden is revealed. Again, the true meaning of Apocalypse. This is the Apocalypse for the old world order. As more of the public awakens, their control continues to slip. They will fight every step of the way, but they cannot stop what is coming, or hide what is being revealed.

So ask yourself what side of history you'd like to be on as this final series of curtains are pulled back, one after the other. Do you still wish that somehow the Trump Alliance will be stopped? You will not get your wish.

If you stand for the freedom of humanity to live in a world that supports their true health and well-being, you might ask to be shown the actual truth, hidden behind all those curtains, instead of the pretty little lies promoted by those that would control you with their banks, their medical cartels, their media, and their old energy technology.

Do not be fooled by their claims to love the environment. They are heavily invested in oil and gas. Do not be fooled by their claims to love health care. They are heavily invested in the corrupt pharmaceutical industry. Do not be fooled by their claims to support prosperity. They foisted their crooked banking system on us on Christmas Eve, 1913. And sunk the Titanic beforehand to take out the 3 major bankers who were against their plan.

That's how little they care about any lives lost in the fallout of their schemes. Did Hollywood tell you about that story? No, it gave you a fictional tale of a lost diamond and a touching love story about a floating hunk of wood with room for only one.

But something else also happened once upon a Christmas night. A rag-tag band of freedom loving Patriots crossed the semi-frozen Delaware and hiked 9 miles in a blizzard to take on the most powerful empire on Earth. Their chance of victory in this war of Revolution, by any mathematical calculation, hovered right around zero percent.

But as Washington himself said:

"The Man must be bad indeed who can look upon the events of the American Revolution without feeling the warmest gratitude towards the great Author of the Universe whose divine interposition was so frequently manifested in our behalf."

Do not bet against President Trump and the Trump Alliance. Divine Providence guides them, like Washington and his Continental Army, in this battle. No one can tell the exact timeframes while we are still in the story, but the route itself is inexorable.

The Titan known as the Federal Reserve was taken down, quietly, overnight, with a single hit from a slingshot.

What is next? When Trump mentioned that light can be used as a disinfectant for diseases in the body, did you make fun of him or choose to look into that technology? The choice, as ever, is yours. The path of ignorance or enlightenment. Both are difficult in their own ways, but only one gets to a place worth getting to.

When light dawns, people awaken. When light dawns, darkness disappears. Darkness and its progenitors had their time for historical rule. There was a genius in their darkness and their methods of control. But when the time is up, the time is up. You don't bet against cycles whose imprimatur predates the plans of any and all mice and men.

And do not bet against Donald Trump or the Alliance that supports him.

The best is truly yet to come.

Where We Go One, We Go All.

2. WE ARE AT HISTORICAL CROSSROADS

"This is not just another four year election, this is a crossroads in the history of our civilization... I knew this day would arrive, it was only a question of when." - Donald J. Trump

Back in 2016, the international media conglomerates declared Hillary Clinton an absolute lock for the Presidency of the United States. How could she not be? She had the support of the vast majority of the mainstream media, Hollywood, Big Business, and every living former President, both Republican & Democrat. Even the Pope was against Trump. The 'official' polls said she had a 99% chance of winning. It would be an landslide in her favor. It was madness to think otherwise.

I came forward with my call. Trump had a 100% chance of winning the Presidency and there was a 0. infinite 0 chance the Clintons would retake the White House.

This might have seemed ludicrous, not only to Clinton supporters (and those who first supported Bernie-- only to witness it get rigged against him and then watch him endorse that rigging for his own personal gain) but also to those rightful cynics out there who knew the Clinton Foundation was deeply entrenched in world politics & big business. Giant corporations and the governments they lobby had paid into the Foundation for influence. There was no way some Reality TV outsider was going to come into the game and defeat a monolith of power that extended all the way up from the criminal underworld, the entertainment industry, to the DC swamp, the intelligence agencies & federal courts, the EU & UN, the Federal Reserve & world banking empire, all the way to the Royal Family and the Vatican.

It would be utterly impossible for one man to do that. No one is that powerful.

And that is true. It would be impossible for one man or woman to affect such a change. Other Presidents have tried. JFK wanted to splinter the CIA "into a thousand pieces and scatter it into the winds" and abolish the Fed so the US Treasury could issue gold backed currency. We know what happened to him. Lincoln also issued greenbacks from the US Treasury, doing an end zone run around the central banking system. And we know what happened to him. Individual political threats to the corrupt world power system of usury fractional reserve banking and war profiteering (along with a host of other insidious things that keep humanity operating in a lower frequency survival state) could ever be eliminated with the consummate ease of a single bullet. As such, what could one individual or even a small group do versus such organizational power at the highest levels? Darkness would always reign at the top of the pyramid. It's the way of the world. Always has been, always would be.

Another, broader perspective, would be that history is not the tale of the unending reign of darkness, but the story of the gradual fall of tyranny. And though the tale is told across epochs, when the fall of tyranny finally arrives, it does so so with a quickness. Along the way, there have been peak moments, major chapter changes and significant act breaks. The American Revolution, which birthed this country and seeded freedom movements across the globe, was one of them.

There was no way the Revolutionary War ever should have been won by the Continental Army. It was a preposterous proposition on the face of it. They were a rag-tag bunch, understaffed, under-equipped, and massively outnumbered against the most powerful Empire the planet had ever known. The British sent 400 warships in their armada to the New York harbor in 1776. The US had exactly zero warships. The Continental Army spent the entire first season of the war losing battles and in strategic retreat. It was not until the winter of 1776, when the army was on the verge of disbanding and conceding inevitable defeat, that Thomas Paine road off on horseback from his place in the field to print up his 'American Crisis' pamphlet, urging the troops to continue the fight, after having stirred up the initial concept of rebellion with his 'Common Sense.'

He wrote: "These are the times that try men's souls. The summer soldier and the sunshine patriot will, in this crisis, shrink from the service of their country; but he that stands by it now, deserves the love and thanks of man and woman. Tyranny, like hell, is not easily conquered; yet we have this consolation with us, that the harder the conflict, the more glorious the triumph."

The enlisted men read this and chose to stay on through the winter. Washington made the tactical decision to cross the icy Delaware on Christmas night in a severe winter storm, leading the Continental Army to their first improbable victory. It was a turning point of the American Revolution. The final result was the founding of a country based on freedom, individual liberty, and the Constitution of the United States - the greatest document to govern a nation yet created. Later, this same country would engage in a bloody Civil War to end slavery, an abuse that had existed throughout the world since time immemorial and still exists in record numbers to this day, though not in western civilization. The international bankers may have had different designs on this Civil War, with respect to bankrupting the US and infiltrating it from within, yet the results of slavery's end remains.

The American Revolution proved the seemingly impossible could happen in the cause of freedom and with the inspiration and guidance of Divine Providence. That first victory in Trenton was fought against highly trained Hessian troops. But the Hessians were mercenaries, fighting for money. The US troops, though outnumbered, fought for freedom and had something infinitely more powerful than money on their side.

Now, there are many who will claim that since those early, heady days of Revolution, of Declarations of Independence, of Constitutions & Bill of Rights, that the United States has lost its way and become the very Empire it fought against. These perspectives are not entirely without merit. Many of the Presidents after Washington on fell prey to the designs of the bankers from Europe. Though freedom on the land in battle was won in the revolution, a banking system can defeat a population more soundly than any canon or bullet.

Since the assassination of JFK, a President who was not without his faults, but wished to do the right thing for humanity, the US has been under the thumb of a deeply corrupt control at the highest levels. The United States has been led down a dark road, with the ultimate aim to eliminate it as a sovereign nation, to make way for a one world global rule, with the EU & UN as model format stalking horses. The US was the last beachhead of freedom. With this country gone there would be nothing left to conquer, nothing left in the way of their insidious plans. Certain European countries might be somewhat of an issue, but none were world super powers, and as such, how could they thwart these designs? The EU had already mostly subverted them.

These dark plans were not some recent invention. They extend back through the centuries, interlinked via bloodlines and secret societies. Many of the 'secret societies' weren't that secret, after all. Skull & Bones, the Bilderberg Group, and the Trilateral Commission were newer versions of the older societies from centuries ago. Did they have any unifying aim beyond their interest in personal genealogy and keeping the public in the dark about their true aims? What exactly were they trying to keep secret, anyway? They'd already stated they wanted a global one world order that they'd be in charge of. And perhaps a lot less people on earth so we'd be easier to manage. The Bushes, Clintons, Obamas, the bureaucrats of the EU, the Big Business lobbyists that funded them, they were all on the same team, regardless of political affiliations. And they all agreed on one thing:

THEY HAVE TO STOP TRUMP.

Why would all of these gigantic worldwide interests be dead set against one political figure? Politicians have always been available to be bought, or simply killed if they go off script. But somehow this one rogue figure, with all odds against him, an impossibility at every level, not only got into the White House, but was foiling every one of their plans and rewriting the world screenplay at warp speed. And there was virtually nothing they could do about it. All of their old tricks, their fail safes, were failing. If things didn't change, they were about to permanently lose control over planet Earth. And that hasn't ever happened since... well... ever.

In the battle of Good versus Evil, both in stories and in real life, Evil has always been able to threaten Good with the destruction of innocent life. It's the classic Good Guy showing up to save the town and the Bad Guy grabbing a child. "Put the gun down. Don't do what you're about to do or I will kill this child, who you love." The Good guy can't look into the child's eyes and watch her get killed, so he drops the gun. The movie never ends at that point, but it is a standard beat, a key move in Bad Guy protocol.

The Powers that Be know well that the fight has come to their doorstep, though much of the public may not. That's why they've deployed everything in their arsenal to stop the Trump Alliance, from the big business and banking fronted media, to the intelligence networks, international criminal syndicates, and much more. I say the Trump Alliance because do not think for a moment that Trump is acting alone in any of this. He has a military and intelligence Alliance that has been planning this for years in exacting detail. In fact, they were the ones who asked him to run for the Presidency in the first place. He will not be assassinated like JFK or Lincoln, as his protections both on the ground and above are almost beyond comprehension. That's why he is so calm in the eye of the storm, with all of the treacherous aforementioned elements against him.

With the war for human freedom being fought, it was a given that some lives would be lost. The dark team plays for keeps. They're not giving up control without fighting to the death. Ideally, it would be someone else's death, but no stakes are too high for them to risk in this fight.

Mind control and pharmaceuticals are a hell of a combo. The Nazis learned in WW2 what one could do with a shattered human psyche. You could program the fragmented personalities which formed to deal with the trauma. These altar personalities often have no memory of the other fragments. Combined with the effects of certain psychiatric drugs, it is easy to create an 'active shooter' among many other things. Contrary to the official story, many of the Nazi scientists from the concentration camps of WW2 were not jailed from the Nuremberg trials. Quite a few were seeded into intelligence operations like the CIA and other world agencies.

The vast majority of active shooters are not random people who just snap and decide to shoot up their school. They are traumatized individuals who are activated for specific terroristic purposes. Sometimes in the role of a patsy, with other shooters involved, and sometimes as the main shooter them-self. Either way, the threat to the good team is ever there: You keep doing what you are doing and we will shoot up more schools and public places. You don't want their blood on your hands, do you?

The threat is thus high that the further the light team advances against the dark's plans, the more innocents could die. Indeed, there's no number of innocent lives lost that would give the dark team even a moment of pause, as long as they themselves are not affected. They even had massive underground bunkers where they could wait out a nuclear conflagration, in high style, no less. But not anymore.

Law abiding citizens legally buying weapons which are directly registered and traceable to them has never been a significant issue as far as criminal acts go. Criminals get their weapons on the black market, untraceable. Crime stats coming from NRA members are virtually non existent. The United States won its independence because it had an armed populace that would not bow to tyranny. The dark team the Trump Alliance is currently at war with would like to see a completely disarmed general public because it has plans to eliminate the US as a sovereign entity and institute an unelected one world government. They knew a lot of patriotic Americans would not be for that, at all. And they didn't want them to be both against it and also armed.

Think about how much more difficult it would have been if the Jewish population in WW2 knew they were being sent to concentration camps, and if even a small percentage of them were armed and decided to do something to stop it. Yes, they would likely not have won, but they would have been vastly harder to take, even if it were just a small number that had the means to fight back. Tyranny prefers an unarmed populace, always. Gun confiscation has preceded every major genocide. Communism and it's cousin socialism have been responsible for the deaths of 100 million citizens in the 20th century. I'm not saying everyone should want or have a gun, but calls for disarming registered law abiding citizens do not have the interests of freedom at their core. One day we will evolve beyond the need of guns. But we are not there quite yet. I look forward to that time.

The Opposition the Trump Alliance is fighting has long done everything in its power to stifle the growth of the human spirit. Fluoride in the water supply, chemically processed foods, aerated metals released into the atmosphere, mercury in vaccines to developing children, indoctrination via the educational system and debt slavery via that same system, you name it. Designer viruses? You betcha.

The Corona Virus was designed as a biological weapon with far more serious consequences than it is currently exhibiting. The plans for its use were intercepted and for the most part mitigated, however its use as an attack is now being used against its would be employers. There's a shadow battle being fought and it's stepping into another, much higher gear.

Before Trump entered office his enemies claimed him to be a total buffoon, a moronic-failed-yet-rich-businessman, but also 'literally Hitler.' He would definitely crash the economy and get us into WW3. He's the Universe's Public Enemy Number One. And anyone who supports him is a racist, sexist, redneck Nazi. You don't want to be one of those, do you? Good. Now go back to sleep and watch another John Oliver sketch.

After taking office, Trump created the best economy in US history (one which allowed us to weather the Covid storm), the lowest black and hispanic unemployment of all time, enacted prison reform, reformed the tax code & brought manufacturing back, restructured the bad trade deals & international accords set to bleed the country dry, began the reform of pharma & the medical system, cleaned out the corrupt bad actors in the intelligence agencies, and built the wall to stem the tide of human & drug trafficking, creating a safer and more secure country for ourselves and our children. Textbook sound leadership. The first politician to actually keep all of his campaign promises.

"But he's racist! MSNBCNN told me!"

First of all, no he's not. But he did creating a massive African American coalition that wiped the Democrats off the map in 2020-- pre-steal, that is. The black community that hasn't been hoodwinked by the DNC can see what Trump was actually doing for them after he took office. Many (though not all) are waking up. The era of the Democratic Plantation is fading fast. Trump promised building and prosperity and he followed through, big time. And no amount of bought and paid for Hollywood celebrities can change that.

Donald Trump, way back before he was running for President, when he was just a guy building hotels and creating jobs, gave a number of black entrepreneurs business loans to help them get their organizations off the ground. When they came to pay him back, he told them to keep it. He just wanted to see them do well. That is Donald Trump, the same guy who legally battled the old world country club standards in order to have Jewish and black individuals freely admitted to his new club in Florida. Totally racist this guy, I tell ya. As soon as he ran for President, of course.

Now, we are met at a key point in this war for Freedom, and not merely Freedom's clever disguise. This Second American Revolution amounts to a World Revolution. Across the globe, other country's citizens are taking to the streets, and in many places, incredibly, they are waving American flags. They know what we represent at the core of our national destiny, though many here who have taken a long march through our own institutions of higher learning may not see it that way themselves. We are the last, best hope for a free world, governed with the interests of humanity at heart.

But nothing is happening!

Oh, really?

There are 200,000+ sealed indictments on the books, thousands of which have already been opened. Any one indictment can contain multiple parties.

12,000+ CEOs have resigned since Trump signed the executive order for the seizure of assets of individuals involved in human rights violations. Some of those resignations are unrelated, however, most of these big dogs have not stepped down in their prime just because they felt like it. This is an unprecedented number and it's some of the biggest names in business. The same goes for all of the DC players who have stepped down or announced they're not running for re-election. The Swamp is being drained and with a mighty suction. Conservative constitutional judges have been appointed across the land in major numbers. The preparatory phase is nearly complete.

Now, a big move is ready to be made. We're no longer a rag-tag army taking a last ditch boat trip across an icy river at midnight.

The Federal Reserve is being restructured from within to transform the entire control system around currency. Spoiler alert: There will be a new asset backed currency instituted that is actually worth something. Usury fiat currencies will go the way of the dinosaur, along with the IRS income tax system, the revenue from which does not go to where the public thinks it does.

The Plan to defeat this millennia old order of tyranny and control will not be a walk in the park. In a sense, nothing in world history has ever been harder to accomplish. Yet it will be done, and in the most effective way possible, with as minimal a loss of life as possible. Order not Chaos rules now. This is, at its core, a spiritual movement. The forces that support it are beyond strictly human understanding. It is the edict of Life itself that this new era is ushered in.

At its most primal foundation is the protection of the innocence and safety of children. Human trafficking has darker ends than almost any sane citizen could wrap their minds or hearts around. The Trump Alliance has made the removal of human trafficking the primary cause since Day One of the administration. They set immediately to it and the numbers reflect that, worldwide. They haven't stopped a moment in this battle to preserve the sanctity of all human life.

What is coming can not be stopped. The world Corona Virus situation is working against those that would have weaponized it. With this temporary world quarantine the playing field has been altered radically, allowing for a major house cleaning in the safest possible fashion.

You can fight against the Trump Alliance, but you will not win. In fact, you will deeply regret it when the battle is over and you see what was actually being fought for. The old world order is about to lose its control over this world and all of its people.

Now, We the People are going to form an even more perfect Union. Many see these times through a mirror darkly. But soon enough, we will know as we ourselves are known. And the truths will be, as they say, self evident. As ever, the legacy media will be the last to let you know. But the quarantine here now should tell you the game has changed dramatically. There is nothing to fear in it. The best, by far, is yet to come.

In the battle between Good and Evil, did you really think Evil would triumph in the end, though the odds against Good might appear insurmountable? Now, the long prayed for era has arrived. The tide turns for the Good with a remarkable power the world over. The enemies of human freedom have emptied their weapons and their bank accounts in vain. Their time in the seat of power swirls down the swamp cleaning drain.

We are at the Crisis at the end of Act 2 of the Greatest Political Story Ever Told.

"And let me conjure you, in the name of our common country, as you value your own sacred honor, as you respect the rights of humanity, and as you regard the military and national character of America, to express your utmost horror and detestation of the man who wishes, under any specious pretenses, to overturn the liberties of our country, and who wickedly attempts to open the floodgates of civil discord and deluge our rising empire in blood.

By thus determining and thus acting, you will pursue the plain and direct road to the attainment of your wishes. You will defeat the insidious designs of our enemies, who are compelled to resort from open force to secret artifice. You will give one more distinguished proof of unexampled patriotism and patient virtue, rising superior to the pressure of the most complicated sufferings. And you will, by the dignity of your conduct, afford occasion for posterity to say, when speaking of the glorious example you have exhibited to mankind: Had this day been wanting, the world had never seen the last stage of perfection to which human nature is capable of attaining."

- General George Washington - March 15, 1783

3. DARK TO LIGHT

We must take note of the key historical markers as we pass them in this 5D chess game. Covid-19 is an obvious one. As was the Trump impeachment fail and the Mueller fail. The firing of FBI Director James Comey was certainly a notable marker. The introduction of Q, the Alliance's intelligence countermeasure to the mainstream media's propaganda dissemination, figures in very strongly. Obviously, Trump's election win on 11/9/16 and his inauguration on 1/20/17 (when he was 70 years, 7 months and 7 days old) are among the most significant.

However, despite all the noise from the Covid Plandemic and the continuing false flag events from the international Deep State Cabal, we must not fail to recognize and assess one the other key markers that has been nearly swept under the rug by the events which followed it: The removal of master pedo honeypot Jeffery Epstein from the chessboard.

Without a doubt, the arrest of Jeffrey Epstein (and eventual disappearance, however you read that) is an ultra-significant marker in the international chess game between good & evil. In a sense, this game has been on-going for thousands of years, but since June of 2015, when Donald Trump announced his candidacy for President, things have really hit warp speed.

There have been many other markers in this battle, such as Dec. 23, 1913, when the Federal Reserve was founded, or Nov. 22, 1963, when President John F. Kennedy was assassinated. And, of course, the infamous 9/11.

Many of these old markers involve the light side losing badly, or at least appearing to lose badly. It seemed as if the dark would always prevail. They held all of the big cards and, in fact, owned the property rights to the casino itself. Many placed their bets accordingly.

A marker that had a lot of pre-game hype, on more of the Y2K doomsday tip, was Dec. 21, 2012. This was the end of the Mayan Calendar, and supposedly heralded some kind of major Apocalypse, Quantum Shift, or at the very least, a seriously heavy long weekend.

When it came and went without a blip, it was dismissed as just another New Age scam. Clickbait, nothing more.

The truth is, that date was another major marker. It was a graduation of sorts for the human race, and just like in an actual graduation, something significant had happened, and it would change things, but as far as right away that very day, it was back to normal life, business as usual, albeit with a paper degree in hand.

But things had changed, energetically, behind the scenes.

From the 2012 marker on, the dark team would be at a disadvantage. Whereas, once, they owned all the casinos and even the dealers, now they would have to play straight up, one-on-one, according to the established rules of the game; rules they had once flaunted and mocked, because there was one set of books for them, and another for everyone else. Sure, laws of the land existed, and could be applied to their opponents, but not to them. Tell it to the Judge, because they owned the Judge, and they owned him/her with blackmail-- of the worst kind.

One of the most effective forms of blackmail has been sex with minors/children, and some things far worse than that, though we won't go into that now. The general public has a built-in response to protect children, starting first with their own children, then extending to children at large. Crimes against children have a way of annihilating political differences and uniting people against an obvious, inarguable evil.

At the turning point of the 2016 election, a lap-top was seized by the NYPD from the soon-to-be-convicted Anthony Weiner (aka Carlos Danger), husband of Hillary Clinton's top aid Huma Abedin. The word on the streets was that hardened NYC cops, who had supposedly seen it all, wept when they encountered what was on that lap-top-- under a file marked "Life Insurance."

The NYPD threatened to go public if the FBI, then headed by James Comey, didn't re-open the case on Hillary Clinton, based on this newly seized information. Comey, a lifelong fixer for the Clintons, knew what had to be done. He announced they were re-opening the case. It was a shocking development, so close to when the ballots would be checked on election day. Trump supporters celebrated, while Clinton's reeled in temporary shock. But then, a mere week later, Comey announced to the world that the FBI had gone through the thousands of files and emails at hyper-speed and there was nothing to see here. Case dismissed. The Comey fix was in. After all, that was his job.

Every power player in old school Washington knew that Clinton would win the election. It was an absolute given. The MSM had proclaimed it from Day One. Big Business and Big Washington were behind it. Political players all across the globe were already in bed with the Clinton Foundation. Anyone that might be a potential whistle-blower on any dark deeds was a one-off, easily silenced by a "two bullets to the back of the head suicide," had blackmail already in place, or a healthy pay-off in fame and fortune dialed in, Hollywood-book-deal-style.

Once Clinton was in office, they could make all of this disappear with ease. They would again control the highest office in the land. In fact, a Clinton or a Bush had held the Presidency or Vice Presidency every year since 1980, other than Obama, and he was campaigning for Clinton. Another legacy 8 was a dead solid lock. And if the voters didn't like it, too bad. Ask Bernie Sanders how that worked out for him.

And Donald Trump? Well, they would deal with him after they got in office. And they'd make such an example out of him, no one would ever try this again.

But then, the miracle happened. Trump won. How could this possibly be? This wasn't in the script. And the dark had always held the script rights and rights to all subsequent sequels.

The big power shift from dark to light had taken place.

"If that bastard wins, we'll all hang by nooses! You better do something about this. You better fix it!" - Hillary Clinton wrote to Donna Brazile in an email, after a public interview with Matt Lauer didn't go according to plan.

Hang by nooses? Why would anyone put losing an election in those terms?

In the Inspector General Report, related to issues concerning the Weiner lap-top, it was written, very briefly as a note: "Initial analysis of lap-top. Thousands of emails. Hillary Clinton & Foundation. Crime against Children."

When Trump was elected, one of his key appointments was Jeff Sessions. Even Trump supporters, by and by, have had mixed takes on whether this was a good or bad appointment. Sessions did recuse himself from the Russian Collusion Hoax, but he also went straight to work combatting child sex trafficking, as evidenced by arrest numbers that skyrocketed both here and abroad. The administration went after the lower level feeder organizations first, the ones that supplied the higher ups, those less protected by webs of blackmail and elite political power.

Back in 2011, Peter Schweizer published "Throw Them All Out," a detailed examination of political corruption as it is actually practiced in the halls of Congress. In his investigation, Schweizer found one single member of Congress against whom no allegations could be held-- who had never taken a dime that was not his, had never cut any backroom deals, had never, simply put, played the game.

That individual was Jeff Sessions. Though there has been much discussion about what side Sessions is playing for, especially with Trump's negative tweets about him, disinformation is also necessary and Sessions record on child trafficking speaks for itself. However, they don't call it 5D chess for nothing. The game has many double and triple agents. Only in its end game results will all of the players and their moves be made clear.

In 2017, the Department of Justice quietly began its investigation into Jeffery Epstein, under the direction and oversight of Jeff Sessions.

Epstein was himself a factor in the 2016 election. Back then, the public had heard about his "Lolita Island," aka Pedo Island, aka Orgy Island. Former President Bill Clinton had ditched his security detail and taken 26 trips to this island on his own. Hillary had taken 6.

Epstein made the claim during his initial deposition for pedo-crimes in 2008 (of which he was convicted and cut a deal) that he was the Co-Founder of the Clinton Foundation & the Clinton Global Initiative.

Epstein had gone from a college drop-out–turned calculus teacher, turned junior stock broker– to an overnight Billionaire. He naturally knew all of the hot shots in New York, where being a billionaire like Donald Trump puts you on a pretty short list.

Trump's opponents have tried to take some words said about Epstein 17 years ago and the fact that he took a flight from Florida to New York on one of his planes, as a means to tie Trump to the honeypot crimes Epstein built his fortune on. The stuff you'd put in a "Life Insurance" file.

They have nothing on Trump or they would have used it in the 2016 election, when they still controlled nearly all the judges in the land. As in 2016, all they have are words he said, framed in a context to make him look bad. In the second Presidential debate, Trump said: "There are words and then there are deeds."

It is the deeds which will be answered for. The "Crime Against Children." And nothing can get them out of that.

Regarding Tump, he is not in the flight log to Epstein's 'Lolita Island' - not even once. He hitched a ride from Daytona to NYC, with Epstein's son, once. Trump, upon learning of Epstein's assault of a 14 year old girl, banned him from his clubs and hotels for life. At Epstein's first arrest, Trump voluntarily went to the police and prosecutor for a statement and they commented that he "could not have been more forthcoming."

This play has been a long time coming. If you thought that the NXIVM case, with Allison Mack singing like a canary, was going to unravel a network of sex crime web works, then this is that times 1,000.

Not everyone in Epstein's little black book is guilty. He was a rich power broker and ran in a lot of circles, celebrity and otherwise. But the people who took a trip to Pedo Island made one fatal mistake: They took their phones with them.

The Dark Team never thought that the technology created for control and surveillance of the general public would be used against them. After all, they controlled intelligence operations like the CIA, and the FBI were their fixers. And they had many a blackmailed judge in their pockets.

They never accounted for patriots and good actors in intelligence, military, politics and the police. Nor the power of an awakened public, who now had somewhere to turn to to report crimes. The dark joke from their team used to be: "Who you gonna call?" Because there was no one to call for Justice. They had that game sewn up, from the inside out.

That era is over. The NSA is being used against them now. Many corrupt members of the DOJ & FBI have been fired. Just look at a list of the bad actors who have been sacked since Trump took office. Then look at the record number of CEO resignations. Then look at all of the new Judges Trump has appointed.

Like rats on a sinking ship, those caught up in the Epstein/Maxwell scandal will turn on each other or look to cut a deal, once they understand what will eventually be revealed.

It's darker than most anyone could imagine. I said before the 2016 election that if the public knew the true nature of the crimes Trump's opposition had committed, these individuals would not be able to walk the streets. There are certain things that people will just not stand for.

We know that many have fallen for the media psy-op projection of these crimes onto Trump. It's simply not true and no amount of projection can make it true. However, the time is fast approaching when the dark deeds of certain political and entertainment heroes, people some thought should be in charge of the fate of our children, will be brought into the stark light of day. In an arena that no one can ignore.

Many will need therapy when they see how far down this rabbit hole goes. Not everything will see public light, but enough will so that this never happens again.

Buckle up. The day is coming when the number of former Clinton and Biden supporters, and those that funded them, will drop to absolute zero.

The Dark will not win this game. They are down to their last hand.

They no longer own the casinos. Their desperate bets can buy them but moments now, when once they controlled Ages.

In the hand of Light is the final Trump.

And it will be played.

"Long established customs of hurtful character could formerly fence themselves in, and do their evil work with social impunity. Knowledge was then confined and enjoyed by the privileged few, and the multitude walked on in mental darkness. But a change has now come over the affairs of mankind. Intelligence is penetrating the darkest corners of the globe. It makes its pathway over and under the sea, as well as on the earth. Wind, steam, and lightning are its chartered agents. The fiat of the Almighty, 'Let there be Light,' has not yet spent its force. No abuse, no outrage, whether in taste, sport or avarice, can now hide itself from the all-pervading light."

-Frederick Douglass, July 5th, 1852

"But whoever causes the downfall of one of these little ones, it would be better for him if a heavy millstone were hung around his neck and he were drowned in the depths of the sea. These stumbling blocks must come, but woe to the man through whom they come!"

Justice is no longer blind.

4. PEACE IS THE PRIZE

In a shouted question on the White House lawn about the Nobel Peace Prize, President Trump's response was:

"Peace is the prize."

Trump has waged peace. No President in memory attempted to disrupt the war-for-profit economy the way Donald J. Trump has. In any other administration, we'd be in a war with North Korea and Iran right now. And not the kind you watch comfortably on TV. And yet, he refused to be pushed into war with Iran because of an unmanned drone being shot down. And he became the first US President in history to cross the line into the DMZ in North Korea to broker peace with that nation.

President Obama did win the Nobel Peace Prize. He also bombed the Middle East for 8 straight years, often with inaccurate drone strikes that killed civilians, while somehow managing to strengthen terrorism in that region instead of curbing it. It was a record number of bombs. In that sense, his name suited him. It also created a refugee crisis that Europe is still reeling from.

It's no secret that the vast majority of the mainstream media, not just the Fake News, but all facets of the entertainment industrial complex in general, is pot committed in the war against Donald Trump. And anyone who understands multi-national mega-corporations and the Federal Reserve system of creating money, could tell you that the 6 corporations that own 90 plus percent of the media are comprised of the same players on the board of the Fed, as well as the ones who stand to profit the most in international war games. They also own the Big Tech companies, which play a gigantic role in how news and information reaches people. The fact that they have all of these chips, and all of those game board assets, and yet still are losing to Team Trump (despite the 2020 election optics) should tell you something about what's really happening behind the scenes.

War is not simply a matter of money. After all, their money is not based on any hard assets such as gold (that era is long gone) but created out of thin air. The more important aspect is control. And nothing keeps that game running as a finely oiled machine like non-stop war, with an occasional break every few years to reboot the system.

Donald Trump is a game changer the likes of which we have never seen, but he is not acting alone. Surprisingly, considering all I've written, a great deal of his insider support comes from military intelligence, patriots who swore an oath to the Constitution of the Republic of the United States and took that oath seriously. No military man or woman who has seen the horrors of combat wants to send their troops into a war that serves no purpose, or worse yet, has a corrupt motive at its core.

Trump's supporters know that the Old World Order will fight tooth and nail to maintain power. We also know that there are citizens railing against Trump who watch the MSM's non-stop attacks on Trump and take it all to heart. They truly believe that Trump is a horrible human being, dead set on doing awful things, or at the very least a raging out-of-control egomaniac. Racism, sexism, etcetera, etcetera. It's been repeated so often, it has to be a fact at this point. And if you offer evidence to the contrary, you're a nazi, a fascist, or a white supremacist. Even if you're black, you're now a black white supremacist. How's that for a twist? Or at best, you're just a dumbass Christian, which by the way, is the only religion you're encouraged to disparage. If you say anything at all negative about any other religion you are a total racist bigot.

After all, the TV did say all the smart people were against Donald Trump. The fact that he fills stadiums everywhere he goes, full of Americans from all walks of life? That's just an optical illusion. It was the Russians that made 2016 happen. Not voters.

It's got to be true. Trump just HAS to be bad. But what is he really doing that is so bad, bad enough that every late night comedian in the land has to attack him around the clock as if their paycheck depended on it? Which it does.

He has improved the economy by taking the US tax rate from one of the least competitive in the world to one that has motivated companies to return their manufacturing to this country, thus creating more jobs. Basic math. It used to be that a company could outsource everything to a place with a better tax rate and cheap labor costs and sell it all back into the US with no tariffs. Meanwhile, all USA-made products are tariffed in other countries.

Our international trade deals were broken and Trump fixed them. Other deals like the Paris Accord, were not designed to actually solve the problem of "climate change," but to loot the US, while funneling money to unelected bureaucrats. They didn't do this because they were stupid. They knew exactly what they were doing. They wanted to cripple the US economically and create a pathway to greater control worldwide, with the model of the EU and the UN as their stalking horse for a new system of governance.

The USA, with its determination to remain sovereign, was the last beachhead to conquer. Had the Clintons re-taken the White House, it would likely have been fait-accompli. But the Spirit of the country had other ideas in mind.

Now the EU model is collapsing in Europe, as countries no longer wish to be beholden to their crooked game. They want to determine their own destiny. The populations of these countries had their own good intentions used against them. Now many of them want their own Donald Trump, not as a personality, but as someone with the wherewithal to protect the citizens of the country, while providing opportunity and prosperity.

The EU, with the help of the Obomb-a-thon and international manipulators like George Soros, forced the migrant crisis on countries like Sweden, France and the UK, without taking the preservation of those cultures into any account. Naturally, Obama did not act alone. In many ways, he was just a well-spoken pawn in a much bigger game. His parents and grandparents were both involved in the CIA. That should give you an idea who he really represented, and it wasn't We the People. But he sure could give a rousing politically correct speech. Almost made you forget the other stuff. But history doesn't forget.

Immigration is great, when people come into the country legally and with a desire to assimilate into their newly adopted homeland. There will always be a certain amount of non-documented immigration we can look the other way at. Someone wants to go around the system so they can work here to send some money back to their family? I understand that impulse. But when a country is bombarded with immigrants beyond their capacity to deal with them systematically, with the majority sent into a welfare system which the citizens must pay for, at a certain point that becomes how you crush an economy and demoralize a populace.

That hasn't happened in the United States, though some people naively seem to be rooting for it, however, they don't fully understand what it means. Being for open borders doesn't make you a nice and spiritual person. It means you don't understand how a successful country that people want to immigrate to functions.

Yes, the US has a checkered past in some respects, partly because of the war-profiteering of political criminals like the Bushes and their like. But never forget that the Clintons were the proteges of the Bushes. The Republican/Democrat divide is often a subterfuge. Though, now that Trump is a Republican it has a bit more meaning as far as the in-fighting goes. The US is going to regain its good name going forward.

Were the Native Americans treated terribly when a new culture came here to set up shop on land they were already living on? Absolutely. And in many respects, their way of life was a model for how to honor Mother Nature and live in tune with the earth, though they did have their issues with internecine warfare amongst the tribes. They were a warrior culture, which was not unusual for that time period. But the truth is, the modern world was coming to this continent and nothing could stop it. If it wasn't Europe, it would have been China, or another empire. It was an impossible situation for the Native Americans, but one that in some fashion or another was going to happen.

It is right to mourn the loss of that way of life. I'd rather be in a teepee right now than typing these words and working up another movie, but you have to live in the time you are in. The United States has had its birth pains, with things such as slavery. But we fought an internal war and passed laws to end that in Western Civilization. Meanwhile, slavery still exists in far greater numbers than the 1800's in other civilizations that didn't take those same steps and make those sacrifices to end it.

The European refugee crisis got kick started because of unnecessary wars for profit and control in the Middle East. The Trump administration going forward (into the eventual second term) will put to an end that model.

But you can't just end war without promoting its prosperous alternative. And look what happened under Trump. The economy was running smoothly, minority unemployment at historic lows and the stock market at historic highs. A strong economy under a free market that promotes innovation is also the avenue to new energy tech being introduced, on a platform of the old energy, of course. There has to be a transition and it doesn't happen overnight. Not because the sky is falling, Green New Deal style, but because petroleum is a resource that will eventually be phased out by far better technologies.

The monetary system will also be reformed. And the players that funded all sides of every war in memory, will be taken off the game board and out of power. That process is happening now, but it's happening in a manner that keeps outright chaos in check. We aim for a smooth transition. But nevertheless, it can not be stopped regardless of how it transpires.

You can still listen to their programs & broadcasts, and maybe if you have eyes to see and ears to ear, sense the galactic frustration that comes from losing the puppet master strings of a hustle they thought would never end.

And maybe you can even pretend for a hot minute that someone else really won the 2020 election, despite the historic great progress under Trump. But deep down, you know and you know and you know, that he's going to be back again.

Bigly.

And that's a good thing.

Donald Trump doesn't need one of the Old World Order's fake honors, like a Wizard of Oz wind-up clock substitute heart.

The Nobel "Peace" Prize.

Peace is the Prize.

5. A NEW ERA DAWNS

Prior to Donald Trump taking office, the best economists CNN could buy predicted the economy would tank like never before. They said Trump was a megalomaniacal failed businessman who had no idea what he was doing and would take us all down with him. This was despite the fact that Trump graduated from the Wharton School of Business, rose to the very top of the real estate and construction business, as well as the industry of media & television, with 396 out of his 400 businesses successful enterprises, a remarkable track record by any measurement.

They also said manufacturing jobs would not be coming back. The then President Obama agreed with them. Yet, what happened? Manufacturing came back en masse (after tax reform & renegotiated trade agreements) and the unemployment numbers, prior to the Covid plandemic, hit historic lows, with the economy booming like never before.

The stock market was meant to collapse when Trump took office, yet it consistently broken its own records. It was almost as if Trump held the 'magic wand' to building & prosperity that had eluded his predecessor. Obama's stock market also rose, however that was from printing trillions of debt-based dollars out of thin air to bail out Wall Street and the "too big to fail" financial entities. Thus, Obama doubled the national debt in 8 years and the GDP stagnated at 1.5% in his final year.

The privately owned fiat currency banking system is not the answer to prosperity or the key to unlocking our economic potential as a nation. These central banks have become, historically, more powerful than the governments they finance. These same banking interests have funded both sides of every modern war. Without this funding, and some might say intentional planning and instigation, these wars never could have happened. The cost in human lives has been immense.

It's therefore understandable, given the water under the bridge to date, that people would have a blanket distrust for all things government and lump Trump in with the rest of the criminal politicos who have sold out humanity in their quest for personal power.

But to those paying attention, it should be understood that we are in the early phases of a massive Reformation in the world of politics, currency, intelligence organizations, and the media.

What once could be kept in the dark, under a 'rule by secrecy,' is no longer possible. It's said that sunlight is the best disinfectant. Well, if you thought the first years the 2020's were "interesting" (regardless of what side of the political fence you are on) you ain't seen nothing yet. Invest in disinfectant.

White Hats have always existed within intelligence, military and business circles, but never have they had the tide of history backing them and propelling them forward. Now we will see what happens when information can no longer be hidden. We will see the just rule of Law return to the land, along with the implementation of an economic system designed for the individual citizen to thrive within, instead of one intentionally hamstrung by elites to line their own pockets and maintain their control.

Some may think that President Donald Trump is simply out to enrich himself and others in his club and that the moves his administration made do not benefit the average person. This point of view is pushed 24/7 by well-entrenched factions of the mainstream media, a media which is owned by giant international corporations in bed with the central banks. They take direction from what you might call rogue elements within organizations such as the CIA and from the international Cabal that orchestrated the founding of these intelligence organizations to begin with.

A previous President made noise about these exact things (secret societies, the CIA, and the FED). His name was John F. Kennedy. We know what happened to him. Trump has a different destiny, however, as this is an entirely different era.

It turns out the Swamp does not appreciate being drained. Because in the draining, all power and control and protection said Swamp offers is also drained. Many 'important figures' are destined for jail, for everything from money laundering, to treason, and in some cases, much worse than this, when the child trafficking crimes of the higher ups come into the full glare of public light.

There have been record numbers of pedophile and child trafficking arrests since Trump and his team took office. This has been the dirty secret in Washington and Hollywood, and frankly all over the world, for far too long to fathom with an open heart.

Does anyone seriously think the broad scale corruption that is being revealed would have taken place if Hillary Clinton, whose entire career is an epic poem to corruption, had moved back into the White House? Alongside, of course, the other half of the political hydra that is her 'husband' Bill Clinton. They of the beneficent Clinton Foundation, kindest of all money laundering charities. It takes a village. And they took many.

A lot of career politicians have gotten filthy rich off government jobs whose salaries do not reflect the windfall they came into after taking office. Where did all of this loot come from? It's called Pay-to-Play and the Clintons were masters of it. Unfortunately for them, money tends to leave a trail, no matter how much they'd prefer to wash said trail away. BleachBit, anyone?

It doesn't take a genius to see that, under a Clinton admin, it would have been business as usual. The scandals would have been fastidiously swept under the rug by professional fixers like James Comey, formerly of the FBI. And the mega-corporate lobbyists would have continued to run their pay-to-play schemes in tandem with the politicos. And, of course, terror factions like ISIS would have flourished. After all, the agents that funded them behind the scenes would still be in power.

Nowadays, ISIS is in a total collapse. They've lost all of their Middle East strongholds, because they were fought in a manner designed to defeat them. All they have left are their sleeper cells, which wreak havoc in several of the poorly governed countries of Europe, countries which struggle to properly run their own systems, because they answer to the globalist bureaucrats of the EU and not their own citizens.

But this, too, will soon change. There is a groundswell in many of these places for their own version of Donald Trump, a populist leader with the fortitude and wherewithal to return the power to the people, where it belongs.

Fortunately, in the United States, we already have a Donald Trump. And we have his leadership because, on a greater level than many realize, we actually willed this into being. The long Era of Secrecy and Control is being dismantled at its very cornerstones. In doing so, new cornerstones will be put into place, ones with a foundation built on integrity, freedom, and the best interests of all of the people at heart. No longer will the government be a front operation for those maneuvering in the shadows.

Is Trump some perfectly realized being? Absolutely not. He is as fallible as any of us. But his word is his bond. He is as dedicated as any leader in the world to fulfilling the promises he campaigned on.

You may hold onto the notion that Trump was out to take healthcare away to enrich some crony capitalists, but this is not the case. The MAGA movement is sincere at its heart, which is what provides its great strength, its momentum, and ultimately its longevity. Trump is not owned by lobbyists, unlike his political opponents. He financed his own campaign and was beholden to no outside moneyed interests. He can't be bought, in other words. How many other politicians can say that?

In fact, only someone with Donald J. Trump's precise set of skills and life experience could have pulled the sword from the stone and entered the dragon's lair to defeat such an immensely well-organized and well-funded beast that was the entrenched political system.

Some very well-intentioned people thought Bernie Sanders could have been that man. And indeed, the populist candidate Bernie did collect money from the people of the village and ride off on his donkey to the dragon's fiery lair. But he stopped just short of the cave, feeling the heat of what he was up against. He then returned with singed clothes to the village and endorsed the dragon! No refunds y'all. He ran on fighting a 'rigged system' and then he bowed to that very same rigging, even when it was against his own campaign.

Socialism never works, by the way. Its chief aim is to centralize power in a vast bureaucratic government, where the citizens are 'equalized' but disempowered vis-a-vis the all-powerful State. It leads to a totalitarian regime in the end and a general poverty is its bellwether. See every time it has ever been implemented, and Venezuela for some recent results. It is effective in small doses only, under a system driven by free markets in which the best ideas compete for implementation and individuals are encouraged to innovate and grow within that system.

So, we find ourselves here. In the second act of an entirely new play. There is great promise ahead, though times may appear dark. In actuality, it is the greatly increasing light that is revealing what has ever been there and thriving in the shadows.

One of those things is 'dark money.' There have been untold trillions spent on unaccounted for programs that did nothing to improve the lives of the people. That money went to the plans and back-up plans of players whose interests ran counter to the interests of humanity. When this spending is cut off at the roots and returned in a productive way to the eco-system of American life, there will be a new renaissance which all of the people will participate in. The political purge in Saudi Arabia is a canary in the coal mine of what will happen in the US, however, it will be accomplished within the modus operandi of the Justice System and military tribunals.

The plans are long and the plans are broad, and like all great plans they may take longer then expected to accomplish from our perspective. But from another perspective, they are happening at the speed of light.

You can expect the Reformation to accelerate to warp speed moving beyond the historic election of 2020, with the vote fraud at its roots.

Hollywood and Washington, kissing cousins that they are, will continue to air out their dirty laundry so that it can be cleaned and replaced with something with far better thread counts.

Trump will continue to represent what he has ever stood for: Building & Prosperity and Law & Order. Neither of these dual concepts are racist, sexist or xenophobic. A great leader both protects and enriches the people of his land. When those interests are in order, he or she can extend the horizons beyond their own borders to the world at large.

Trump may sometimes seem like one of the biggest fans of Trump, but he deserves to be. He is also humble in ways people often don't recognize. And he arrived at a time when he was truly essential. He answered the call at a remarkable crossroads of History, and now we are on a new timeline where all things are possible.

We will see a reformation of our economic system.

We will see a reformation of our intelligence organizations.

We will see a reformation of our local and federal government, all the way from the election process to term limits and above all else, to personal accountability.

We will see a massive reformation of Big Pharma, an industry whose pockets have been lined by keeping people sick, and in some cases, actually engineering illnesses, rather than healing them. This will have a significant carry over effect in the medical community at large.

And lastly, we will see a gigantic growth in new energy technologies, as the free market is unchained from the fetters of multinational conglomerates that buy out patents and stifle the emergence of the inventions that can compete with them. We will see a comeback of the original Tesla, and not the simply company that hijacked his name.

Take, if you will, a step away from the media culture that has a vested interest in the old world order, and consider for a moment what a truly free humanity might be capable of. The World Wars of yesteryear required an insane amount of money and human resources. When the financial instigators of those wars are removed from power, we will see humanity emerge into a remarkably positive new dawn.

Trump is part of it, but he is only one man. The movement is much bigger than him and it has only just begun. It cannot be stopped or derailed, it can only be momentarily slowed down. But make no mistake, it is going in the direction that Life itself has decreed.

Where We Go One, We Go All.

6. FREEDOM FROM MIND CONTROL

The Hegelian Dialectic.

Problem-Reaction-Solution.

It should come as no surprise to anyone following the spiritual-political story unfolding on Earth that things are heating up to a boil following the 2020 US Presidential election. This election was the last chance for the international Deep State Cabal & their bloodline families (and those that control them in realms non-physical) to regain their grasp on the puppet strings of the citizens of the world and the political and economic systems that govern them.

"They never thought she (Clinton) would lose," is true indeed. It sent a titanic shockwave through the DC swamp and by extension all world governments, many of which had bought into the pay-to-play apparatus of the Clinton Foundation. The mere fact that Clinton did lose, with the mainstream media, big business & DC, and the incumbent administration pushing their chips all-in on her installation (voter fraud and all) was, in a word, a miracle. However, it was a miracle many of us saw coming. The Universe operates in cycles and on December 21, 2012, a nearly 26,000 year cycle completed and We (both the Earth and ourselves as individuals) transitioned into a New Era in which Light would predominate over Dark.

"Dark to Light" is another memetic trope from Team #17. It is very appropriate. It is, in fact, a foregone conclusion. The end result is certain. It is only a matter of how we get there from here.

And we are not there yet. The Old Guard, the historic rulers of this world, are not going to let their control go easy. In truth, there's nothing that they would not do, no action too dark or too criminal, to maintain their power. Mass slaughter is a given. Many at the top of their occult pyramid already engage in ritual sacrifice, and have done so in an historical line since the Biblical days of open Baal worship. Do you think there's anything that's going to give them pause now? There isn't. They will do absolutely whatever they can get away with– however, wherever, whenever.

They would have assassinated President Trump long ago if that option was a possibility. In reality, it has been attempted many, many times. However, Trump's protections are not only of this world, on the ground and in the air, but also in other dimensions and in realms unseen. A galactic and spiritual protection you might call it, and if you give it some thought, it is really the only way this could work. When the best mind-controlled assassins in the world can't get to you, over this long a stretch, there's a big reason for it. And this drives the Cabal insane. The assassin's bullet, or poison, or car-bomb, or fill-in-the-blank-style-hit, has ever been their go-to with uppity leaders who got too big for their britches. And now with Trump, their biggest nightmare incarnated and the once and future shot-caller in Whitehouse, their go-to move has been taken away from them. They have been neutered, at least in this particular respect.

However, they still have the technique of mind-control and their constituency of individual sleeper cells ready to activate under that modus operandi. Though it existed well before WW2, mind-control (sometimes known as MK-Ultra) took a gigantic leap forward in technology as a result of the Nazi concentration camp experiments. Many know that after the War, Nazi scientists were installed in the intelligence operations of organizations like the CIA, and its counterparts around the world. Operation Paperclip, it was called.

When you hear of a school shooting, or any active shooter in a public place scenario, or for example, the knee-on-the-neck murder of George Floyd in Minneapolis, with subsequent public riot, you must consider, given the nature of the war being fought for control on the world stage, how these things really work. A police officer, a soldier, an entertainer, a 'random' student, these are just socially designated labels. The reality is, they are all people, and any one of them can be mind-controlled. It is a science-based technique. A mind-controlled individual has different altar personalities, some not aware of the others. They can go into blackout or amnesiac states, and they exist as sleeper cells, ready to be activated at a moment's notice, for whatever the cause.

The opponents of the Trump Alliance need chaos. Their treasured secret societies have long designated their rule as Order out of Chaos. They need to stoke the fires of a race war. Having a cop on video, breaking the rules of his profession blatantly, knowing he was being filmed, fits right into the problem-reaction-solution pattern. Perhaps, it wasn't that. Perhaps it was an organic event. However, the fact that the two men in question, Chauvin and Floyd, worked together for many years doing security at the same club is a red flag. The fact that it happened right after Democratic Presidential nominee Joe Biden was heavily criticized for saying that if you don't vote for him "you ain't black" is another red flag. It is not a certainty that the Chauvin/Floyd murder was an organized operation, but it does, however, have the all of the hallmarks of one.

The bigger question is this: How prevalent is mind-control in our society and what can we do to counteract it? Obviously, it exists on many levels, from television and movie programming, to the academic system, which often promotes an anti-patriotic Marxist view of US history, all the way to influencers on social media. Fortunately, though it is controlled by Big Tech and often censored, social media also gives opposing viewpoints to the mainstream narrative a chance to air out their ideas. All it takes is the courage of your convictions and an active awareness of the game being played. And it's a big game. For all the stakes.

The Far Left viewpoint is that the United States is an evil empire, with an endemically racist and sexist culture and structure, run by rich old white men, and that only a socialism-themed revolution can save us from the corruption of these capitalist war pigs. Any prosperity that exists (or is created through this system) is ill-gotten gains. However, there is a secret hatch door to this way of thinking. If you accept this modern liberal point of view, then you are a good guy/girl, fighting the good fight, the one who cares about equal rights and battles against racism. You get a gold star for being woke and subsequently any rewards or benefits you reap from living in this selfsame economic system are your just rewards. It's a good deal. You get to enjoy living in the land of the free, or at least the most free relatively speaking, reaping the rewards of the free market, while still wearing your woke Che Guevara shirt. Forget about the fact that Cuba under the Castro regime was a military dictatorship, a reign of terror. And if a current riot in an American city or two is not so much about the details of what transpired, but more about the fact that the local Target just got busted open in a consumer free-for-all, you can look the other way at that or even grab a couple lamps for your apartment. Power to the People.

The more accurate reality, however, is that you're getting played. The Dark Team that organizes these mind-control driven false flag events and race-division-promoting riots thinks that you are stupid. That is why they spam the same techniques over and over again. Even in the age when one can quickly determine via the internet that the Same Damn Guy organized both Occupy Wall Street and the Unite the Right in Charlottesville. It's agitprop theatre. The Hegelian Dialectic.

They want us divided. Divided by race. Divided by sex. Divided by religion. Divided by political affiliation. Because when we are no longer divided, their rule is over. Where the money comes from is clear. George Soros is often mentioned as a figurehead and he is indeed a notable one. But one name is not as important as the fact that the central banks have ever been able to print all the money they've needed since they own the printing presses, digital or otherwise. It is simply a matter of laundering the funds. And organizations like the CIA have always been able to take advantage of 'dark money' through their operations in the drug trade and human trafficking. When these things become known facts and not mere conspiracy theories, both sides of the political spectrum must demand justice. It is essential that we unite against the agents of tyranny and not fall into their well-designed divide and conquer traps.

In the era of Dark to Light, they can't hide the true nature of their activities very much longer. The Trump Alliance is playing 5D chess, taking them out financially and taking down their rat-lines. However, the opponent is a worthy one. They are well-entrenched and will fight savagely, to the death. Because it is their death that awaits them if and when they lose. Just up ahead, around the next historic bend, are federal courts and military tribunals, jail cells and executions for treason and crimes against humanity, and epic falls from grace for both politicos and some well known purveyors of Hollywood entertainment. The Bell is Tolling and it tolls for them.

We can expect more false flags in the wake of the 2020 election. We saw how they went all-out on election fraud and ballet harvesting. Covid-19 was their last ditch big maneuver. It has fizzled in some respects, but they will play its aftermath to the hilt. They will claim Donald Trump is responsible for every death, even though the majority of the numbers are from nursing homes, and general numbers have been inflated by terming non-Covid deaths as Covid. There was money in it for the medical cartels, so they weren't going to miss out on a dime of that.

The plan was to crash the economy, create chaos, force stay-at-home voting ripe for fraud, pin every negative effect of the plandemic on Trump, even though he responded like a champ, as he always does. Their plans will ultimately fail. Their plans will not only fail, they will fail catastrophically. What is taking place on the world stage is not some random event. It is a cosmic lesson. It is a lesson that the story of human history has been ever proceeding toward. The closer we get to the finale the more events take on a magnetic feel. It is the fall of tyranny and its dark methods of control. It is the awakening of the individual to true spiritual freedom and an awareness of the essential unity of all life.

The Dark Team has no real out at this stage, no avenue to final victory. Like two chess masters playing a game for the soul of humanity, both the Dark and Light Teams know that Dark will lose the game. They see the moves further ahead on the chessboard. Darkness/Tyranny will ultimately get checkmated. The only move the Cabal has at this point is to stall the game, extend it a bit longer, and hope against hope that Light will make a mistake. Light will not make a mistake.

President Donald Trump is not a racist. He has ever been a champion of the rights of black men and women. He has been given significant awards for it during his career as a businessman. He fought against the old country club system to allow blacks and Jews into his clubs. He gave black business owners loans and when they came to repay him, he said keep the money, I just want to see you succeed. He has held Black America Summits at the White House. Under his administration black unemployment hit historic lows. He reformed the prison system, giving second chances to inmates who earned that opportunity. He radically changed the game for how a modern Republican President is viewed by black citizens. He did and will continue to do the real work.

This should not come as a surprise. The Republican party was created to abolish slavery. The Democrat party wants Black America to stay on their plantation and in their welfare system. They are not promoting economic freedom and opportunity for their black constituency the way that Trump did. They know that if they lose the black vote it is all over for them. When the real results come in, we will see that despite their attempt to import illegal votes and stuff ballot boxes everywhichway they could, digital and otherwise, it was a DJT landslide in 2020. And that's a fact.

Race baiting (their tried-and-true go-to) gets spammed over and over again. They have no choice. It is both their political language and their political weapon. Where it does not exist, they will create it. They will use every tool at their disposal, especially mind-control. It's a no-brainer, pun intended.

Is America perfect right now and entirely racism free? Of course not. Are there bad cops out there, capable of acts of violence, even criminal violence? Yes, but they are in the extreme minority-- far, far less than 1%. The average police officer is a steward of Law & Order and essential to maintaining the peace in society. After all, who are you going to call if there's a break in at your house, or if there's a robbery or assault on the streets? The town priest? The mailman? Lady Gaga?

The anti-Trump Left desperately needs their narrative to prevail. Racism, Sexism, Health Care For All (ie: bad health care under huge taxes) and The Sky Is Falling Climate Change Green New Deal. They want a New Deal, alright. They want a New Deal in which they will be in total control over every aspect of your life and your pocketbook. Not going to happen.

Patriots are in Control. And what comes next is going to be stunning. This isn't called the Greatest Political Story Ever Told for nothing. On the other side of this grand battle for control we're currently entrenched in are the answers to the problems that have plagued humanity throughout history. Patents to be unlocked. New technologies in energy and health. A new monetary system. The end of the war for profit industry.

But wait awaits, most importantly, is human freedom. We are about to truly awaken and wipe the sleep of history from our eyes, wipe every tear away, so to speak. Irish author James Joyce famously wrote: "History is a nightmare from which I am trying to awake."

In a way, we are all the children of a mind-controlled history, it is only a matter of to what degree. Yet, it is our collective destiny to awaken. One of the most significant hashtags of this movement, characterized by the Trump Alliance and brought to you be the number 17, is:

#TheGreatAwakening.

The awakening process is currently happening and it cannot be stopped or mind-controlled or rioted away. It is worldwide. However, the United States is at the forefront of this event, because of what Trump in the White House represents. However, the heroic Nigel Farage deserves credit for first picking up the torch of freedom in his historic battle with the EU.

The US has already won one impossible war for freedom. We declared Independence over Tyranny and achieved the first major victory for that cause. Along with other countries in Western Civilization, we then ended slavery, though many others in the world did not follow our lead, as they preferred the profits of slavery over their own people. Now We the People are going to take back the United States of America from the despots of crime and tyranny. And this time every country will follow our lead.

Evil thought it had this planet all locked up. Safely hidden away in the cosmos in a permanent quarantine, away from the Creator's prying eyes.

They are about to find out what it means to lose control in real time to the Universal Freedom Fighters of this movement, which is galactic in scope.

Hold onto your hats, Patriots.

It's about to get Biblical.

7. DECLARING A NEW INDEPENDENCE

In the 2016 Presidential Election, Donald J. Trump entered the Casino Royale- the international bloodsport coliseum of world politics- and he wagered everything to his name. He wagered everything he and his family had built over decades in multiple industries, pushing his chips all-in on one colossal bet for the Destiny of the United States.

What would compel a man to wager not only his own great fortune, but the fate of his entire family, risking a terrible demise should he come a cropper in this titanic bet? Do you think his political enemies would have let him walk out of the Casino with his life if his wager had fallen short? Not a chance. He would have been made an example of, so that no one would ever try this again. In times of old, he would have been beheaded, like William Wallace, his skull spiked on London bridge and his severed limbs sent to the four corners of England.

It should be noted that Trump's matrilineal bloodline is Scottish, through his mother Mary Anne MacLeod. It should also be noted that the very Bible he was sworn in on at the 2017 inauguration, was a Bible from a revival in Scotland on the Isle of Lewis, known as the Hebrides Revival. But that is a story for another time.

The point is that Donald John Trump has the absolute courage of his convictions. Despite his opponents mocking him endlessly, pointing out both his real and invented personal foibles on a 24-7 news-propaganda cycle, he was the one willing to walk through the door of the Casino Royale and lay down the biggest bet anyone could place. And he did it without wavering or trembling, knowing that he might not ever rest again in this life until his quest was completed or death took him, whichever came first.

When one wagers one's "life, fortune and sacred honor," the whole of the Universe watches. What could compel someone to trade in an established good life, a life of literal fame and fortune, for the opportunity to be crushed into powder by an ignominious and almost unfathomably well-entrenched enemy?

The answer lies in another moment of history, in the birth of a nation, whose founding document was a Declaration of Independence over Tyranny, and a reliance on Divine Providence to guide it on a journey to an incredible, impossible victory.

The expressions on the faces of the signers of the Declaration, knowing they risked the death of not just themselves but their wives and children, was reported as "undaunted resolution."

"We must hang together," Franklin said, "or surely we will hang separately."

But the signers of the Declaration did not enter that room with such undaunted resolution. In fact, they had been discussing all day what to do, knowing there would be no turning back once their names were on that parchment. However, they were not alone in that room.

An unknown man, it was noted, arose and gave an electrifying speech. The room was locked and this person had no traditional means of appearing before them. And yet, there he was, giving one of the most extraordinary oratories in history at a moment when the courage of the founding fathers was wavering.

Many believe this man was Saint Germain, also known as the Wonderman of Europe, an enlightened figure who lived many years beyond a normal human lifespan and had performed notable works of both alchemy and scientific invention. It was said that at the moment of his ascension he chose to return to earth in a body instead of moving into the realms of spirit. His aim was to help free humanity from its historical prison, and thus, at this most critical juncture, when the fate of a nation and a people hung in the balance, he had a means to be there in that room, via what might be termed bio-location.

And these are the words he spoke to the assembly:

"Sign that document!

Gibbet? They may stretch our necks on all the gibbets in the land-they may turn every rock into a scaffold-every tree into a gallows, every home into a grave, and yet the words on that Parchment can never die! They may pour our blood on a thousand scaffolds, and yet from every drop that dyes the axe, or drips on the sawdust of the block, a new martyr to Freedom will spring into birth!

The British King may blot out the Stars of God from His sky, but he cannot blot out His words written on the Parchment there! The works of God may perish-His Word, never!

These words will go forth to the world when our bones are dust. To the slave in the mines they will speak-hope-to the mechanic in his workshop-freedom-to the coward-kings these words will speak, but not in tones of flattery. No, no! They will speak like the flaming syllables on Belshazzar's wall-

THE DAYS OF YOUR PRIDE AND GLORY ARE NUMBERED! THE DAYS OF JUDGMENT AND REVOLUTION DRAW NEAR!

Yes, that Parchment will speak to the Kings in a language sad and terrible as the Trump of the Archangel. You have trampled on mankind long enough. At last the voice of human woe has pierced the ear of God, and called His Judgment down! You have waded onto thrones over seas of blood-you have trampled on to power over the necks of millions-you have turned the poor man's sweat and blood into robes for your delicate forms, into crowns for your anointed brows.

Now Kings-now purpled Hangmen of the world-for you come the days of axes and gibbets and scaffolds-for you the wrath of man-for you the lightnings of God!-

Look! How the light of your palaces on fire flashes up into the midnight sky!

Now Purpled Hangmen of the world-turn and beg for mercy!

Where will you find it?

Not from God, for you have blasphemed His laws!

Not from the People, for you stand baptized in their blood!

Here you turn, and lo! a gibbet! There-and a scaffold looks you in the face. All around you-death-and nowhere pity!

Now executioners of the human race, kneel down, yes, kneel down upon the sawdust of the scaffold-lay your perfumed heads upon the block! Bless the axe as it falls-the axe that you sharpened for the poor man's neck!

Such is the message of that Declaration to Man, to the Kings of the world! And shall we falter now? And shall we start back appalled when our feet press the very threshold of Freedom? Do I see quailing faces around me, when our wives have been butchered-when the hearthstones of our land are red with the blood of little children?

What are these shrinking hearts and faltering voices here, when the very Dead of our battlefields arise, and call upon us to sign that Parchment, or be accursed forever?

Sign! If the next moment the gibbet's rope is round your neck! Sign! If the next moment this hall rings with the echo of the falling axe! Sign! By all your hopes in life or death, as husbands-as fathers-as men-sign your names to the Parchment or be accursed forever!

Sign-and not only for yourselves, but for all ages. For that Parchment will be the Text-book of Freedom-the Bible of the Rights of Man forever!

Sign-for that declaration will go forth to American hearts forever, and speak to those hearts like the voice of God! And its work will not be done, until throughout this wide Continent not a single inch of ground owns the sway of a British King!

Nay, do not start and whisper with surprise! It is a truth, your own hearts witness it, God proclaims it. This Continent is the property of a free people, and their property alone. God, I say, proclaims it!

Look at this strange history of a band of exiles and outcasts, suddenly transformed into a people-look at this wonderful Exodus of the oppressed of the Old World into the New, where they came, weak in arms but mighty in Godlike faith-nay, look at this history of your Bunker Hill-your Lexington-where a band of plain farmers mocked and trampled down the panoply of British arms, and then tell me, if you can, that God has not given America to the free?

It is not given to our poor human intellect to climb the skies, to pierce the councils of the Almighty One. But methinks I stand among the awful clouds which veil the brightness of Jehovah's throne. Methinks I see the Recording Angel-pale as an angel is pale, weeping as an angel can weep-come trembling up to that Throne, and speak his dread message-

Father! The old world is baptized in blood! Father, it is drenched with the blood of millions, butchered in war, in persecution, in slow and grinding oppression! Father-look, with one glance of Thine Eternal eye, look over Europe, Asia, Africa, and behold evermore, that terrible sight, man trodden down beneath the oppressor's feet-nations lost in blood-Murder and Superstition walking hand in hand over the graves of their victims, and not a single voice to whisper, 'Hope to Man!'

He stands there, the Angel, his hands trembling with the black record of human guilt. But hark! The voice of Jehovah speaks out from the awful cloud-'Let there be light again. Let there be a New World. Tell my people-the poor-the trodden down millions, to go out from the Old World. Tell them to go out from wrong, oppression and blood-tell them to go out from this Old World-to build my altar in the New!'

As God lives, my friends, I believe that to be his voice! Yes, were my soul trembling on the wing for Eternity, were this hand freezing in death, were this voice choking with the last struggle, I would still, with the last impulse of that soul, with the last wave of that hand, with the last gasp of that voice, implore you to remember this truth-God has given America to the free!

Yes, as I sank down into the gloomy shadows of the grave, with my last gasp, I would beg you to sign that Parchment, in the name of the God, who made the Savior who redeemed you-in the name of the millions whose very breath is now hushed in intense expectation, as they look up to you for the awful words-You are free!

And now the Parchment is signed; and now let word go forth to the People in the streets-to the homes of America-to the camp of Mister Washington, and the Palace of George the Idiot-King-let word go out to all the earth-

And, old man in the steeple, now bare your arm, and grasp the Iron Tongue, and let the bell speak out the great truth:

FIFTY-SIX TRADERS, LAWYERS, FARMERS AND MECHANICS HAVE THIS DAY SHOOK THE SHACKLES OF THE WORLD!

Hark! Hark to the toll of that Bell!

Is there not a deep poetry in that sound, a poetry more sublime than Shakespeare or Milton?

Is there not a music in the sound that reminds you of those awful tones which broke from angel-lips, when news of the child Jesus burst on the shepherds of Bethlehem?

For that Bell now speaks out to the world, that–

GOD HAS GIVEN THE AMERICAN CONTINENT TO THE FREE–THE TOILING MILLIONS OF THE HUMAN RACE–AS THE LAST ALTAR OF THE RIGHTS OF MAN ON THE GLOBE–THE HOME OF THE OPPRESSED, FOREVERMORE!"

These are the stakes that Donald Trump and the Trump Alliance are playing for. In this bet, nothing less than everything must be wagered. Victory is a certainty because the Hand of Divine Providence has guided these matters. But never forget that it took individual hands to sign that document and an individual to walk through the doors of the Casino Royale and place that all-in bet.

Say what you will about Donald Trump and his family, but they have guts galore and the courage of their convictions. And such patriotic courage has never been more necessary.

The Trump Alliance is All-In.

Where We Go One, We Go All.

And We're Going All the Way.

8. NEW SHERIFF IN TOWN

The sporting organizations have begun their games again, in particular major league baseball, however at this juncture there are cardboard cut-outs in place of human fans in the stands and the players take a knee before the game, paying homage to the George Soros funded Black Lives Matter organization, which has nothing to do with black lives, but is a Marxist-themed agent of demoralization and destabilization. And thus, that is to what and whom your well-paid sporting heroes are taking a knee to. Not so heroic in that light, are they?

BLM is not about the consideration of black lives, otherwise it would target Planned Parenthood, which executes more black lives in the womb than any other ethnic group. BLM is about stopping Donald Trump. The same with the Covid Plandemic. There's a reason that Hollywood, the DC Swamp, Big Business Conglomerates & International Bankers, the Rogue Intelligence Agencies, and the entire collective apparatus known as the Deep State are aligned against Team Trump.

It's because there's a new Sheriff in town. And this Sheriff is not only appointed to his position, but anointed to it, by powers that can only be termed as metaphysical– both connected to and unified by their origins in the Source of Life itself. This is not a power that can be defeated within the working of men or even by extraterrestrial means. This is the Storyteller Itself, the originator of the Universe and Multiverse, dictating a new passage in the annals of life- a new chapter, as it were.

In this new chapter, Evil is being comprehensively revealed for the control it has held over the Earth for thousands of years. The actions of Evil, both behind the scenes and in front of them, are termed as crimes in the legalistic sense. Crimes against Humanity, in the broader sense.

When True Law emerges in the land, with the proper authority backing it, criminals become very upset. When those criminals have had the run of things for thousands of years and thought their plans could never be countered, they are rather more than upset. They are enraged and terrified. In order to assuage their terror, they convince themselves they will soon have the world back under their control. Order out of Chaos has ever been their game. Along with Divide and Conquer. However, with each passing day their old methods of control lose their power and effectiveness.

President Donald J. Trump is by no means acting alone, however he has been appointed Sheriff for this crucial moment in time- when the criminals of the world who hide their dealings in the shadows are revealed to humanity at large, then apprehended and arrested. Some will be executed, most others taken off the stage in another manner, but all will lose control over both the purse strings of the world and the mind-control aspects of the media that have kept the public dancing to their tune. They will also lose control over medicine and the energy & tech sectors.

Trump is archetypically similar to other key leaders from history, such as Washington and Lincoln. In many ways, we are currently in a combination of the American Revolution and the Civil War. Yet, Trump is also like unto Cyrus the Great, whose arrival in Babylon was prophesied by Isaiah 150 years before his birth. Belshazzar, the arrogant playboy king of Babylon had been partying in the temple with a thousand of his closest politicos and advisors, when Cyrus and his troops drained the protective moats around the city and surreptitiously surrounded the former ruling forces while they were in a debauched celebration. It was here that the Writing on the Wall appeared. The prophet Daniel was summoned by Belshazzar to interpret the writing, which had mystically appeared before the assembly.

Belshazzar offered Daniel half of his kingdom to interpret the words on the wall. Daniel replied that he was sorry to say that Belshazzar did not have half a kingdom to give. For the writing on the wall said: "You have been weighed and found wanting. Your kingdom is no longer."

Cyrus was a builder, like Trump, who prided himself on taking cities without spilling a drop of blood, either his enemies or his own troops, much like a modern day corporate take over. Tactics and strategy (think Sun Tzu) were paramount. When he'd take control, he'd then rebuild the city, providing a better way of life than the playboy kings or despots that preceded him.

When Cyrus approached the steps to the Temple, it was Daniel who came down them to greet him, handing him the parchment that predicted his arrival well over a hundred years prior. The parchment read:

"This is what the LORD says to his anointed, to Cyrus, whose right hand I take hold of to subdue nations before him and to strip kings of their armor, to open doors before him so that gates will not be shut:

I will go before you and will level the mountains; I will break down gates of bronze and cut through bars of iron.

I will give you the treasures of darkness, riches stored in secret places, so that you may know that I am the LORD, the God of Israel, who summons you by name.

For the sake of Jacob my servant, of Israel my chosen, I summon you by name and bestow on you a title of honor, though you do not acknowledge me.

I am the LORD, and there is no other; apart from me there is no God. I will strengthen you, though you have not acknowledged me,

so that from the rising of the sun to the place of its setting men may know there is none besides me. I am the LORD, and there is no other.

I form the light and create darkness, I bring prosperity and create disaster; I, the LORD, do all these things.

You heavens above, rain down righteousness; let the clouds shower it down. Let the earth open wide, let salvation spring up, let righteousness grow with it; I, the LORD, have created it.

Woe to him who quarrels with his Maker, to him who is but a potsherd among the potsherds on the ground. Does the clay say to the potter, 'What are you making?' Does your work say, 'He has no hands'?

Woe to him who says to his father, 'What have you begotten?' or to his mother, 'What have you brought to birth?'

This is what the LORD says– the Holy One of Israel, and its Maker:

Concerning things to come, do you question me about my children, or give me orders about the work of my hands?

It is I who made the earth and created mankind upon it. My own hands stretched out the heavens; I marshaled their starry hosts.

I will raise up Cyrus in my righteousness: I will make all his ways straight. He will rebuild my city and set my exiles free, but not for a price or reward, says the LORD Almighty."

Cyrus was tasked with creating the Second Temple. Trump is now tasked with creating the Third Temple. It was no mistake that Trump was the President who finally moved the Embassy in Israel to Jerusalem, though many other US Presidents had promised it.

It should be clear to most by now, that the recent Presidents (the Bushes, Clintons, and Obama) have not answered, metaphorically speaking, to God Almighty, but rather to Lucifer, the agent of deception and division, the rebel that defied God and sought his own counterfeit kingdom. These Presidents, and by extension those behind the scenes that puppeteer them, are the Belshazzar of this story. When the writing on the wall appeared, Belshazzar soiled his shorts, so to speak. The God he thought did not exist had made His existence known, in absolute terms. Belshazzar's rule was no longer. He died that very night.

The agents of Lucifer and Baal, and however else you might want to term them, are losing their power now at the speed of Light. The words are beginning to appear on the wall for them, but they do not yet have the wisdom to interpret them. Thus, only the world stage play, enacted for all to witness and experience, will be able to teach them.

It is true that the Bible has been significantly edited over the years. At the Council of Nicaea, for example, reincarnation was removed from the Book. And yet, despite the editing and other mechanisms of control (such as the Vatican) much truth has survived within the written words, and that is no accident. These are Living Words.

It may appear as if darkness is actually gaining more control these days, particularly if you watch the mainstream media. However, what's actually happening is that darkness, and it's modes of historic control, are being revealed to all humanity, where once they were hidden. Darkness can no longer hide in the shadows and under rocks. It must now face the light of day and answer for its actions.

The Baal worshipers in Biblical times were child sacrificers. That has not changed since then, they have only become experts at hiding their doings, sometimes even in plain sight, mocking the public with their occult rituals at sporting events and the like. That is where the 'ball' comes from in sporting events: Baal. Though there are many good individuals who play professional sports, and some that even might qualify as heroes, we cannot expect them as a whole to light the way out of the dark world we are now exiting. They answer to those who cut their enormous checks: the businessmen that own the corporations that hire them. It's clear the NBA, for one, answers in large part to China, not exactly a friend to the USA at the moment.

We cannot blame the People of China or of any other lands for these actions, for they also seek freedom and the pursuit of happiness, like anyone on Earth. But the fact is that the United States in this current epoch is leading the way to world Freedom. The US is the last beachhead. Were it to be conquered there would be no hope of true freedom for any country or individual going forward. The US has a sacred destiny, birthed in the American Revolution and coming to fulfillment in this present age. The reason that Trump cannot be defeated (or assassinated like JFK) is that he is Divinely protected. It's as simple and as amazing as that. He has been anointed (like Cyrus) to his post and all of his tasks will be completed. This Sheriff wears a badge pinned on him by God. You may not believe this, but you will see it play out.

The New Sheriff in Town means that true Law & Order is going to be enforced. Anyone involved in hidden criminal activities, anywhere in the world, will not like this. In fact, they will despise it with every fiber of their being, like they despise Donald Trump. They despise him because they know what he represents and what he is doing. They feel betrayed by him because they thought he was one of them. Someone out entirely for the self, with no guiding morality to steer in the direction of God or Truth.

The Golden Rule of Christ is to treat your neighbors as both yourself and as God, because they are one and the same. Those that have taken the Luciferian path, to temporal fame and fortune, or simply to the satiation of their physical lusts, have betrayed this one truth. They have sold out their fellow human beings for their own (very) short term gains. But now Karma, on not just a world stage- but a galactic and spiritual one- is coming home to roost. Try as they might, they cannot avoid it.

The Writing is on the Wall. Cyrus and his troops are at the temple perimeter. He has drained the moat and has Belshazzar and company surrounded. He snuck up on them while they were engaged in a decadent feast. Was it the blood of our children they were feasting on?

They thought they could hide forever in history, away from the prying eyes of any spiritual authority. They had their many thousands of years, but their time is up. The eyes of Spirit are upon them now and Spirit has a plan that cannot be altered or defeated. It is currently playing out to perfection.

Weinstein, Epstein, Maxwell. Human Trafficking arrests. CEOs resigning en masse. Intelligence Agencies being cleaned out. The Swamp being drained. Corrupt trade deals rewritten. The Wall being built. The appearance of Q to guide the public. The takeover of the Fed by the US Treasury. These are the Writings on the Wall.

You are being tasked now to wake up and join the Revolution of the Good, as Freedom Fighters for Humanity. It is far better to join the tide of Spirit now, than be deluged by it later.

Evil and Darkness will be comprehensively defeated and cleared from the Earth, like the cancer they are. A New Era, guided by the precepts of Spirit, and planted like seeds by the Founding Fathers of the United States America, will Dawn in this historic moment. Nothing can stop what is coming. And like Trump often says: The Best is Yet to Come.

Trump will re-win the Presidency in the final accounting. This is a certainty. The Dark Team will exhaust every card they possess trying to stop this impending reality. But Lucifer does not hold the Trump Card. The Patriots do. God does. And God Wins.

It can only go One Way in this great story. It is the Greatest Political Story Ever Told. Primarily because it is a spiritual story. Those who take part in it, will ever know they were part of something truly special. Something no mere sporting event could ever aspire to.

Put your name on the permanent roll call for all that is Good and

Righteous. It is the legacy you leave for the children of this world and the worlds to come.

"Turn to me and be saved, all you ends of the earth; for I am God, and there is no other.

By myself I have sworn, my mouth has uttered in all integrity a word that will not be revoked: Before me every knee will bow; by me every tongue will swear.

They will say of me, 'In the LORD alone are righteousness and strength.' All who have raged against him will come to him and be put to shame.

But in the LORD all the descendants of Israel will be found righteous and will exult."

Isaiah: **45**.

Where We Go One, We Go All.

9. PIONEERS OF PEACE

Your favorite President was nominated for the Nobel Peace Prize for his moves to broker peace in the Middle East. While there is very much work still to be done there, steps are actively being taken in that direction.

You may have noticed that Trump also brokered peace with North Korea, when that could easily have been a nuclear conflict. He also avoided an armed conflict with Iran when many governmental forces were pushing him in that direction.

How come the guy the media said was going to be another Hitler kept fostering peace around the world? Shouldn't he have initiated wars somewhere if he wanted to live up to his enemies great prophesies?

There was another guy who actually won the Nobel Peace Prize. That guy dropped a record number of bombs on the Middle East during his administration-- over 100,000-- many of them inaccurate drone strikes that killed civilians. That shakes out to a bomb every half hour, 24 hrs a day for 8 years. Ladies & Gentlemen, your Nobel Peace Prize winner: President Barack Obama. Send him to Saturday Nite Live for a lap of honor.

The actual war Trump fights is right here at home and he has no choice but to do so. His enemies start fires by arson and call it climate change. Apart from causing much needed chaos-- the fires also bring in Federal Relief money for certain bankrupt west coast states in dire need of it. Apparently, climate change doesn't have a Canadian passport because it knows exactly where to stop nowadays, with pinpoint accuracy.

Why that selfsame climate change behaves remarkably like a certain designer virus that can distinguish between a riot and a rally or a hair salon. So smart these two, you would think they were given political training before they were set loose on the world.

I have been writing for years now that Trump's opposition would empty every weapon at their disposal to stop him from winning the 2020 election. Maximum chaos in the streets was required-- with brutal Antifa-style violence a given. Did anyone notice that Antifa's logo is virtually identical to the Nazi Germany Antifacista one? Different time period, same tactics. Who are actual Nazis again? You're going to have to remind us one more time. At least get a new logo, for f-sake.

Trump's opponents intentionally tanked an economy that was breaking records with each passing month. They couldn't have Trump cruising into this election with a record prosperity in the marketplace. Enter Covid19. It was supposed to be far more deadly than it has turned out to be-- at least according to the pre-viz Bill Gates and company did a year beforehand, when they predicted (and presumably planned for) 50 million dead.

And, of course, we know they went all-out for voter fraud with the write-in ballots. Biden was even told by the last election's loser Hillary Clinton not to concede on election night. Cue the trucks with write-in ballots and the endless tallying that followed. Along with the Dominion algorithm.

How difficult is it really to track every ID and citizen with a single vote with today's technology? Yet one side doesn't want a voter ID. They don't want a fair election where you must be a citizen to vote and you only get ONE vote. And you have to be currently alive.

Make no mistake-- the Democrat candidate Creepy (or Sleepy, take your pick) Joe Biden could not have 'won' this election on a straight vote without fraud. He had zero chance of doing this. Fraud was the only way in for him, and the scary thing is that a lot of anti-Trump people out there gladly looked the other way at this fraud just to get Trump out of office. They would thus annihilate the very foundation of the Republic because they didn't like who the People chose according to the established rules of the game.

The Russia scam, the Mueller scam, the impeachment scam, the virus scam, the arson, the rioting & looting, the 24-7 cycle of fake news propaganda, and all of the compromised celebs pushing a Hate-Trump agenda-- they would stop at nothing, absolutely nothing to disrupt what is inevitably going to happen.

One side kneels at sporting events and thinks that virtue signaling is actually accomplishing something real-- when it is only narcissistic vanity. Another side sees a real problem and tackles it head on. Trump created historic record low unemployment in the Black and Hispanic communities. Trump reformed the prison system, with his Second Chance Act. Trump held many Black America Summits in the White House and was the most popular Republican leader in that community since Abraham Lincoln, if you consider the real numbers.

Yes, many celebrities and talk show hosts and sports figures will tell you this isn't true, that Trump is racist. But they completely ignore conservative blacks and black Trump supporters as if they didn't exist. While Biden claims that "they ain't black" if they support Trump.

We know who the real victims of the mental disease of racism are, as well as those who desperately need to keep the American public divided and at each other's throats. Enough people from all walks of life have rejected this conditioning, such that there's no way back to the old world they'd like to trap us in. Try though they might, they will not get their race war.

Ask yourself, why must this old system fight so hard against this one particular political leader? And how come, with all of the weapons at their disposal, they are singularly incapable of stopping him? When Trump says he's going to do something, sooner or later down the timeline it gets accomplished. The record speaks for itself. However, when someone has been brainwashed, nothing you show them (such as Trump's good deeds) will have any meaning to them or even be accepted at any kind of face value. They must vehemently deny it all in order to maintain their worldview.

Well, I can tell you, the world has other plans for humanity and it doesn't care about your media indoctrination or your Trump Derangement Syndrome. It's going to happen with or without you. One way or another.

In mythology, the precession of the astronomical or celestial ages is often couched in stories of gods in battle, such as those of the Greek's Mount Olympus. The old god inevitably fights to maintain control, as the old age transits to the new. Chronos ate his children in an attempt to keep his cycle going longer. But the new god always manages to escape-- whether in a basket on a river or by hiding in a cave, or something along those lines. There are often key helpers there to insure his safety at the crucial moments.

One can try to kill the new god or age but it never works out in the end. Chronos must make way for Zeus-- as the current age of Pisces must make way for Aquarius. A nearly 26,000 year cycle ended in 2012 and a new one began, launching more specifically on Dec. 21, 2020. The Age of Light is gradually taking over from a much darker cycle. We can no more stop this than we can stop the sun from rising. However, like the gods of mythology, there will be inevitable battles to try to stop the inexorable from actually occurring. We are seeing all of this now.

At the same time, we are seeing a greater opportunity for peace than ever before. Where the Middle East goes-- so goes the world. If a lasting peace can be achieved there, it can happen anywhere. Right now, the United States (despite the mirage of the Biden 'presidency') is the beacon for the destiny of the world, and for civilization in general. An old order, whose activity can best be described as deeply criminal, is going all-out and all-in to stop this. And they must. Because they will lose everything if the Letter of the Law is actually enforced. Unfortunately for them, they do not have the precession of the ages on their side. Light is increasing-- making it harder and harder to hide what was once obscured in the shadows.

Their tactics involve the implementation of Marxist revolutionary ideology along with round-the-clock media mind-control regarding what's actually happening. They also formerly had the banking system at their beck-and-call, but they are rapidly losing that chess piece. Unfortunately, they will take some good people down with them, as well meaning individuals get caught in the crossfire. However, each person can always call on the guidance of the Creator of this grand play we are all enacting, and along with your better angels, you will find you can be in the right place at the right time and avoid any violence and mayhem in the streets.

This Story only ends one way. Biden (or whoever they replace him with) will not continue as President. I'm sure he will gladly renew his Netflix subscription and stay at home watching Cuties on an endless loop. As long as we keep him away from sniffing and feeling up little kids in the White House that is fine by us. As for Kamala Harris, she of the prison industrial complex and all too recent family slave-owning background, she can always hang around and back another fake race-baiting scam like Juicy Smollet. Have bleach, rope and hired extras will travel.

Those of us who have not been brainwashed and have done our homework as to what is transpiring will meet you on the other side of history. Like the Prodigal Son, we will love you just as much even though you got this one wrong. And it was a big one to get wrong. Yet, every moment another person wakes up. What triggers their awakening is always personal and it can come at any time. We encourage everyone to drop the division-sowing of Marxist ideologues. Because as ye sow, so shall ye reap. Where you can't find the division and the hate in freedom-loving patriotic Trump supporters you will project it onto them, everywhere you go. It's an ugly way to live, in my opinion, yet I know the vast majority are simply good people who have been played for fools by the aforementioned cultural forces. The Marxists called them 'useful idiots' for a reason. Don't be one.

We patriots take it in stride because we know what is in our hearts. We respect all life as One and answer to the promise of our country's founding documents. We know that this nation, under God, shall have a new birth of freedom-- and that government of the people, by the people, for the people, shall not perish from the earth.

One day soon enough you will have another leader-- one not as bombastic as President Donald J. Trump. That man or woman will be more delicate in their sensibilities and more gentle in their manner. Everyone will agree on this individual's peaceful and pleasant diplomacy. But that time is not now. Right now we are currently in a reboot of the American Revolution and Civil War all-in-one, and Trump is our Washington and Lincoln. He is our Commander-in-Chief in this battle and that is what is currently required. There is not a man alive who could have run this gauntlet like him. And like Washington before him, he is a strategic genius guided by Divine Providence. Not the buffoon his detractors claim him to be. Were that so, then they lost to a buffoon. What does that make them?

Though I may oppose them, I know Trump's opponents are skilled and there is a genius in their darkness. I do not for one moment underestimate them. Yet, they are currently being-- and will ultimately be-- defeated.

Like I've said before, you don't have to like it, you can even hate it, but you will be forced to accept it. Or you can join the Patriots who support this freedom movement. The glory of this triumph will eventually be ours. We fight not just for this country, but for the world at large. A true and lasting freedom and peace will reign in every land and amongst every people.

The pathway there is through Trump. You might not believe it, but it can't happen without him back at the helm in this current historical moment.

Trump was twice nominated for the Nobel Peace Prize, but there is no need for him to win it. This isn't about prizes and false honors. If you can give an individual who dropped 100,000+ bombs a peace prize then your prize means nothing. It means less than nothing.

I agree with Trump on this matter:

"Peace is the Prize."

The grave that Trump's enemies are digging for him-- and by extension us-- they will crawl into. The coming world is not one that they will inherit. Not by the means that they are employing. Our revolution-- unlike the Marxist one that is always followed by a reign of terror-- has a global peace as its ultimate end.

How we get there remains to be seen, but where we go one, we go all.

You wanted to live in interesting times, didn't you?

"To replace the old paradigm of war with a new paradigm of waging peace, we must be pioneers who can push the boundaries of human understanding. We must be doctors who can cure the virus of violence. We must be soldiers of peace who can do more than preach to the choir. And we must be artists who will make the world our masterpiece."

- Paul Chappell

10. A MORE PERFECT UNION

What I have learned about with some on the Left with the whole nazi/white supremacist thing is that it's like a weird fetish to them. It doesn't matter what you do or say, you just have to stand back and let them get off on it. Because they are going to do so whether you like it or not. Just distance yourselves from the eruptions and let their own dopamine do any necessary calming work after the fact.

Renounce it, denounce it, announce it, any of the nounces-- it won't matter and it won't make a single bit of difference. Denounce their fantasy issue a million times and you will have to do it once more, and once more again.

"Tell us that you're not a nazi, you nazi!"

It's so absurd, unseemly and irrational, but fetishes can be like that when you really commit to them.

So, just let them do their thing and pleasure themselves to the nazi/white supremacist hologram. It might not be your kink-- but it's theirs, so let them have it. Do you really want to stay up at night worrying about Gavin (founder of Vice) McInness's Proud Boys? Like they are some dangerous group at large.

The only real white supremacist organizations with any legit power are the Aryan Brotherhood-style prison gangs and those of their ilk. But no one is going to mention them or ask anyone to denounce them because they are actually real. They're so real they might actually do something about it if you call them out. So, there will be no tough talk posts on them. Not one.

The KKK and Antifa were declared terrorist organizations by the Trump administration. But apparently, according to Joe Biden, Antifa isn't an organization, it is an idea, you see. Ah yes, so if you lost your business to Antifa looting, vandalism & rioting and/or were pulled out of your car and beaten half to death, that was an IDEA that did that to you. Feel better?

In other news, Joe Biden was against the Green New Deal even though he is also for it. He's not sure where he went to college, but I'm sure he did very well there. And his son Hunter is a totally upstanding gentleman with an equally upstanding bank account, no need to check any of the international records there. Joe said so.

Trump wants to open the country back up, Biden wants to keep it closed. Voter fraud is not a real thing, even though it clearly is. If the election steal that happened in broad daylight (and at night) blatantly right in front of our faces in the 2020 election isn't resolved, then we don't have a country anymore. Waiting for the next election cycle isn't an option. What would be the point if the system is still rigged? An intervention (Divine, or otherwise) is now necessary. The fate of the free world depends on it.

Biden is a very old man. He does not have the stamina to be the President or to run a country, or even a roller rink, for that matter. Nothing could be clearer than that. I even feel a little sorry for the guy myself, though given what he has done, I shouldn't.

The best thing that ever happened to the Democrats was the Covid Plandemic and that is exactly why it was deployed. I will give them that. With their backs against the wall, they went for broke and got biological on our asses. It was supposed to be a lot worse, but even as it did pan out, it gave them a leg to stand on to enact their criminal election steal.

Unfortunately (for them) a one-legged Biden hopping around on his post-Covid platform is not going to be enough.

PS... Yes, yes, we know, you still think Trump is a White Supremacist. We just don't take your fetish seriously and neither do the record number of voters who happen to not be white who turned out for him. They paid attention to reality and not some fever dream from 1930's Germany. Look out, look out, the White Supremes are coming!

So, if you marxists could just finish up quickly, we have the room booked next for the robot furry polyamorous foot fetishists. Now, those folks are into some really serious kink. Please take your nazi costumes and Trump masks with you. There's a great dry cleaner right around the corner. They'll get those stains out in a jiff and have you ready for your next msnbc episode.

Now, for those following at home, Trump has condemned racism & neo-nazis very strongly and many times, but the media refused to accept it and misrepresented and reframed everything he said to make him appear to be a racist that supports this phony idea of white supremacy. They are still bringing up Charlottesville, which was organized by the same guy who organized Occupy Wall Street, as intentional agit prop theatre-- funded by G. Soros, of course. They are still gaslighting the public that Trump wouldn't condemn neo-nazis and that he called them "very fine people."

Trump was referring to the regular people there to protest the tearing down of the statues, not the hired tiki torch people, who in many ways are relatives of Antifa, in that money flowed from the same source to both of them. Here is what Trump said about that, which the media rabbit-holed and refused to accept as a real statement, along with every Democrat supporter, who still hysterically believes 'he won't condemn them!'

"As I said on Saturday, we condemn in the strongest possible terms this egregious display of hatred, bigotry, and violence. It has no place in America. And as I have said many times before: No matter the color of our skin, we all live under the same laws, we all salute the same great flag, and we are all made by the same almighty God. We must love each other, show affection for each other, and unite together in condemnation of hatred, bigotry, and violence.

We must rediscover the bonds of love and loyalty that bring us together as Americans. Racism is evil. And those who cause violence in its name are criminals and thugs, including the KKK, neo-nazis, white supremacists, and other hate groups that are repugnant to everything we hold dear as Americans. We are a nation founded on the truth that all of us are created equal. We are equal in the eyes of our Creator. We are equal under the law. And we are equal under our Constitution. Those who spread violence in the name of bigotry strike at the very core of America."

- President Trump

The reason racism must be brought into every political debate by the left is because their ideas on paper for running the world are dubious at best and they cannot stand on that platform in any real way and under any kind of microscope. Have you read the Green New Deal? It is ludicrous and completely disconnected from reality. On Joe Biden's website he states he is for it, yet in the debates he said he was against it-- but also that it would pay for itself.

I sincerely love and respect many of the people who are passionately against Trump. But all they really have are their delusions of his racism (which run counter in every possible way to the reality of the President's actions) and this idea of 'free socialism' that will solve all the world's problems-- as promised by every other socialistic regime that has previously failed and led to tyranny and/or societal collapse. Those at the highest levels of this anti-Trump sphere want absolute power for themselves and not We the People. Their ideological forefathers labelled their supporters at ground level (ordinary citizens) as "useful idiots." This was because of how easily they were manipulated to act against their own interests. Appealing to their vanity and their desire to claim the moral high ground was a chief tactic.

So, again and again, Donald Trump's opponents circle back to:

"HE WOULDN'T CONDEMN WHITE NATIONALISM!"

He has done it a hundred times in as clear a language as a human being could ever speak. We have the video clips and we have the transcripts. We show them again and again and they bounce right off some people, hit the ground and roll down the street. Their minds are locked and they refuse to accept any and all previous denouncements. They want a new one right now and that one also won't be good enough. It's quite literally a psychosis at this point.

In the debates, Trump said he would denounce it again.

"Who do you want me to denounce?"

Biden said the Proud Boys. Their chairman is a Black Hispanic man. At this point they can't even throw a real white nationalist organization out there for him to condemn.

The Proud Boys claim they stand in opposition to Antifa, who ran amok in many Democrat run cities, assaulting people and trashing businesses and causing mayhem. Trump declared both the KKK and Antifa as terrorist organizations, which they are. Antifa are even so bold as to use the EXACT same logo as the Nazi Antifascists. How obvious does it have to be?

So, Trump has to declare his condemnation of white nationalists a billion times (which will never be enough) while Biden is never put on the spot to denounce and condemn Antifa? Trump was trying to put Biden in that position, since it has been Antifa and BLM (both left funded organizations) that had been out in the streets causing violence. I strongly disagree with the Proud Boys going out there to stop them. It is a job for the National Guard in conjunction with the police (who are stood down in many Dem run cities) and maybe even the Marines.

What side used street violence against citizens to put over their agenda? These leaders need to be put on the spot to condemn this over and over again-- just like Trump was asked again and again to condemn white supremacy. That was what Trump was trying to do in the debates, though I admit it did not work, because all that the left wanted was another chance to pick apart and parse his words out of context.

When he condemned the evils of racism and white nationalists in Charlottesville in the clearest possible terms, the media selectively edited the condemnation out and falsely claimed he said they were very fine people. We have the full tape and transcript and we have shown it over and over. It was the exact opposite of what they claim. It doesn't matter.

They don't care about a denouncement or condemnation-- what they want is for this subject to be on the table forever, so that we can't focus on reality and the details of policy and running the country on the platforms of Law & Order and Building & Prosperity.

Trump created the best economy in memory and what he has done for the black community is unparalleled-- and it is only going to get better. Black people who are awake and not under the spell of the media recognize this because it affects them directly. They don't care about delusional liberals and their virtue signaling social media posts condemning white supremacy.

That does absolutely nothing for their real lives. It is pure narcissistic vanity on the part of the ones doing the posting.

Economic gains and opportunity. Prison reform. School choice. These are the only things that matter. The rest is bullshit.

The Dems will talk forever and ever about racism and then do nothing. They may increase the welfare state and promote broken families, which is the worst possible thing for the black community or any community. But that's their approach. That's why they call it the Democratic Plantation. That's why the movement is called Walk Away. And many are, with many more to follow.

Back when Trump was a businessman and not the leader of the free world, he gave a number of black entrepreneurs business loans. When they came back to repay him, he said keep the money, I just want to see you succeed. Does that sound like a racist? Donald Trump is loved by this community, who see clearly how he fought for them. Donald Trump has gotten more funding to historically black universities than any President in history. So racist. So totally racist.

The left/media/liberal/anti-Trump nonstop claims of racism are lies. But they traffic in these lies and build up their political currency on them. Trump is taking action in real life, inside the political bloodsport arena, to make things better for minorities. What the hell is anyone else doing? Virtue signaling on the internet? Get the hell outta here with that prima donna bullshit. Accomplish something real within the system or GTFO.

We have waited long enough for an agent of real and positive change. Now we have one and he is not going away. He will 100% return to the White House (wherever that might be). His opponents will be forced to accept the reality that their leaders (like Biden) have done nothing of consequence for We the People in all their years in office. They have lined their own pockets and empowered themselves. Period.

The Biden-style political dinosaurs are finished. They are over and they are never coming back. You can feel sorry for the Bidens of the world, if you must. Trump ran over him like a Bull in a China (intended) Shop in the real election. It might be painful to accept this fact for some.

I understand that Biden has recovered from a childhood stutter. That is admirable. I sincerely wish him the best somewhere far away from the controls of the US economy and defense systems.

So, for now, some can take their self-congratulatory victory laps about how they are so-not-racist and everyone else is.

Team Trump will be here firmly ensconced in reality waiting for you on the other side of the stolen election, which we have already won.

Trump will be President for the full 8 years. This is written. It will not be unwritten. Invest in therapy and Kleenex as needed.

"And as I have said many times before: No matter the color of our skin, we all live under the same laws, we all salute the same great flag, and we are all made by the same almighty God. We must love each other, show affection for each other, and unite together in condemnation of hatred, bigotry, and violence. We must rediscover the bonds of love and loyalty that bring us together as Americans.

We are a nation founded on the truth that all of us are created equal. We are equal in the eyes of our Creator. We are equal under the law. And we are equal under our Constitution."

- President Donald J. Trump

RECONCILE

Antifa uses the same logo as a Nazi paramilitary unit. Reconcile.

The KKK was a militant white supremacist Democrat organization instituted after they lost the Civil War to the Republican led party, which was created to end slavery. Reconcile.

Joe Biden eulogized KKK Grand Cyclops Robert Byrd at his funeral. Reconcile.

Hilary Clinton called KKK mass recruiter Robert Byrd a political mentor. Reconcile.

George Soros, who funds both Antifa and BLM, helped the Nazis confiscate property from his fellow Jews during WW2. He called it one of the greatest moments of his life. Reconcile.

Margaret Sanger, founder of Planned Parenthood, spoke at a KKK rally, where she stated black people were "human weeds and reckless breeders spawning children that never should have been born." Reconcile.

Do you disavow and denounce these people? History has clearly shown you who they are.

American Patriots understand this history. We know who we are fighting for and what we are fighting against. Equality and freedom for all under the Constitution. No one must be above the Law. The criminals in politics and business do not like the proposition that the Law can be used against them. They thought it was for the little people only. They will fight to the death to prevent a just law enforcement from happening. They will lose this fight.

You cannot dissuade Trump supporters or push us off the line. To us it is a spiritual battle between Good and Evil. Patriots are of every color, creed and orientation and from all walks of life. We do not care about your attempts to marginalize or mock us. We know exactly what we stand for and who the real racist/tyrants are. And we know well what projection is.

We have the numbers and we have history and truth on our side. Every moment another individual wakes up from their slumber and joins us in this fight for freedom against the old power structure, whose dying media is their last and best weapon.

Only 5% of the US population fought in the Revolutionary War. But that was enough to defeat the biggest Empire the world had ever known. It was a miraculous victory.

But the Empire was not vanquished in one war. They circled their wagons and came back with other tactics-- namely infiltration instead of invasion. And a covert banking system.

So, now we are met at the Second American Revolution and the Civil War and perhaps even WW3 all in one. It is a war fought primarily with information. Its outcome is certain-- though the path on the ground can only be lived day to day, by the individuals that are here.

We want you to wake up and fight with us for true freedom-- but we cannot force you. We can only show you the door and put a key in your hand. You have to go through it on your own and with your own intent. You may lose some friends in the process-- but would you rather have truth and the light on your side, or more media brainwashed friends? They will come around eventually anyway.

The choice as ever is yours. The winners and losers of this battle have already been decided.

I denounce the anti-freedom street violence tactics of Antifa, as well as their entire organization. They are the very thing they claim to be fighting against. I hope the money was worth it, because it doesn't spend well in jail.

"Our cruel and unrelenting Enemy leaves us no choice but a brave resistance, or the most abject submission; this is all we can expect. We have therefore to resolve to Conquer or Die. Our own Country's Honor, all call upon us for a vigorous and manly exertion, and if we now shamefully fail, we shall become infamous to the whole world. Let us therefore rely upon the goodness of the Cause, and the aid of the Supreme Being, in whose hands Victory is, to animate and encourage us to great and noble Actions - The Eyes of all our Countrymen are now upon us, and we shall have their blessings, and praises, if happily we are the instruments of saving them from the Tyranny meditated against them. Let us therefore animate and encourage each other, and shew the whole world, that a Freeman contending for Liberty on his own ground is superior to any slavish mercenary on earth."

- George Washington

11. A SACRED VICTORY

That day has arrived, long awaited and fought for, and intrinsically connected to other essential moments in US history-- most specifically the American Revolution, and the writing of the sacred documents that were the cornerstone of that revolution and representative of the true birth of our nation.

When our founding fathers were considering whether or not to sign the Declaration of Independence, knowing full well it could mean a death sentence for themselves and their families, a mysterious stranger rose and gave an impassioned speech:

"The words of this declaration will live in the world long after our bones are dust. To the mechanic in his workshop they will speak hope: to the slave in the mines freedom: but to the coward kings, these words will speak in tones of warning they cannot choose but hear...

Yes, as I sank into the gloomy shadows of the grave, with my last faint whisper I would beg you to sign that parchment for the sake of those millions whose very breath is now hushed in intense expectation as they look up to you for the awful words: You are free."

Every one of those men arose and signed that document and the revolution began in earnest. That document was also co-signed by the wives and children of those men, because their lives were at stake, as well. These were not just hollow words on a piece of parchment, they were world-defining inscriptions, sacred declarations that were divinely inspired, and later to be coupled by the Constitution and the Bill of Rights.

These declarations of the rights of all human beings, as given by our

Creator, were the terms those early revolutionaries were fighting for, and not simply the land itself. That is what 'Make America Great Again' represents, in case the message on those red hats was lost on anyone.

But what about slavery, some might ask, how does that fall in line with the equal-rights-for-all proclamation? Well, what wound up happening? What country chose to fight a Civil War and bleed a generation's blood into the soil to live up to the words on that parchment? That's right, it was the United States of America. You might notice to this day, that there are many countries such as China, India, Africa and places in the Middle East, who have not yet joined the US in ending the terrible practice of slavery. That will change.

While others might ask, what about the American Indian, the Native American? Wasn't this land stolen from them? It is a good question, worthy of being asked. The answer is that the United States of America had a destiny that was designed to be fulfilled long after its founding. A crossroads moment would arrive when the USA would be the center of a battle for the human rights and freedom of the entire world.

In order for this destiny to be fulfilled, the country was required to develop, at something akin to warp speed, into a great power in the world. And at some point after that, a momentous moment would arrive, when a historic battle would take place, fought as much with information as weapons, for the Soul of a Nation (seen this anywhere?) and the Freedom of a Nation. The results of this battle would determine the fate of the world and humanity. This does not excuse the evil actions of individuals of that former time, or specific things that happened to the Native Americans, but that is a story for another day. Suffice to say, their warrior spirit is intimately involved in the events transpiring on their sacred lands this very hour.

Tyranny or Freedom. It is that simple. That is what is at stake. A unified reverence for all life everywhere, or a humanity in chains, led by a godless elite bent on absolute power for themselves, with an utter disdain for anything sacred, and a foundation based on death and the occult.

I revere the Native American culture. Though they had many issues with inter-tribal warfare, they had and have a profound connection with the Spirit of Life and the Land, referred to by many as Mother Nature. Because of this inherent strength they were asked to do the near impossible: to witness everything they held sacred appear to get taken away and get crushed to dust. To get pushed up right to the precipice where all hope appears lost and everything has been destroyed. And then, to reach deep within, to that reservoir of Spirit beyond this world, and make a vow not to be defeated, whether in life or in death, and then to turn the corner and incredibly come back. To be reborn in the ideals that made the culture great originally, and like a phoenix from the ashes, bring that wisdom forged in destruction into the new. And not simply like it was before, but greater than it ever was.

"This is not simply another four year election. This is a crossroads in the history of our civilization." - Donald J. Trump.

This was not an exaggeration. This very moment was instilled in the destiny of our nation at its very founding. A Second American Revolution was actually built into the first one.

"This is a struggle for the survival of our nation. And this will be our last chance to save it. This election will determine whether we are a free nation or only have the illusion of democracy. I knew this day would arrive. It was only a question of when. And I knew the American people would rise above it and vote for the future they deserve. The only force strong enough to save our country is Us. Our great civilization has come upon a moment of reckoning..." - Donald J. Trump.

This battle was not just against the enemies of freedom, who hate the sacred trust of our founding documents, but a battle as to whether we could awaken enough US citizens to what was at stake before the key elections of 2016 and 2020 took place.

As you all well know, not everyone voted to "Make America Great Again." The enemies of freedom had a compromised corporate media at their disposal– and all of the famous faces that work for them– as well as countless blackmailed politicians, intelligence agents, lawmakers, and last but certainly not least, an entire worldwide banking system which had already usurped much of the power from the United States already, as the founding fathers predicted it would.

The Creator likes a good story. And coming back from the brink of defeat against impossible odds, to triumph magnificently and miraculously for the best of all possible reasons, makes a pretty good story, wouldn't you say? And to live that story instead of just reading about it is all the more magnificent. We are, all of us, in that story right now. This period of history will be studied for generations to come, just like the original American Revolution.

The hardest part as far as the vote was concerned was overcoming the mind control aspects of the media and the 'cult of cool' of Hollywood. Most people are so busy with their lives that deep dives into researching every aspect of an historic moment was not possible. They were working and raising their families. The TV was delivering most of their news, with social media following a close second.

And so it was via the aqueducts of social media, as compromised by Big Tech as they are, that a great current of the truth would have to flow through. It would be up to the people themselves whether they could break past the sea of noise of both Fake News & Real News and uncover the truth behind what is happening. The one thing we had versus the enemy is that in this era, truth predominates over deception. It has an advantage. This was not always the case. There are many factors behind why now is the moment for this quantum event, and not some other time in history, but put simply, this awakening involves the closure of a very long cycle (near 26,000 years) and the beginning of a new one.

The whole world is watching, regarding the aftermath of the 2020 election and what it represents. Though there are many who are against Trump and who bought into a deceptive narrative, and yet others who are apathetic, because they feel the whole system is corrupt and both candidates were bad– a very strong numerical majority of citizens made their decision and it was for Trump. No voter fraud can change those real numbers.

To make this just a little easier, the Universe gave you Joe Biden. A transparent joke, falling apart mentally and so obviously compromised by pay-to-play deals with foreign interests, particularly communist China, it might as well have been written in the sky in neon letters.

And yet, many dismissed this as simply not true and dug even deeper into their Trump derangement syndrome. Denial is strong and the Marxist education many received joined forces with a media culture designed to reject patriotism and the unity and power which comes from that--

especially when that patriotism is rooted in the United States of America, whose destiny and rights were God-given and planted deep into the soil for a time such as this, where they would burst forth into the sunlight for all of the world to see.

Make no mistake, the enemy was committed to conquering your mind, above all else. Where your mind went, your body would follow. They had every tool possible at their disposal. And as such, we cannot blame our brothers and sisters who fell under this spell. As the victories of freedom continue, we must welcome them back into the fold and fan the flames of their own awakening, comforting them with a truth without judgement. Often those that awaken later understand the enemy better than most, because they were so deep into that world before they came back.

Which is why you see individuals like Brandon Straka or Candace Owens having such an impact. A gay man and a black woman. These designations within identity politics were supposed to be clear givens for the Democrat vote. Not anymore. Straka founded the Walk Away movement and Owens the Blexit movement. Those two movements, along with many others, are having a tremendous effect on the enemy, breaking through their Rules for Radicals warfare utilized so well in the past, with the old Divide and Conquer methodology.

The Rules for Radicals playbook was dedicated to Lucifer. This is not a tongue in cheek dedication. So, if it stands that symbolically Lucifer is on one side of the battle, who do you suppose might be representing the other side?

The former Apostolic Nuncio to the United States, Carlo Vigano, sent a letter to President Trump acknowledging the historic and world-determining battle taking place between the forces of Good and Evil-- with the 2020 election being a key turning point. The enemy has a Great Reset as their plan. A plan for the total subjection of the human race, with socialism via a 'Green New Deal' and medical control as their chief stalking horses. While, We the People have the Great Awakening as its counter strike, led by a Trump Alliance that seeks to utilize the free market and the American Dream as its nexus point.

From the beginning, I have stated that Trump stands for the pillars of Law & Order and Building & Prosperity. In order for the Prosperity pillar to be sound, there must be a true Law enforced, in which no one is above the Law, and the Law applies equally to all.

There is a reason Trump is hated so much by certain players who must commit everything at their disposal to destroying him. Criminals do not like Law & Order when it applies to them. They despise it because it means the end of their power. For far too long they have hidden their dirty dealings in the dark, ruling by secrecy behind the scenes. The Deep State. The Shadow Government. Secret societies. These things are not mere conspiracy terms, though a conspiracy has indeed existed. And it was not to the benefit of We the People, I assure you. It was there to subjugate the People and render them neutered and helpless when the key moment arrived-- whereby they could take total power out in the open. That moment when defeat by the forces of Good was no longer possible.

"The very word 'secrecy' is repugnant in a free and open society; and we are as a people inherently and historically opposed to secret societies, to secret oaths and to secret proceedings... Our way of life is under attack. Those who make themselves our enemy are advancing around the globe... No war ever posed a greater threat to our security. If you are awaiting a finding of 'clear and present danger,' then I can only say that the danger has never been more clear and its presence has never been more imminent...

For we are opposed around the world by a monolithic and ruthless conspiracy that relies primarily on covert means for expanding its sphere of influence- on infiltration instead of invasion, on subversion instead of elections, on intimidation instead of free choice, on guerrillas by night instead of armies by day. It is a system which has conscripted vast human and material resources into the building of a tightly knit, highly efficient machine that combines military, diplomatic, intelligence, economic, scientific and political operations." - President John Fitzgerald Kennedy.

That is a description of the modus operandi of the enemy we face today. We are finishing now what JFK started. His quest was to break the CIA up into a thousand pieces and scatter it to the winds, and to abolish the Federal Reserve and give the power of currency creation back to the US Treasury-- with notes backed by gold, not imaginary fiat usury money created out of thin air.

We know what happened to JFK, but that was a story of another time.

Trump has protections around him that are not just of this world. As such, he will not be assassinated, no matter who makes the attempt or what means they employ. And they have tried many, many times, believe me.

So take great faith in the results of this election, however it ultimately plays out. I guaranteed Trump would be President in 2016 and that miracle of an election came with two terms ultimately attached. What has been accomplished thus far has been incredible, though much of it not reported- or not reported accurately by the compromised press.

The 6 international corporations that own 90% of the media have members that all sit on each other's boards as well as the board of the Fed. They control the players on their payroll that deliver the 'news' to you much like they control chess pieces. Anderson Cooper of CNN is a Vanderbilt. His mother Gloria, and family, were heavily involved in the occult. You can see it in 'artwork' above the bed where young Anderson and his brother are pictured with her. The art depicts a human sacrifice. Would you put that in your child's bedroom when he was growing up? Didn't think so.

And who appeared at the end of Joe Biden's campaign? Lady Gaga. World famous for constant Luciferian imagery in almost every major media spectacle she does, with some notable exceptions when she is in a more 'normal' mode. This is not a mistake on the Biden campaign's part. That is who, symbolically or otherwise, they are aligned with.

The Vanderbilt pool is a place of some interest. It is an empty pool, on their estate in North Carolina. Its likeness appears in the art of Tony Podesta, whose brother John was Hillary Clinton's campaign manager in 2016. Google 'Podesta Art' and you will find imagery of ritualized child abuse. And that is putting it in the most comforting terms, because it gets a lot worse than that.

They thought that the people wouldn't believe it, that they wouldn't accept that something so dark could be taking place under our eyes. And yet, they shoved it in our face with their 'art' events at every turn. Even Stanley Kubrick tried to do his part with Eyes Wide Shut, which displayed some of the occult rituals of the elite. But they cut 24 minutes out of Kubrick's film and he didn't live to see it finished.

So, yes, this is not a mere conspiracy theory to just dismiss out of hand.

Trump went to work on child and human trafficking on day one. The numbers reflect this. Players like Epstein (founder of Clinton Foundation) are now gone. Many more are to come.

Some (not all) members of Hollywood do not seem to like Trump very much. They scream to the high heavens (or to hell) to get rid of him. Why are they so worked up about a President that promoted a strong economy and strong law enforcement? Is there something that a few of them are hiding? We shall see. Do not get too invested into celebrity heroes. Some are very good people and others will break your heart in the days to come.

And Tinsel town has long been in bed with the CCP. This party owns 51% (a controlling interest) of CAA, the biggest agency in Hollywood. That is just one little tidbit of info. CCP China has its tentacles all over that industry and others, such as the NBA.

The people of China (who desire their freedom as much as we do) are waiting on the final results of this election, as are many, many others the world over. Which side will prevail, Good or Evil?

Whose vote will decide this-- the awakened US patriots or the 'woke' and mostly unwitting disciples of Marxism and the entertainment media complex?

The agents of Lucifer (whether you consider that metaphorical or literal) or the Children of Light, as termed by Carlo Vigano?

I think you know the answer. In the end, we are all the Children of Light. This battle has ever had results that were written on stone and in parchment. And the results will not be changed.

God wins. We the People win. And when we do, we enter an entirely new era and history. At first gradually, and then all at once.

It doesn't get any better than this.

Enjoy the show.

God Bless America and God Bless the World.

12. PARTING THE WASHINGTON SEA

In America, during the first American Revolution, Patriots pledged "their Lives, their Fortunes, and their sacred Honor" in their quest for freedom. Many of them felt that Divine Providence was their only path to victory.

Also in America, there were those loyal to the Crown, who felt this band of misfits was transparently doomed to failure against the biggest Empire on Earth. Therefore, they placed their bets on England, and even signed up to fight on that side in some instances.

Then, there was a third, smaller side. This faction claimed: "King George and George Washington are both equally corrupt! Don't support either of them. The common man never wins!"

Being in the first category myself in this Second American Revolution (whose 'shot heard round the world' was Donald Trump coming down that escalator to announce his candidacy in 2015) I understand all about fighting against the second type. They have symbolically staked their claim for the British Crown and under the established terms of the game, we must officially defeat them, on the political playing field this time.

Yet, it is the third group I find particularly pernicious. They are much smaller in number, but they have a way of pulling nascent patriots off the field with their tactics of demoralization and cynicism. In terms of past eras, there is much to be cynical about, hence there is ground for them to stand on with their point of view.

But what their view doesn't account for is the moment when great change is truly possible, when the right leader and movement has actually arrived. Remember, George Washington and his band of misfit Patriots defeated the invincible Empire of that day. Washington had traitors, even amongst his own personal guard, but he knew his quest was guided by a higher Source, wherein the impossible could be made possible.

Regardless of what anyone's beliefs are today, atheists included, what matters is that these Founders staked everything on an essentially spiritual belief, not a political or materialistic one, and they built an entire Country on this belief.

That is why their cause succeeded, and why, in this very moment today, the eyes of the entire world are watching to see what comes to pass in the USA.

"We hold these truths to be self-evident, that all men are created equal, that they are endowed by their Creator with certain unalienable Rights, that among these are Life, Liberty and the pursuit of Happiness.

--That to secure these rights, Governments are instituted among Men, deriving their just powers from the consent of the governed, --That whenever any Form of Government becomes destructive of these ends, it is the Right of the People to alter or to abolish it, and to institute new Government, laying its foundation on such principles and organizing its powers in such form, as to them shall seem most likely to effect their Safety and Happiness...

And for the support of this Declaration, with a firm reliance on the protection of divine Providence, we mutually pledge to each other our Lives, our Fortunes and our sacred Honor."

Today, we only have a United States of America (and our Constitution & Bill of Rights and the sacred freedoms they entail) because the Continental Army won the First American Revolution against unimaginable odds.

Perhaps, back then the numerical majority did not support the revolutionary effort. People like to be on the side that wins. But enough of the right ones did support it. And supporting the effort meant waging your life on it and your family's life upon it.

In this moment of history, the battle is being fought on fields of kinetic warfare, but it is primarily a war of information for the hearts and minds of the people. In that sense, each and every person is involved in their own unique way, even those observing from the sidelines, playing Switzerland while they see what happens.

When Washington's side was victorious, the majority came around almost overnight. The miracle had happened and there was no point in denying it.

People like to be on the winning side.

Donald J. Trump and the Patriots are the winning side of the Second American Revolution. To some, this may seem laughable, especially at this late hour, yet I tell you, when the tide turns, it will turn in a single day.

That is all it will take to turn from Biden appearing to still be President--> to everyone knowing that Donald Trump has secured his second term. The timing of that one day is a mystery to most, but it is as inevitable as the sun rising, and it gets closer and closer every moment, until it finally happens.

It will be the shock felt around the world.

I don't mind having opponents on the other side of this battle. I might even like it. It's that third party I find tricky. Those with enough knowledge to seed doubt on both sides, but not enough to get in the real fight for freedom when it is on their very doorstep.

In the end, we will bring virtually everyone around. There might be a small percentage who are too far gone to wake up. They will be a sad group, indeed, but there's only so much one can do.

Miraculous victories guided by Divine Providence have a curious way of turning hearts on a dime. We did it once with this great Country and we are destined to do it again, in the 2020 election and in what transpires in its aftermath.

Enjoy the great transformative energies which have come in the wake of December 21, 2020, including its Star of Bethlehem Great Conjunction.

You are living pages out of an incredible historical moment when the tide turns and everything changes in a profound and stunning way.

Embrace the inherent possibilities of that, whatever side you are on.

"In the beginning of a change the patriot is a scarce man, and brave, and hated and scorned. When his cause succeeds, the timid join him, for then it costs nothing to be a patriot."

- Mark Twain

The Red Sea Moment

Pharaoh and company didn't see this one coming. If they were warned, they mocked it. And much like today, it doesn't get reported until after it happens. And by then, it's too late to stop it.

"As Pharaoh approached, the Israelites looked up and saw the Egyptians marching after them, and they were terrified and cried out to the LORD. They said to Moses, 'Was it because there were no graves in Egypt that you brought us into the wilderness to die? What have you done to us by bringing us out of Egypt? Did we not say to you in Egypt, 'Leave us alone so that we may serve the Egyptians'? For it would have been better for us to serve the Egyptians than to die in the wilderness.'

But Moses told the people, 'Do not be afraid. Stand firm and you will see the LORD's salvation, which He will accomplish for you today; for the Egyptians you see today, you will never see again. The LORD will fight for you; you need only to be still.'

Then the LORD said to Moses, 'Why are you crying out to Me? Tell the Israelites to go forward. And as for you, lift up your staff and stretch out your hand over the sea and divide it, so that the Israelites can go through the sea on dry ground. And I will harden the hearts of the Egyptians so that they will go in after them. Then I will gain honor by means of Pharaoh and all his army and chariots and horsemen. The Egyptians will know that I am the LORD when I am honored through Pharaoh, his chariots, and his horsemen.'

And the angel of God, who had gone before the camp of Israel, withdrew and went behind them. The pillar of cloud also moved from before them and stood behind them, so that it came between the camps of Egypt and Israel. The cloud was there in the darkness, but it lit up the night. So all night long neither camp went near the other.

Then Moses stretched out his hand over the sea, and all that night the LORD drove back the sea with a strong east wind that turned it into dry land. So the waters were divided, and the Israelites went through the sea on dry ground, with walls of water on their right and on their left.

And the Egyptians chased after them— all Pharaoh's horses, chariots, and horsemen— and followed them into the sea. At morning watch, however, the LORD looked down on the army of the Egyptians from the pillar of fire and cloud, and He threw their camp into confusion. He caused their chariot wheels to wobble, so that they had difficulty driving. 'Let us flee from the Israelites,' said the Egyptians, 'for the LORD is fighting for them against Egypt!'

Then the LORD said to Moses, 'Stretch out your hand over the sea, so that the waters may flow back over the Egyptians and their chariots and horsemen.'

So Moses stretched out his hand over the sea, and at daybreak the sea returned to its normal state. As the Egyptians were retreating, the LORD swept them into the sea. The waters flowed back and covered the chariots and horsemen— the entire army of Pharaoh that had chased the Israelites into the sea.

Not one of them survived."

THE HOUR IS NOW

Playtime is over. No one on either side of the political aisle should now be surprised to find President Trump utilized the full force of the powers afforded him as Commander-in-Chief of the US Military when in office.

If you thought we were going to roll-over for the attack on the United States which this election fraud categorically was, you are living in an alternate reality which will not last much longer. Calling it an attack from China is not completely accurate, as it is really Deep State operations out of China, as reflected by intelligence operations like the CIA and their central banking cohorts, whose tentacles extend worldwide.

Nevertheless, CCP money owns a large part of cultural institutions you may have heard of such as Hollywood, major universities like Harvard and many others, and of course, far too many US politicians to name at this point. JFK called it: "Infiltration instead of invasion."

President Trump took away their financial power by folding the Federal Reserve in the US Treasury. That is the head of the snake. He has also cut off the dark money (via drug & human trafficking) that has fueled CIA operations. Since the CIA has been described as the secret police of the central banks, can you now see that we have already been in an undeclared war ever since President Trump took office?

Now, we are reaching a crux moment of engagement. It is infinitely beyond petty politics at this point, or two dimensional thinking like Democrat and Republican. Both parties have agents that have been compromised and blackmailed, along with judges and other key figures in the system. There comes a time in the game, regardless of the cards you have, when you must go all-in. This is that time. I have been stating that the Trump Alliance holds a royal flush, and this is true, but it is not because of anything in the political world. It is much bigger than that.

This is the battle for the Soul of a Nation. Some may consider that merely a metaphor, but if you spent time behind the scenes with those at the top of the pyramid on Team Anti-Trump Central Banker, you'd find their occult ceremonies extend well beyond the world of metaphor. They put their occult symbolism all over their money, and the mock-sacrifices they display in 'art shows' by Marina Abramovich and others are not-so-mock when the curtains are closed and the cameras are off.

So, if we are (symbolically at the very least) referring to a clash between Lucifer and God for the Soul of a Nation (and by extension the world) what side have you placed your bet on and aligned yourself with? If these religious concepts are too, well, religious for some, then it should be noted that Lucifer really represents Deception, Separation, and Control to the point of absolute Tyranny. The counterpoint which is God then represents Freedom and Unity, with any workings of a Government Under God to be operated transparently and beyond secrecy for the good of We the People.

This is what the Founding Fathers fought for. They built the cornerstone of this Country on the ideal of One Nation Under God, Indivisible, with Liberty and Justice for All.

"The very word 'secrecy' is repugnant in a free and open society; and we are as a people inherently and historically opposed to secret societies, to secret oaths and to secret proceedings." - President John Fitzgerald Kennedy

Whether it is officially declared or not, we are in a State of War over this election, insofar as the acts committed during it and the ramifications for the entire world determined by its outcome. There's been a lot of hot air from the agents of deception (and those that believe them) about Trump being a dictator. While this is patently untrue, the one good thing about it may be that no one, especially his enemies, should be be surprised that he utilized the full scope of his powers and position as Commander-in-Chief.

Do not forget one of the key moments in US history which gave us a Country to begin with. General Washington and a band of underfed soldiers short on supplies crossed a frozen river on Christmas night and hiked 9 miles in a blizzard in order to kill their enemies at dawn.

Commander-in-Chief Donald Trump is the heir to General Washington. The pot stakes have reached their limit and the Alliance is all-in. Oppose it at your peril. Our occult enemies may have pledged their souls to Lucifer, but the Patriots of the United States have pledged their allegiance to a Higher Power. And when we win this war, which we will, all glory is to God, not ourselves, because God is the architect of this Victory.

Merry Christmas.

"Providence, to whom we are infinitely more indebted than we are to our own wisdom, or our own exertions, has always displayed its power and goodness, when clouds and thick darkness seemed ready to overwhelm us. The hour is now come when we stand much in need of another manifestation of its bounty however little we deserve it."

2- George Washington

13. DIVINE POLITICAL PROVIDENCE

Deception cannot prevail in the Age of Light. And be certain, in this grand and dramatic election story, it is Justice which will prevail.

The politicos and globalistas, who exist to serve themselves and not We the People, had their moment and staked their claim to the destiny of the United States. Dominion was their calling card and "In God We Trust" was definitely not their motto.

True, there were some good insiders in DC, but very few showed any heart or moral courage when it was all on the line. The small number that did, I applaud them.

Now it is God's turn. It would only be just, naturally, to let both sides play out their hands and to now reveal all remaining Trump cards in this Casino Royale showdown.

The Enemy is very good at staging events and false flags. They put on a good show, they tug at the emotional heart strings. If human lives need to be lost or sacrificed, that means little to nothing if their ultimate agenda is served.

However, we also live in a time of rapid communication via technology and the sharing of information across all borders instantaneously. Within days of their 'Capitol Breach' event, anons and patriots, who number in the hundreds of millions plus globally, released a tidal wave of videos and other information destroying the hoax for all with actual eyes to see.

For those without eyes to see, or only eyes for the corporate media's crafted interpretation of events, you will always remain the last to know what is truly going on. And you will be the ones shocked, devastated and in fear when the reality you were told is happening is suddenly not happening, and is then replaced by something else: namely the Truth that has been hidden from you all this time. Perhaps it is a darker Truth than you are willing to face. Nevertheless, it must be revealed and faced head-on.

President Trump has officially stated that he is focused on a peaceful and smooth transition of power and that everyone should remain calm and adhere to Law and Order. He also stated that he would not be at a January 20th inauguration.

And yet, with only 12 days left in his term, Pelosi and others were panicking and screaming for impeachment and the 12th amendment. What were they so afraid of? Wasn't Biden a sure thing that was about to assume power in just a few short days? Why all the fear mongering?

Was there something they knew or something about to be made known? I have often stated that President Trump is always 17 steps ahead of them and that anything they might do in a false flag attempt would ultimately be used against them.

There are DNI reports in play, lap-tops from hell and other places, Durham prosecutions, sealed indictments, declassifications, FISA activity, all sorts of powerful face cards in this all-in poker game still at large.

President Trump was the Commander-in-Chief of the US Military. Are his opponents concerned that he did something within his legitimate powers while still in office that could deeply affect their little fiefdom?

Are Joe Biden's media-induced followers concerned that something might be revealed about him that will destroy all of his credibility and leave you wishing you could flush your vote for him down the toilet?

In another era, darkness might prevail in this meta-historical moment, but not in this one. The outcome is secure.

As far as the light around the election fraud goes, it will only be increasing. It cannot and will not be stuffed back into a box, Pandora or otherwise.

In answer to a rhetorical question from above: Yes. They should be afraid. When the People know who they are and what they have done, many of them will not be able to walk down the street.

To those still under the media spell this message is not really for you. You will not face these truths until there is no other avenue left for you and no denial possible any longer. So be it.

This writing is for the patriots and warriors of faith. Do not lose heart for an instant, for this is a graduation moment for you and for your perseverance to stand for the truth and for what is right, even if the whole world seems against you and the task at times impossible.

Nothing is impossible when God is involved. President Trump, like Washington before him, is guided by Divine Providence on this mission. He is a human being and not without his personal flaws, if you want to call them that, but you could say the same thing about each and every one of us. He answered the call when it came and has shown incredible fortitude and strength throughout the entire long journey, along with his family. He is a true hero and history will remember him as such.

He also has support for what he is doing that would be unimaginable to some and protections in place that secure his safety. This next phase is the moment he has prepared his whole life for. Send him your support and prayers, along with those who work for him, who are on the front lines. Remain calm while what must take place is put into action. It is the only way it could be done.

There has always been a Plan, since before Trump took office, and the Plan is unfolding in perfect timing & execution. Things may not happen on the dates we expect or in the manner we desire, but they will happen as they are intended to ensure a successful outcome for America and for We the People, worldwide.

This is in the cards whether the Swamp wants it or not. And it is no surprise that they don't want it at all, because it means the end of their dominion. So, if you are a person of faith and you can grasp what is occurring, stand firm and stand tall.

Speak your Truth regardless of what anyone else might say or think. You know what is right and you should make your stance known in this key moment. That is what it means to graduate. Hold the Line and know that Victory is the end result.

And All Glory is to God.

"These that shall reject him, shall be shocked at how he takes the giant down. And they shall say: what is your plan for this giant? And he will take a simple stone (remember the name) and he will hold it up and they will laugh at him. But the plan is so brilliant, says the Lord, that it could only have been given by me." - Kim Clement's prophecy of Trump presidency.

"So do not be afraid of them. For there is nothing concealed that will not be disclosed, and nothing hidden that will not be made known. What I tell you in the dark, speak in the daylight; what is whispered in your ear, proclaim from the housetops." - Luke 12:4

WHOSE RIGHT HAND I HAVE HOLDEN

My Trump/Cyrus temple coin from Israel arrived. You know what that means? Cyrus/Trump has drained the moats and secretly surrounded Babylon/DC with his military forces.

Meanwhile, Belshazzar and a thousand of his princes & politicos are partying in the temple, celebrating their victory, while desecrating the sacred artifacts and mocking God with their debauchery.

It looked like a fait accompli. Nothing could stop the clever usurpers. They were in total control. Until Cyrus showed up. Like Donald Trump, Cyrus the Great was a builder and a brilliant strategist, known for conquering cities without shedding a drop of blood, but rather by outmaneuvering and out-thinking his opposition.

And it certainly didn't hurt that Cyrus was anointed by God to deliver the Jews and rebuild the Temple. Cyrus was not initially a religious man. He was a very unlikely candidate for anointing, to be sure, but by his calling he ultimately became a man of God. Sound like someone we know? Someone that prophets were calling a Cyrus all the way back in 2015, and even before that. When Donald Trump moved the US Embassy to Jerusalem on December 6, 2017, he was honored with this coin in Israel:

"This special coin was produced to praise the Jerusalem Declaration of President Donald Trump as a continuation of King Cyrus's Declaration. As part of a historical and divine process towards the Rebuilding of the Third Temple."

The main reference to Cyrus in the Bible is in Isaiah 45. And what number President is Donald Trump?

"Thus saith the LORD to his anointed, to Cyrus, whose right hand I have holden, to subdue nations before him; and I will loose the loins of kings, to open before him the two leaved gates; and the gates shall not be shut; I will go before thee, and make the crooked places straight: I will break in pieces the gates of brass, and cut in sunder the bars of iron: And I will give thee the treasures of darkness, and hidden riches of secret places, that thou mayest know that I, the LORD, which call thee by thy name, am the God of Israel. For Jacob my servant's sake, and Israel mine elect, I have even called thee by thy name: I have surnamed thee, though thou hast not known me."

The arrival of Cyrus in Babylon was prophesied by Isaiah 150 years before Cyrus's birth. It was Daniel who came down the Temple steps and gave him the scroll with his name and prophecy on it.

Daniel also interpreted the "writing on the wall" for Belshazzar the night the moats were drained, unbeknownst to Mr. B, of course.

The writing said "God has numbered the days of your reign and brought it to an end. You have been weighed on the scales and found wanting."

Biden & Harris (and their controllers) have been weighed and found wanting. Their kingdom is no more. Commander-in-Chief Trump has drained the moats of Washington DC, so to speak, and the Military forces of the United States will now carry out their duty to protect and defend the Constitution from all enemies foreign and domestic.

In Trump 2.0 there will be a new United States of America. It will no longer be the United States Corporation, a captured operation since 1871, and further via the Federal Reserve Act in 1913. There will be a new monetary revaluation, with currency backed by gold and part of a quantum financial system.

This will fulfill what President John f. Kennedy started, along with the dissipation of the CIA, the secret police of the central banks.

In the second administration of Donald J. Trump (an entirely new administration) the Third Temple will be built. Cyrus authorized the build of the Second Temple. King Solomon built the First.

Israel and the USA have a twin destiny. They go together like Cyrus and Trump. In fact, USA is right in the middle of JerUSAlem. The United States is the only other country in the world whose founders consecrated the land to the Living God and based their Laws on the Rights of the People as given by their Creator.

Did they think they were going to usurp this Country and seize its Destiny for themselves with a treasonous criminal fraud?

Try they did. Fail they must. Their arrogance, like Belshazzar will be their undoing. For a spoiler alert, Belshazzar did not survive the night, after he was given the writing on the wall. But first, his loins were loosened. Which means two things. One, he was disarmed. Two, he shat himself in mortal fear when he realized what was happening.

Washington DC and other places will soon need an emergency delivery of Depends. Because Cyrus is back in the person of Donald J. Trump. And once again, he has out-thought, out-maneuvered, and out-everything-ed his opponents while they were busy celebrating, mocking him and God and us.

Well, guess what? Some people are about to get to know the US Military and Special Forces very intimately in the coming era. Gitmo is expanded and ready for new occupants. It even has a geriatric unit, because when they go there, it's a one-way ticket. We are all about to be introduced to the Plan. And it is truly brilliant because it comes from above.

The Swamp will be drained. And yes...

It's Gonna Be Biblical.

"I will raise him up in my righteousness: I will make all his ways straight. He will rebuild my city and set my exiles free, but not for a price or reward, says the Lord Almighty."

14. GOD WINS

"I caught 'em. I caught 'em all. We have the cards. They don't."

- 2 Term President Donald J. Trump

Though I often refer to President Trump, this is really not about him. He is a faithful servant to the United States of America, but moreover to the One who truly called him. Though he may not have known it at the time, he does now.

This is about God's Plan. And yes, that Plan is in alignment with a Military Operation that has been in the works since the assassination of President John F. Kennedy.

The Plan is about Draining the Swamp. Have you heard that catchphrase a few times? For those with ears to hear, can you hear the drainage taking place under the dark tunnels of DC at this very moment– tunnels that were used for unspeakable evil.

Donald Trump is an anointed leader like Cyrus the Great. Cyrus drained the moats of Babylon and took the city in a single night. No counterattack was possible, because his Plan was not only strategically brilliant, it was "in the cards" from a Higher Source.

Do not kid yourself that this treasonous (at the highest level) criminal election fraud, which was an Act of War against the United States by Enemies Foreign & Domestic, was somehow successful and now the brain damaged puppet they call 'Joe Biden' is going to permanently take over as de facto leader of the world.

Patriots are in control. The US Military is in control. Laugh all you want, but Space Force Guardians are in control.

This is not the first Revolutionary War, where ordinary citizens are tasked with charging the enemy in a field with bayonets. This is cyber-warfare. Satellites and the dissemination of information via technology are the main weapons.

General Flynn called citizen patriots in this Second American Revolution digital soldiers, engaged in irregular and asymmetrical warfare. That is accurate. But this is, above all else, a spiritual war. A battle between Good and Evil for the Soul of a Nation-- and by extension the World. Because where the United States goes in this battle, so goes the World.

Where We Go One, We Go All.

Spoiler alert: The war has already been won in the spiritual realms. Now we are enacting it in the physical, temporal realm. Like a stage play, the main story has already been written, but there is still flux and flow as to how the actors perform the scenes, as well as the minutiae of the overall performance.

Anyone who has ever acted in or been involved in the theatre knows that each performance of a play is unique, a lot of things can go right or wrong on any given night, but the actual script stays the same. There is improv possible within those contexts, or mistakes that could happen. A light could fall from the rafters and hit an actor. And yet, come what may, the Show goes on and the actors all gather and take a bow afterwards.

The outcome of this grand story is 100% secure because the Author is God. Whether we feel like we are onstage in this Show or in the audience, or a little bit of both, we are all going to see this Story through together.

The bigger picture is that humanity has awoken, or at least enough of humanity has. The majority of the world knows beyond a shadow of a doubt that this 'election' was a fraud and that 'Joe Biden' is not a legitimate leader. There will be no putting the genie back in the bottle or convincing us all to go back to sleep, and continue watching the corporate media for news, while looking to Hollywood stars (paid actors) for direction.

That old world is dead. A new world is emerging from its ashes like a Phoenix. There is no possibility whatsoever that Biden/Harris can lead the awakened human population for any significant time moving forward.

It doesn't even matter that they "inaugurated" Biden. It was a fake inauguration, via a fraudulent vote and under the auspices of the 1871 United States Corporation, which is now a defunct and bankrupt organization.

When Donald Trump is re-inaugurated it will be in the line of succession following Ulysses S. Grant, the last President before the corporate takeover of the United States.

So, in a way, Donald Trump was the Last President of the Old US Corporation and will be the First President of the New United States of America which follows in its wake.

That's how big the historical moment you are living in is. That's why we say that it's going to be Biblical.

This moment in history is aligned with the birth of the United States and the dream of the founding fathers, who consecrated this land to the Living God, deriving all rights as given from the Creator, and who then went to war with the biggest Empire on Earth, relying solely on Divine Providence for their Victory.

Well, here We the People are again. In the culmination moment of that journey, a moment that will deliver not a birth, but a rebirth of a Nation.

Make America Great AGAIN.

The only way to make it great again is to free humanity for good this time. The only way to do that is to take down the Deep State Swamp in ONE FELL SWOOP. By the Grace of God.

Angelic Armies are working in conjunction with human armies, which are working in conjunction with the citizens of the world. If you aren't a military operative, you do not need to pick up a weapon. No violence whatsoever is required. No storming of Capitols or anyplace else.

All that is needed is that you stand up and stand your ground. Declare your Truth before the World and stake a claim for the rights of all humanity.

WE'RE NOT GONNA TAKE IT ANYMORE.

SLAVES NO MORE.

We're not wearing your masks. We're not bowing to your media lies and deception. We are not disavowing President Trump.

We are not turning our backs on the prophets of God, and most especially we are not turning our backs on God itself.

In God We Trust!

This is not about In the Vatican We Trust. Or in Hollywood We Trust. Or In Corporate Media We Trust. Or In Central Banks We Trust. And it's certainly not In Congress We Trust.

"There is no distinctly native American criminal class except Congress."

- Mark Twain

All of the above are captured operations. They appear strong, even invincible to some, like Goliath did to the people of his day.

But David did not fear Goliath. He laughed at him. David trusted in God. And he was a hell of a marksman with a slingshot, to boot.

"My David I have set aside for this Nation."

- Kim Clement in 2014, regarding the coming Trump Presidency.

Nothing Can Stop What is Coming.

This is all in God's Plan for humanity and for the world. So, oppose it at your own peril. However, anything the politicos and globalistas do will have no effect on the ultimate outcome. They already lost. And yet, it looks to many like Donald Trump has left the Oval Office forever.

They probably would have said the same thing about Sun Tzu or Cyrus, right before they realized they were played by a master.

The shadow government opponents of the United States are about to lose everything. They are going to lose their money. They are going to lose their power. And many of them will lose their lives.

We are all here as witnesses. First, we will witness the collapse of their plans. Then we will witness what they have been up to all of this time in the dark. And dark it is. Most of them at the top were occultists, and it's all-too-true that some of them used children in sacrifices or ritually abused them. They did the same thing to their own children, to mind-control them, so can you imagine what they would do to children not in their family?

They were able to hide in the dark and rule by secrecy because the average person could not accept that something so dark and abominable could actually occur in this world. However, this has been going on since Biblical times with Baal worship-- and it has continued up to the present. This activity was used for blackmail and also to advance within the ranks of the Swamp.

The nature of evil and darkness is such that only the most ruthless and amoral can advance. Anyone with a shred of humanity would balk at a certain point and thus could not reach the pinnacle of the pyramid of rule. Anyone with a change of heart along the way would not be able to back out. They'd be eliminated for knowing too much. It's like the Mafia that way.

However, now we are in an "Untouchables" moment. The world criminal Mafia is being taken down. It will be done legally, by the book, and by the Constitution.

What happens next now remains to be seen and to be lived. It's part of the fun, for those in the know. For others, it may be a rocky rollercoaster ride.

It doesn't matter what happens in the small picture. The media can program Biden 'inaugurations' and press events, with flying trapeze acts and sparkling fireworks shooting out of Joe Biden's ass, while he soars through the air in an attempt to nail the landing.

Update: I have been informed by my imagination staff that the fireworks will be shooting out of the ass of Kamala Harris, because no one on either side of the political aisle should rightly be subject to the other visual.

But let's face it, Biden events have all the thrills and chills of a Metamucil commercial. The guy is so boring, watching him for more than 10 seconds is like reading a phonebook in hell. Donald Trump has always been Prime Time TV. Whether you loved him or hated him, everyone tuned in.

Even Biden's supporters can't stand to listen to the schmuck for any extended period. I know they likely think he's going to get replaced by Kamala, probably via prison shiv in a Starbucks bathroom sometime soon, but that's neither here nor there.

I conclude by telling all Patriots and Trump supporters, many of whom are broken hearted right now: Do not get hung up on timeframes and this day or that day, watching the pot waiting for it to boil or not boil.

Nothing the Enemy can do can change the outcome. While they have their media they can still stage and interpret events for the remaining gullible public, but they cannot un-write what God has written.

How does it end?

God Wins is how it ends.

Every road leads to Rome and every road leads to that outcome.

The United States will experience a National Renaissance, which will transform into a World Renaissance. There will be a new Quantum Financial System to go along with it.

If you are wondering about Q, it was/is a Quantum computer employed by a small number (less than 10) of patriots in military intelligence and others, who have gamed out this meta-historical moment, taking all possibilities and moves and countermoves into account for maximum success.

And also for:

"A smooth and orderly transition of power."

The transition of power will be from the Luciferian Deep State Swamp, with its usury fiat banking empire, its deceptive media, and its blackmailed agents in intelligence and politics, back to We the People.

We the People have awakened and cannot be defeated now. God is on our side and Lucifer is getting chained up and dropped in the Pit, for a thousand years or more. You can take that either literally or figuratively, but the end result is the same:

The Best is Yet to Come.

And All Glory is to God.

So, give us your last bet shot Team Puppet Biden.

Give us your last best Media Spectacle. We've got our Popcorn.

And no death of any true freedom fighter, from JFK to Bobby Kennedy to Martin Luther King, and back to the original Patriots of the First American Revolution, to Patriots for the cause of human Freedom the world over, all the way back to the Alpha and Omega of freedom fighters, Jesus Christ, will ever have been in vain. It all led to this.

Now We Win. For them. For Us. And for the children of today and tomorrow. As it was in the beginning, so shall it be again.

"Like anybody, I would like to live a long life. Longevity has its place. But I'm not concerned about that now. I just want to do God's will. And He's allowed me to go up to the mountain. And I've looked over. And I've seen the Promised Land. I may not get there with you. But I want you to know tonight, that We, as a People, will get to the promised land! And so I'm happy, tonight. I'm not worried about anything. I'm not fearing any man! Mine eyes have seen the glory of the coming of the Lord!"

- Martin Luther King

15. WINTER WHITE HOUSE CLEANING

A Hollywood-style "inauguration" or the real thing?

Who has the true authority here? The Media or We the People?

In the Media We Trust - or - In God We Trust?

80% of the American People voted for Donald J. Trump. He has the authority of the People and the moral high ground because the facts are that he won legitimately under the rules of the game in the old system.

The other side (both the pawns and their controllers) committed an Act of War against the United States of America by their attempt to steal the Presidency through the Dominion voter system (Foreign) and the mail-in voter fraud (Domestic).

The Military has sworn an oath to defend the United States and the Constitution against All Enemies Foreign and Domestic.

If anyone thinks this was all over on Jan. 20th, 2021 at high noon in DC (which was in reality built over a Swamp) they are out of their minds.

This will end when it ends, when ALL of the moves are made.

This is a game of 5D chess. For all of the stakes. For the Fate of the world. Washington DC was fenced in and surrounded by 30,000 troops. Does that seem like just another day at the office?

The Biden team should go ahead and entrench themselves as deep as they can into the Swamps of DC. They pressed play on their 'virtual inauguration' and now let's see if they can digitally take over the whole of the United States of America with their little dog and pony show.

Let's see them all gather in one place and attempt to hold that ground and rule going forward.

There is no chance.

They are all going to Gitmo. They are guilty of treason at the highest levels and they will pay the price.

No matter how this Story plays out or how many twists and turns are still left, that is what happens in the end.

If it looks to Trump supporters like-- "Oh, no! We lost! It's all over!"-- I will be here laughing and laughing and laughing.

Nothing is over until WE say it is over. Was it over when the Germans bombed Pearl Harbor?

LOL.

They have their timelines and WE have ours. And God has a timeline as well--> the only One that matters.

Does anyone think the whole awakened planet is just going to pack up and go home, go back to sleep and give up on freedom because Sleepy Creepy Traitor Joe has a video tape certifying his stolen election, which we are, in fact, not obligated to take seriously in the slightest bit. It is a fugazi. The guy is a criminal fake to the highest degree. He can rule in hell if he wants, but not in Heaven or on Earth.

Joe Biden and Harris have zero authority. I openly mock them and everything they stand for. They can do absolutely nothing about it.

If some people don't like this point of view, that's too bad. I will only be getting louder and louder and more vocal in support of the Real and Just President of the United States, Donald J. Trump in the coming days.

When this is all cleared up, then I will go back to making movies.

Of course, I have my popcorn ready for the next few months. This is fun to me (as serious as it truly is) because I know that no matter what happens in the small picture, the big picture is absolutely secure. The crimes that took place in the 2020 election will be brought to Justice. That is 100%.

The 2018 EO on Foreign Interference in a US Election is the stone that will bring the Giant down. The stone which they laughed at when

President Trump held it up.

The Giant is the worldwide Deep State, or Shadow Government, or Cabal, however you wish to term it.

This Story is Biblical because it involves Good and Evil, God and the Devil, the Jews in freedom and exile, the Red Seas (metaphorically, in our time) parting, a Purim gamble moment, all of the great themes in that Book wrapped into One in the Greatest Political Story Ever Told.

Great Stories have Great Endings, so hold onto your seats.

One the best devices in a thrilling story is the false ending. And if you can do two false endings, you really have a masterpiece.

I give you advance notice that we are definitely in store for a false ending or two. And the conclusion will be truly majestic.

The conclusion is Stars and Stripes Forever. It's going to be something for the ages. And the Dawn of a New Age.

So, for those of you who haven't given up and don't plan to, have no worries. Stay calm and stand firm. Trust the US Military and trust Donald J. Trump. He didn't write that EO for no reason.

The Enemy is a master or false flags and staged operations. Hollywood, it should be obvious, is under their command, at least for the time being. So expect some continued staged productions from them. Their time is, however, fast running out.

They have the low ground, we have the high ground. If they dig themselves in deeper to their low ground, it will be easier to put a lid on them, as Juan O Savin has said.

These last few moments and strategic plays will be helpful in smoking out the remaining rats. When people think they have finally "won"– then they really show you their true colors.

Trump even said on the Charlie Rose show back in the day that he'd like to see what it's like for a short period to lose everything (or appear to lose everything) so that he could see who is loyal.

We will find out beyond the shadow of a doubt in this timeframe who is loyal to the core in this freedom movement and who is not.

Let the chips fall where they may. But never forget: GOD WINS.

The Winter White House at Mar-a-Lago or the Dark Winter White House in DC. Where would you rather be?

"Former" President Donald J. Trump as always is in the right place at the right time, with the right cards. And yet, if he is the former President, why did they still try to impeach him again in DC? Do they know he hasn't truly lost power?

And why does DC look more like a military prison camp than the seat of US governance?

The reality is that DC has ever been a captured operation, owned by the Vatican and the City of London, and modeled as an independent city within a city like those two entities, complete with occult obelisk and all.

But now that the 1871 USA Corporation is bankrupt and defunct, what exactly is Joe Biden in charge of and who is really running the Show at this point? It would appear (on TV) that Biden is zipping off a record number of executive orders, undoing all that President Trump has accomplished, while putting America Last in his new insane agenda.

And yet Biden and Company took an independent private flight to the "inauguration," where he did not receive the nuclear football, as is protocol. His whole admin to date has the feel of a B-movie filmed on a Hollywood backlot, with multiple rough-cut edits floating around the studio offices, all in desperate need of a voice over to fill in the missing narrative, like Apocalypse Now.

BIDEN (VOICE OVER)

"Castle Rock ... shit, I'm still only in Castle Rock... Every time I think I'm gonna wake up back in the White House. When I was home after my first cloning, it was worse. I'd wake up and there'd be nothing. I hardly said a word to my VP, until I said 'yes' to an impeachment. I'm here a week now... waiting for a mission... getting softer. Every minute I stay in this room, I get weaker, and every minute Trump squats in Mar-a-Lago, he gets stronger. Each time I looked around, the walls moved in a little tighter."

The White Hats have the Deep State in the hurt locker now. Messing with their insider trading deals on Wall Street, knowing they have a new

Quantum Financial System on-line, knowing the old Federal Reserve and Central Bank system is going the way of the dinosaur in a tar pit.

The new system will be based on gold, much of which has been seized from the Vatican and the Crown. Ye ole Obelisk ain't what it used to be. Sell, sell, sell those 666 stocks while you still can, folks.

Meanwhile, much of the default world doesn't know whether it is currently stuck in the endless re-runs of a former reality show or on the precipice of a new dawn. It has been an instructive lull moment.

The Shadow Government puppeteering Biden (and he is nothing more than that, an empty vessel) is being forced to reveal to everyone what they represent and what plans they've had in mind for We the People. They have to show their cards.

A crooked, rigged stock market in which corporate entities get government funded bail-outs when their criminal schemes fail. GameStop? Yes, the Game has Stopped.

A Covid-based medical tyranny wherein everyone can be tracked and controlled by submitting to bio-tech injections and "where are your papers?"- style travel injunctions.

A blatantly obvious cratering of small businesses while allowing international big box outlets to stay open and thrive.

"You gotta know when to hold 'em, know when to fold 'em. Know when to walk away, know when to run."

It was (or should have been) clear to all that the weaponized Covid virus was used to crash President Trump's economy and force him out of office, via mail-in ballot election fraud, used in conjunction with the Dominion Voter System.

But it also should have been clear that the Trump Alliance saw this coming a million miles away and planned accordingly for it.

There was a 2018 Executive Order put in place for exactly this occurrence, which works hand-in-glove with the Insurrection Act, which, yes, President Trump did in fact sign, abdicating power to an Interregnum Government controlled by the US Military, with Chris Miller a key figure at the helm, along with Lt General Charles Flynn, brother of General Michael Flynn.

But none of this is true according to the Mainstream Media, owned by the same companies married to the central bank system. If they don't report it, it isn't true. Whatever they report on their controlled outlets is the actual reality and everything else is a conspiracy theory. Until it isn't.

According to the EO on Foreign Interference in a US Election, and the previous one on Crimes Against Humanity (see child trafficking) all personal and corporate assets can be seized should the guilty parties fall under the aforementioned orders.

So, if the White Hats in US Military Intelligence are holding the Trump cards of a new financial and governance system, along with the power to shut down the entire operation of the Deep State Obelisk Empire-- with its funny-money based on nothing and its unimaginably dark occult activity of sexual abuse and sacrifice (yes, adrenochrome is real)-- then why would they wait so long to play those cards?

The truth is, the new world is coming, and is in fact already here, but the transition is designed to be smooth and peaceful for the general public to the greatest extent possible. In order for it to be smooth and peaceful, a significant amount of activity must take place behind the scenes, before the final cards are laid down on the green felt of the world poker table.

It would not be ideal for the US Military, now that President Trump has stepped aside, to suddenly publicly announce that an internecine war is active and many individuals in the corrupt DC system (compromised as they are by foreign entities like the CCP) are still at large and in desperate need of arrest at this very moment.

The Antifa/BLM riots and other false flags would then violently re-launch and whatever key arrests are outstanding would be all the more difficult to accomplish.

In a word, it would be chaos, which is the exact opposite of the orderly transition of power we are looking for. And the transition of power is from the old captured operation (stacked to the gills with blackmailed agents and rigged to max by the shadow government) back to We the People. As it was in the beginning, so shall it be again.

When the power returns to We the People and the Destiny of the United States of America is fulfilled, the dream of the Founding Fathers and

Mothers will play out on the world stage as something akin to a miraculous intervention joining hands with the birth of a Golden Age.

The Medical and Energy technology that has been hidden and stifled by the old world order, will then be unveiled. Though it is entirely based on working science, and individuals we have even heard of like Nikola Tesla, it will have the initial feel of something out of a science fiction novel.

Perhaps there is an element of science fiction to it, because some of the tech comes from galactic sources. It should come as no surprise that We are not Alone in the Universe.

You could also make the case that there is only One of us here. One Intelligence awake within the multiplicity of every living being. That said, think of the vastness of space. We are not the only game in town.

And this was not just another 4 year election. This incredible unfolding drama, often characterized as the Great Awakening, has attracted attention from far-and-wide, galactically speaking. They have come to see how Humanity will handle the transition. It is a birth moment of sorts, and it is not an occasion to be missed.

If this seems like an overblown fantasy, because the world as we know it is still ticking by in ordinary mundane fashion, that is largely because we are living in the fine grain of the moment, day to day and hour by hour. However, if this historical moment were condensed into screenplay format, and then writ large on the world stage, it would be viewed in an entirely different manner.

We are currently in a transition phase of world-altering importance. What exact timeframe it occurs in, we cannot determine while we are living it, yet you can be sure that from a higher perspective, there is most assuredly a Plan and the Plan is unfolding in all appropriateness.

God has always had a Plan for the United States of America, as a salt and light to the world. In the Story to date, it may appear that Team Lucifer has won the Game. Biden is supposedly the President and the Deep State has everything needed to institute their New World Order. Sovereign Nation States will soon be a thing of the past, now that the last beachhead of the US has been captured and put out to pasture in a CCP electronic cage.

Not so fast, sucka.

Did you think that the Greatest Political Story Ever Told wasn't going to have a false ending or two? That would be criminally negligent screenwriting.

Team Biden might have "won" the January 20th game, but how will they do with the rest of Time?

They will be "Doing Time" is how they will do. And still some will hang from the gallows they built for others.

Which path do you choose this day?

Do you want to live in the old world or the new?

Which do you prefer: The Winter White House at Mar-a-Lago (Sea to Lake) or the Dark Winter House– a fenced-in military cage in Obelisk DC?

The Time is Up for those that are corrupt.

The Egyptians you see today you will never see again.

"Today's ceremony has very special meaning because today we are not merely transferring power from one administration to another or from one party to another - but we are transferring power from Washington DC and giving it back to you, the people.

For too long a small group in our nation's capital has reaped the rewards of government while the people have borne the cost.

Washington flourished but the people did not share in its wealth. Politicians prospered but the jobs left and the factories closed.

The establishment protected itself but not the citizens of our country.

Their victories have not been your victories. Their triumphs have not been your triumphs. And while they celebrated in our nation's capital, there has been little to celebrate for struggling families all across our land

That all changes starting right here and right now because this moment is your moment. It belongs to you. It belongs to everyone gathered here today and everyone watching all across America.

This is your day. This is your celebration. And this - the United States of America - is your country. What truly matters is not which party controls our government but whether our government is controlled by the people. January 20, 2017, will be remembered as the day the People became the rulers of this nation again.

There should be no fear. We are protected and We will always be protected. We will be protected by the great men and women of our military and law enforcement. And most importantly We will be protected by God.

The time for empty talk is over. Now arrives the hour of action.

We stand at the birth of a new millennium, ready to unlock the mysteries of space, to free the earth from the miseries of disease and to harness the energies, industries and technologies of tomorrow."

- 2 Term President Trump's Inaugural Address

Know this: God has not abandoned the United States of America.

The Shining City Upon a Hill will shine brighter than ever before.

The Best is truly Yet to Come.

And though we may have imagined what a new world might be, it is far better than what we have imagined, because indeed, we will not just imagine it...

We will live it.

Where We Go One, We Go All.

16. THEY CAME, THEY SAW, THEY CO-OPTED

One of the most compelling tactics of the Cabal has ever been their method of creating their own opposition or co-opting those that might challenge their position, or attempt to enlighten the populace as to their nefarious rigged system, or the means by which it was achieved.

If, at the very least metaphorically, Lucifer is the Prince of Deception, looking to create and rule over his own counterfeit kingdom in the phenomenal world, then it stands to reason that the 'Rock Star' is Lucifer's version of Jesus Christ. There was only one Jesus Christ, though his appearance in the world may have occurred concurrently in many locations, however there are very many rock stars, with a handful of new ones created each season to join the other old standbys.

This plays into the somewhat erroneous concepts of Right and Left that were fine-tuned in the 60's and which play greatly into influencing the hearts of minds of people across the board today, both young and old. In the 60s many well-meaning people idolized the nascent rock stars as avatars of freedom and positive change, fighting against the corruption of the Establishment or "The Man."

In truth, the rock stars were created by "The Man" as controlled opposition. This does not discredit the value of their music necessarily or the creativity involved in it, but it does underline the entire dynamic by which rock stars come into being. They are birthed by the machine of corporate industry and do not spring into being organically by their own bootstraps. True, their early work which might put them on the map in a local scene could be entirely of their own hand and that of their bandmates, but in order to become a genuine rock star, or any Hollywood-style celebrity, they need to be ordained as such by the powers that be and promoted into their status by the influence of the corporate media, which was created and is controlled by the central bankers who created our current monetary system. If you create and control the issuance of money, it is natural that you will also for the most part control the industry at large.

And that is what Hollywood is known as: The Industry. Much like pilgrims journeying to the Land of OZ, would-be rock stars and their celebrity counterparts make their way to the Emerald City Wizard, looking for the fake-holy halo of celebrity to give them what they seek, which is generally a sense of self-importance, disguised as perhaps a heart, courage, or intelligence. Of course, in Lucifer's world, a quasi-meaningless paper diploma, a shiny medallion, or a plastic heart is what the celeb-seeker really gets. Then they must rationalize that these counterfeit items are somehow of magical importance, since so much was sacrificed in their attainment, and the general public seem to hold them in such high regard. And the financial payout for holding them, like a form of currency with no known provenance or value yet which still nevertheless spends, for the time being. In the final analysis, that currency will be like the Confederate notes after the Civil War.

If you go back to the 60's, many of the original rock stars did not come out of the San Francisco scene characterized by Haight-Ashbury, but first emerged from the Laurel Canyon scene in the hills of Hollywood, where the initial wave of bands were comprised of men and women who were all the children of military intelligence-- military brats, as it were. Now, if only half of them had this background, you could chalk it up to chance, but the fact that virtually 100% of them had it is beyond the pale of mere coincidence. Laurel Canyon was also the location of a semi-secret military/government base in Lookout Mountain, created ostensibly to study footage of nuclear detonations, but in actuality it was a functionary of the kind of mind-control that Hollywood and the Media as a whole specialize in today.

Perhaps it's nuclear background is fitting, because the crafted Luciferian world which the rock star and celebrities inhabit has had a nuclear detonation effect on the psyche of the public at large, who both worship (and sometimes revile) these media avatars and consider them to be the ones who "Made It" - ie: achieved the apotheosis of the American Dream, regardless of what country they might happen to reside in.

But Lucifer always leaves hints as to who is in charge of their souls. Take Miley Cyrus (the once seemingly-innocent Disney youth 'role model' who subsequently exploded into a tongue-wagging dildo sporting sexpot, as is standard ops for Hwood-style sexual exploitation of youth, for however long that youth lasts) and the name of her new album: Plastic Heart.

Is that Wizard of OZ-ian enough for you?

In the journey to Christ, the true way-shower of Unity Consciousness, you receive a real heart, one that pulses with gratitude for the Creator, and knows itself as One with all Creation. In the Luciferian Kingdom, you get a plastic wind-up heart, one that ticks for a limited time, before the owner of said plastic toy is sacrificed to the false god who gave them their 15 minutes. Which is why so many of the rock stars end up as sacrifices or die young. The ones that live to old age are the rare ones of high eminence favored by the string pullers behind the scenes and perhaps those that graduate to certain intermediary positions themselves as puppeteers of other marionettes.

Returning to the original wave of rock stars out of Laurel Canyon, best characterized by Jim Morrison, whose Admiral Father was instrumental in the staged Gulf of Tonkin incident that sparked off the transparently corrupt Vietnam War, the very thing the left wing Hippies of the day were marching against. Morrison himself, the self described Lizard King, pretended to reporters of the time that his parents didn't exist, that they had already died. The media of the day, one would gather, were content to leave it at that, without any further investigation, at least not any that was widely broadcast. This is not to say that the artist himself did not have good intentions, however they can also be co-opted without realizing what has happened. Mind control is tricky that way, and drug use can play a part in it. But Morrison also said that "whoever controls the media, controls the mind." And I expect that he was personally against the control the media had gained over the voices of its so-called rock stars, even if they were publicly speaking out against the war machine's latest effort in Vietnam.

Being against Vietnam was not a difficult position to take from today's perspective. There was a draft in that war, a war which could have been won in a week if the US side was really trying to win it. But of course they weren't. It was an extended operation in taking meaningless hills in the jungle and then giving them back, all in the name of loosh-giving bloodshed and the war economy, it's real reason-to-be.

So, when the Left was against this war they seemed like the sensible ones, albeit also the ones tripping out on acid and fomenting the sexual revolution, which was perhaps good on paper, but which had an unforeseen (or foreseen) impact on the nuclear family. Since the nuclear family is one of the cornerstones of western civilization, its quasi-devastation in today's landscape is best reflected by the prison statistics which show an incarcerated population of 80% of individuals from single mother households. While the child-nurturing characteristics of women are beyond dispute and a necessity in an ideal upbringing, it is the discipline of the father in the adolescent youth-rebellion years which is often lacking. This is, of course, not always the case, but in the world of statistics, it often comes out in the prison wash.

In today's news, Britney Spears is coming to light with the abuse at the core of her child rock star upbringing. We will see what comes to light there, but it is likely what some of us already know all-too-well: the MK-Ultra programming that the Lookout Canyon facility specialized in, as well as some form of ritualized sexual abuse, no doubt, because the two often go hand in hand. A rock star lives a hard life, from the constant performance perspective. A several hour show every other night for weeks or months on end can be phenomenally exhausting. It's no surprise that many rock stars turn to drugs for artificial energy, but some have also been psychologically manipulated in their youth, by what are known as altar personalities, which come into play when someone is traumatized in such a way that their psyche fragments-- and then those fragments can subsequently be programmed.

An exhausted performer can be switched (by trigger words from a handler) to a more refreshed alter personality. Many well known performers and rock stars have named their alter personalities, such as Beyonce and her Sasha Fierce. Fragmented personalities have been used historically from everything from sex slaves, to assassins, to celebrity performers best characterized by rock stars like Lady Gaga or Eminem. The Nazi's perfected this mind control technique in WW2 and named it MK-Ultra. Some of those very 'scientists' were then secretly folded into US intelligence operations like the CIA after the war, in what was called Operation Paperclip.

All of this is to illustrate how these "Stars" were created and co-opted from the start as either witting or unwitting agents by the very "Man" the generally clueless public thought they were somehow fighting against. This also includes the original Hippies, who also first came out of Laurel Canyon, not Haight-Ashbury. The bands those nascent rock star military brats came from were not initially greatly skilled. From a recording perspective, much of their sound was created by the Wrecking Crew, a group of studio musicians who played on most of their albums. Therefore, when these bands (such as The Byrds) played, they were at first not very good live, and the attraction was more oriented towards the Hippies, who were known for their acid-inspired, highly sexualized dances which compelled the crowds more so than the music itself. These early LA music scene Hippies, later called Flower Children up north, were composed mostly of young women, amongst which today's Miley Cyrus, Britney Spears and Beyonce would be well at home.

"They thought we would follow the stars" is a phrase used by a certain counter intelligence operation to the mainstream media. It refers in part to the 2016 US Presidential election, in which the rock stars and celebrities came out en masse to decry the candidacy of Donald Trump. These celebrities knew who made them and who buttered their bread. They were not about to bite the hand that gave them their celebrity, or pull back the curtain on the Wizard of OZ, to reveal him for what he actually is: a sad old schmuck whose powers come almost entirely from deceptive technology and not from any noble inherent values.

When Trump won the 2016 election (which was also rigged against him) it was an absolute affront to the powers that be which created the system which created the celebrities of yesteryear and today. Those powers and the media personalities they control, with something as trite as a paycheck and the faint glow of public worship, reacted with an unbridled rage that extended from November 9th, 2016 until this very day. One would think that now that they have "won" with the ludicrous puppet Joe Biden they would go back to normal behind their green curtains, but the fact is, they know something that most of the general public, who follow the media for their day-to-day guidance and enlightenment on current affairs, don't know: that the battle being fought for control is not over yet. And the results of the stolen 2020 election are not written in stone.

In order to Drain the Swamp, the Swamp needs to be caught in the kind of generational crime that transcends any one administration. The Covid-Election Steal one-two punch is just that kind of crime. It is interesting how many left-leaning folks from back in the day were devout believers in JFK, but later came to hate Donald Trump, because some bought-and-paid-for media actors told them to. And because the Left, supposedly the anti-war and anti-corporate corruption folks, told them to. The reality is, JFK and Donald Trump have the exact same goals: the elimination of the central banks and the dissolution of the crooked intelligence agencies like the CIA, who are in effect the secret police of the central banks.

The golden rule is that he who controls the gold controls the rules. And yet, by the grace of God, it is gold that will destroy the Federal Reserve, when a gold-backed currency is instituted by the US Treasury in a Quantum Financial System.

If we had a Quantum Voting System, the 2020 fraud never could have happened. However, it is my point of view, and that of many others, that the 2020 fraud was allowed to take place. Without such a titanic crime (and the Titanic was sunk to take out the few bankers opposed to the institution of the Fed) then the Swamp could never be drained. To only partially drain it would be of little value, since it would only grow back stronger and more swampy.

This great story, the Greatest Political Story Ever Told, is not over yet, not by a long shot, as we enter the chapter known as the Forensic Audit. However, this discussion has been about our rock stars, celebrated for their creativity, and often rightly so, but unfortunately so often co-opted before they could be the revolutionary agents of positive change they proclaimed themselves to be in the 60's.

While they may have been slightly mocking Jesus Christ in the musical Jesus Christ Superstar, the dime store version of Jesus Christ we see in Hollywood celebrity rock stars will never match the original. Just like counterfeit money can pass muster long enough to spend for a while, it's creators and suppliers and those that try to palm it off, often end up not in palaces but in prisons, where they in truth belong, and not amongst those they so criminally deceived and sought to make fools and beggars of.

I appreciate the craft that goes into creating an artificial world. Those worlds can be instructive as far as storytelling goes, but when it comes to guidance I will always look to that which endures and not that which falls away when it's worth is revealed as mere fool's gold and not the real thing.

And so, Hollywood and it's parent company, the Media itself, can have it's rock stars and celebrities and their bought-off opinions on important matters of the day. While some of them are good people duped by the wiles of the Green Wizard, I will stick to the original in whose shadow they merely strut briefly upon the stage.

"Now when Jesus saw the crowds, he went up on a mountainside and sat down. His disciples came to him, and he began to teach them.

He said:

Blessed are the poor in spirit,
   for theirs is the kingdom of heaven.
Blessed are those who mourn,
   for they will be comforted.
Blessed are the meek,
   for they will inherit the earth.
Blessed are those who hunger and thirst for righteousness,
   for they will be filled.
Blessed are the merciful,
   for they will be shown mercy.
Blessed are the pure in heart,
   for they will see God.
Blessed are the peacemakers,
   for they will be called children of God.
Blessed are those who are persecuted because of righteousness,
   for theirs is the kingdom of heaven.

Blessed are you when people insult you, persecute you and falsely say all kinds of evil against you because of me. Rejoice and be glad, because great is your reward in heaven, for in the same way they persecuted the prophets who were before you.

You are the salt of the earth. But if the salt loses its saltiness, how can it be made salty again? It is no longer good for anything, except to be thrown out and trampled underfoot.

You are the light of the world. A town built on a hill cannot be hidden. Neither do people light a lamp and put it under a bowl. Instead they put it on its stand, and it gives light to everyone in the house. In the same way, let your light shine before others, that they may see your good deeds and glorify your Father in heaven.

Do not think that I have come to abolish the Law or the Prophets; I have not come to abolish them but to fulfill them. For truly I tell you, until heaven and earth disappear, not the smallest letter, not the least stroke of a pen, will by any means disappear from the Law until everything is accomplished."

17. TREASURES IN HEAVEN

As we collectively traverse this foggy hall of mirrors between the old world and the new, many may find this current limbo state confusing or dispiriting. With all that is happening behind the scenes, the main stage of our culture resembles an absurdist drama recycled from scraps of film left on the cutting room floor of a once-popular TV series.

But the juice that made that show hum just isn't there anymore. However, nothing has replaced the old series yet. And most of the audience don't know that backroom deals have been made to cancel the entire production.

Another impeachment charade has now come and gone. Supposedly, President Trump isn't the President anymore, yet they tried to impeach him again, because even when he is "gone" he is still the only game in town.

And while certain among us have long been advised to Enjoy the Show, much of the general public still thinks the kabuki theatre masquerading as reality is the straight dope of the new normal.

In the meantime, a Mission Impossible rubber mask version of 'Joe Biden' is podcasting his 'presidency' out of the Castle Rock White House set, DC is surrounded by barbed wire fencing & deputized US Marshal National Guards, and the Corona virus scamdemic continues to stagger ever onward, even though world death rates have gone up exactly 0% since this supposedly deadly manufactured disease first began to ravage the Earth.

Yes, it's true, we are all living in a B-movie right now.

But think about it, Star Wars and The Matrix are basically B-movies expanded by impressive scale into blockbuster epics. And respectively, those movies are about a Rebel Alliance that tapped into their connection to divinity (the Force) and defeated an Evil Empire bent on galactic tyranny; and a Rebel group seeking to free an enslaved populace which has been turned into human livestock by a machine consciousness artificial intelligence. And how does this second group also defeat their captors? By awakening to their own divinity within the illusion of a controlled Matrix.

"You are the One, Neo."

The theme of these B-movies and the B-movie we are currently incarnated within are one in the same. Awakening to the Divine Source within each and every one of us. Since the One Source at the root of all Life created us, there is no door locked which we cannot unlock, should we sincerely seek the key to unlock it. The key is Unity Consciousness and the Law of One. That is why it is called 'the Great Awakening' and also why 'It's Gonna Be Biblical.' Exactly what was Christ teaching the people of his day?

"Truly, truly, I say to you, the one believing in Me, the works that I do, also he will do. And he will do greater than these..."

Christ did not incarnate to be worshipped as an individual, but to plant a seed of being that would blossom in future generations as Christ Consciousness or Unity Consciousness. He also conquered the two greatest fears of humanity: the fear of a painful, torturous death and the fear that death itself is the permanent end of the individual.

While it is true that death is the end of the temporal ego associated with that particular incarnated individual, Jesus Christ through his death and resurrection demonstrated that by trusting and aligning with the Source of Life itself, the incarnated individual can transcend these two debilitating human fears and enter the glory of life everlasting.

These two fears are important because we have historically been ruled and imprisoned by them. After all, what else can you really threaten someone with other than physical pain or the specter of non-existence via the death of their body? One might suggest the concept of Hell, which has worked for various churches, and that would be accurate to the extent that the concept itself was the threat and not the actual reality of it. Because indeed, we have all experienced Hell already. It is the experience of disconnection from the Source, disconnection from the very Unity Consciousness the heroes of the aforementioned B-movies were seeking to awaken to, in order to free themselves from the tyranny of their persecutors.

You will note that in both movies, it was a machine intelligence or the worship of a deadly machine (the Death Star) which was the counterpoint to the awakening consciousness. The Luciferian Ideal has ever been to create a counterfeit kingdom or an artificial immortality. But since their plans are not in alliance with the Source, they don't have the actual energy to subsist indefinitely in this manner. Therefore, they need an organic energy source to provide the juice for their machine world to continue.

Enter humanity. The Luciferian dilemma is that the source of their energy is the self-same consciousness which can overthrow them should it awaken in full. That is why, in the Georgia Guidestone sense, and the Gates Vaccine Population Control sense, they seek to limit our numbers, while still keeping enough of us around to fuel their sick fantasy world.

Metaphorically (and in some Chuck Schumer cases literally) the people in the Swamps of DC politics are the same Pharisees and Sadducees who contended with Jesus Christ in Biblical times. Today, in modern times, they've tried to assassinate our President Donald J. Trump, both in character and in body. Back then, they did not accept the power of Christ's message of Unity Consciousness. They wanted to maintain their selfish positions on the hierarchy of temporal and vainglorious worldly power.

It is the same today in DC and Hollywood. These people have sacrificed their integrity for the illusion of "specialness" in the world of rule-by-separation and division. When that world is gone, they are gone with it.

They could have listened to Christ and conquered death and the fear of mortality. Instead, they chose to do battle with Him, and by extension with the Source of Life itself.

"These People Are Stupid" means they have chosen an unwinnable battle against an undefeatable Power. The very Power and Energy of existence itself.

It calls to mind the Norm MacDonald joke about Germany going to war with the World:

"In the early part of the previous century, Germany decided to go to war. And who did they go to war with? The World. That had never been tried before. And so you figure that would take about 5 seconds for the World to win, but no, it was actually close."

And that is where we are at this very hour. The Luciferians have chosen as their opponent God, or the Source. They have gone to war with this Source, and at the moment, it looks like it's actually close. Or even that they've won.

After all, look what they've gotten away with. The satanic torture and murder of children in their occult sacrifices. All of the many banker-constructed world wars, including the horror of the second world war-- a gigantic occult sacrifice of humanity in a very real sense. By their actions they were stating: if we can get away with this, there is no God.

It may appear that way from a limited perspective, but what have these Luciferians really won? Have they conquered death and mortality by the Way of Christ or simply dug themselves a deeper Pit? Have they in actuality created their own Black Mirror Hell which they must now experience for themselves?

Yes, they have.

Archbishop Vigano stated that the 2020 election drama was a battle between the Children of Light and the Children of Darkness.

Those who would follow the path demonstrated by Christ-- who illuminated the concept that we treat our neighbors as both ourselves and God because they are One in the same-- are the Children of Light. Those that would follow the Luciferian path of separation consciousness must tread the path of mortal fear, seeking a false machine immortality by way of the subjugation of the illusory other. And who is this illusory other?

It is the Self.

The Luciferians in this election fraud are trying to buy themselves time in a historical world that is no longer there. They are trying to build additions onto their own prisons, which are crumbling to dust before their eyes.

They are going to end up back in the sands of Israel, with the words of Christ echoing once again through their very souls:

"Do not store up for yourselves treasures on earth, where moths and vermin destroy, and where thieves break in and steal. But store up for yourselves treasures in heaven, where moths and vermin do not destroy, and where thieves do not break in and steal. For where your treasure is, there your heart will be also.

The eye is the lamp of the body. If your eyes are healthy, your whole body will be full of light. But if your eyes are unhealthy, your whole body will be full of darkness. If then the light within you is darkness, how great is that darkness!

No one can serve two masters. Either you will hate the one and love the other, or you will be devoted to the one and despise the other. You cannot serve both God and money.

Therefore I tell you, do not worry about your life, what you will eat or drink; or about your body, what you will wear. Is not life more than food, and the body more than clothes?

Look at the birds of the air; they do not sow or reap or store away in barns, and yet your heavenly Father feeds them. Are you not much more valuable than they? Can any one of you by worrying add a single hour to your life?

And why do you worry about clothes? See how the flowers of the field grow. They do not labor or spin. Yet I tell you that not even Solomon in all his splendor was dressed like one of these. If that is how God clothes the grass of the field, which is here today and tomorrow is thrown into the fire, will he not much more clothe you—you of little faith?

So do not worry, saying, 'What shall we eat?' or 'What shall we drink?' or 'What shall we wear?' For the pagans run after all these things, and your heavenly Father knows that you need them. But seek first His kingdom and His righteousness, and all these things will be given to you as well."

Those that would seek to imprison humanity for their own ends will soon experience the hell of their own conceptions and their own separation consciousness. It will not last forever, because God does not imprison aspects of Itself forever, even those that might war against the Unified Source. However, to those individuals involved, the hell of the realization of what they have done will feel like forever, for however long it lasts.

To the rest of us, those that sincerely fought for the Good (which is God) and supported the Alliance in the battle to free humanity from the tyrannical Matrix of the Old World Order, know this:

Every B-Movie blockbuster has a dramatic and redeeming conclusion-- but only after the Hero has experienced the All is Lost moment.

Since Jan. 20th, 2021, Trump supporters the world over have experienced the 'All is Lost' moment. And the Old World Order has exhausted us with its endless repeats and re-runs of shows that weren't even that good to begin with.

But it has also forced us to go within and to not put our faith in anything outside of God, the true Author of this meta-historical moment.

We have been given the map for this time-- both in the Bible and in the Q posts.

Future Proves Past. Where we go ONE, we go All.

If you go within, you will find the doors of the prison have already been opened. The Old Guard is no longer. The once invincible Death Star is just intergalactic dust particles now. Or, are those particles actually a wave?

They are indeed a wave, and one we can ride to another shore of history.

They once believed they could use us as an energy source, kept hidden from the Source of Life itself. But now we will ride the energy wave that comes from the fall of their illusory prison planet-- to the real planet, which is Awakened Gaia and Awakened Humanity. You can call it the 5th dimension if you like, but it is really the world Jesus Christ was showing us the Way toward. He walked a path on Earth two millennia ago so we could follow in his footsteps today.

Juan O Savin stated that the country (and world) was going to go through a near death experience in this election drama. The chief aspect of a near death experience (NDE) is the realization that at the end of any darkness or death experience all is yet truly well, because we are ever safe in the Unity of God. And moreover, we are loved by this Unity for the very individuality we were created to express and to be.

If we simply follow the Golden Rule of Christ regarding our neighbor, we can never go wrong in this or any incarnation.

So, have no fear about President Trump's return. The Biden camp has built their foundation on shifting sand and dust.

The Trump Alliance has built their foundation on the covenant the founding fathers had with The Founding Father: God Almighty.

By their own choices, those that oppose God's Will have already lost.

We may find ourselves seeking dates and time frames while we are yet still in the story, but I will suggest to all that this great drama will move by the seasons.

The Dark Winter they had planned for will be defeated by the Spring. And the glory of the rebirth of this coming Spring will be the rebirth of this Nation.

One Nation Under God. And it will be a rebirth for all Humanity.

"Then, this is a Day of Independence, for all of the munchkins and their descendants. So, wake up you sleepy head, rub your eyes, get out of bed. Ding Dong the Wicked Witch is Dead!"

We are going to show you a new world.

Those who are blind will soon see the light.

A beautiful brave new world lies ahead.

We take this journey together.

One step at a time.

WWG1WGA!

Q

Excerpt from the 'Angel of Liberty' Vision of George Washington:

"Again, amid the fearful noise of the conflict, I heard the mysterious voice saying, 'Son of the Republic, look and learn.' As the voice ceased, the shadowy angel for the last time dipped water from the ocean and sprinkled it upon America. Instantly, the dark cloud rolled back, together with the armies it had brought, leaving the inhabitants of the land victorious!

Then, once more I beheld the villages, towns and cities springing up where I had seen them before, while the bright angel, planting the azure standard he had brought in the midst of them, cried with a loud voice:

'While the stars remain, and the heavens send down dew upon the earth, so long shall the Union last.' And taking from his brow the crown on which blazoned the word 'Union,' he placed it upon the Standard while the people, kneeling down, said, 'Amen.'

The scene instantly began to fade and dissolve, and I at last saw nothing but the rising, curling vapor I at first beheld. This also disappearing, I found myself once more gazing upon the mysterious visitor, who, in the same voice I had heard before, said:

'Son of the Republic, what you have seen is thus interpreted: Three great perils will come upon the Republic. The most fearful is the third, but in this greatest conflict the whole world united shall not prevail against her. Let every child of the Republic learn to live for his God, his land and the Union.'

With these words the vision vanished, and I started from my seat and felt that I had seen a vision wherein had been shown to me the birth, progress, and destiny of the United States."

Enjoy the Show.

No B-Movie lasts forever.

The Best is Yet to Come.

18. THERE FROM HERE

One of the primary characteristics of the meta-historical moment we are all in, particularly in what might be called the Truther community, is a certain persistent feeling, which emerges within as a nagging question of the mind and soul:

Exactly how do we bring this collectively imagined new reality, which we feel is a civilizational imperative, into the day-to-day lived experience of our world? Are we just kidding ourselves that any of this is real? Maybe we are simply the new version of the hippies (but right wing this time) who think we're going to change the entire world with our wishful magical thinking--while the establishment world only digs deeper and deeper into the prison constructs it specializes in.

Where the hell are we really right here and now?

It may seem to some that we're out on a precipice, trying to build scaffolds into some bizarro science fiction territory, which recedes from us every time it seems within reach, like the finish line for an ultra-marathoner, that disappears right before they're about to break the tape, leaving them alone in the woods, wondering if they were ever even in an organized race to begin with.

I have described this situation before as the foggy hall of mirrors. Many are questioning what is real and what is fiction. Our world is cooperating beautifully with this step in the Hero's Journey, giving us layered absurdities in the political sphere, such that it is perfectly reasonable to wonder whether some of the supposedly most important and powerful figures in the United States government (like the current "president") are actually actors wearing elaborate rubber masks. Can you imagine any other era in history when vast numbers of people all across the globe could seriously question whether the 'leader of the free world' is either a clone, CGI, or some actor in a rubber mask operating the 'White House' out of a Hollywood set?

The mere fact that this question is being asked should assuage any concerns about whether or not we are in science fiction territory already. Phillip K. Dick would have balked at such a plot point in this post election drama as too over the top. And while we're at it, could someone please straighten out Joe Biden's nose so that we can follow it properly? The 'masked president' has wandered off the pages of history into blank white page territory, where nothing has been written.

We can't rely anymore on the "it is written" certainty of some of the age-old words of organized religion because we have collectively leapt out of the bindings of those books and landed on a blank parchment that extends infinitely in all directions.

Have all of our historic touchstones deserted us right when we needed them the most?

Not necessarily, if you know the Author behind all authors. We are indeed creating a new world, a new age, but in order to do so we must zero out our boards, so that what we create is not limited by the fears of the previous ages. The Luciferian order requires us to live in a world of fear so that they can control us like cattle by this very fear. And you know what happens to cattle-- they end up on the dinner plate.

Yet, what is there really to be afraid of? It should not be death because that is built into the structure of life. And in truth, our birth is actually more of a death experience, and our death is more of a birth experience. Birth creates limits and borders around our spirit so that we can incarnate as a body and enter a particular storyline-- while death releases us from these borders so that we can be our unlimited and unified selves once again.

Incarnating is something we want to do. We choose it as both a service to the God that created us out of the only material that exists, Itself, as well as because we enjoy these stories in time like nothing else. It is the Art of

Creation, the Art of the Deal, if you will-- the very essence of creativity and joy made manifest. In that respect, even a bad story is a good story, if you can understand that essential conceit.

Imagine it like this. In the movie Total Recall, the Arnold character decides he wants the recall experience and he selects the details of the 'vacation' he intends to enter once he signs up and sits down in the recall chair. No matter what 'happens' to him in this imagined experience, no matter how real it seems at the time, he is always safe back in the office. The game he plays within the recall construct is not real in the way he thinks it is at the time, nor is the avatar he inhabits. However, what is real is that he is having an experience.

To extend this metaphor, our recall character is also connected to other players having the same kind of experience. We populate each other's games. Again, the only thing 'real' is the individual and shared experiences. Everything beyond this is completely imaginary. We are all safe in the office chair the whole time.

We are these recall characters and we are all safe in God's Office, no matter what happens in this particular game. That does not mean that nothing matters and we can operate from the Luciferian "Do What Thou Wilt is the Whole of the Law" modus operandi. We are sharing this game with other players and while they may be safe from a spiritual perspective, we do not want to give them hurtful or painful experiences while they are active in the game. Because what we give them, in a roundabout way, we will ultimately give ourselves, since we are intrinsically connected to each other.

Where We Go One, We Go All. You might have heard this before.

So, back to the new world we are seeking to create together within this game. Our creative abilities are limited by our ignorance or our fear, with fear being the more powerful of the two. The Luciferians know this. They are, in a sense, inside the matrix of the game, looking to control it and us from within. There is a genius to their dark methods. They see the ones and the zeros of the matrix and they want us to be a zero. However, in truth, we are actually the One.

The One that created us has no limitations, but more importantly, the One has no fear. It has no fear because it exists eternally and there is nothing to contend with it, beyond Itself. So, if you ever find yourselves in fear, tune into the One which is your Source, beyond all worlds and words. Nothing can ultimately harm or extinguish your being. You are safe. The only thing you can have is a bad experience, a painful experience, if you will, but it is only temporary, within an ultimately imaginary game.

That which is real is eternal. If something is not eternal, it is an illusion. The temporal world is an illusion. Our characters in this world are also an illusion, because they are also temporary. That is okay. In fact, it is great, because none of us would wish to play one character endlessly forever. We might want it to last longer than it does at times, but remember that birth is really death and death is really birth. It is a good thing that we don't linger too long in these illusory worlds, however precious they are. They will always be here when we get back, because they aren't really here. Not in the way we think they are.

But back to our current meta-historical moment. What does it mean that we find ourselves battling these seemingly entrenched dark forces, while attempting to create this new "5D" world, this Golden Age of our deepest desires? Are the Luciferians even real? And what about the things they are doing and have done to children? What about the banking system they have caged us in within? What about all of their control methods? The pharmaceuticals, the chemtrails, the media brainwashing, etc, etc, etc? Is any of it really real?

The Luciferians are as real as we are within this game. And their methodologies are as real as anything else here as far as that goes. They want to maintain their counterfeit kingdom and extend the game indefinitely within a single life, so that they never exit the total recall matrix. They have their own fears, which are what you might expect, that there will be karmic retribution for what they have done. They are essentially right about that. They will have to experience the selfsame experience they subjected the illusory 'others' to. The darkness they have created for the other they will experience themselves, because indeed, there is no other.

There is only One of us here.

We all play by the same rules, it is simply a matter of the degree of perception. What makes the Luciferians so dark are the extremes to which they have taken their internal sickness. But we have all in our own ways touched on similar thematics. Have you ever tried to control someone, someone you perhaps felt was weaker or lesser than you? If, for example, you saw a homeless person, wretched in their circumstances, and beside them was a rich businessman or famous celebrity or what-have-you, and if for even a moment you felt that the celebrity was somehow intrinsically better or more 'important' than the person lying in filth with nothing but the clothes on their backs, then it is truly only a matter of exaggerated degrees before you get to the state of mind that drives the Luciferians. They think they are "better than." They live the "better than" perspective within this game, taken to psychopathic extremes.

But what makes someone better than someone else? Is it because they have something to give you? Is it because they have something you want?

No one is more important than anyone else in this world because these 'things' people think they have, they don't really 'have' in the sense that they can keep them for any significant period of time. The moment you think you actually have something it is already leaving you with a quickness.

"Do not wear yourself out to get rich; do not trust your own cleverness. Cast but a glance at riches, and they are gone, for they will surely sprout wings and fly off to the sky like an eagle."

The most precious jewels of this world are the jewels of experience. A shared moment of joyous laughter between friends is more valuable than a mansion. At the end of Citizen Kane the rich man was living in a mansion that was more like a tomb, and what he longed for more than anything was an experience of joy from childhood. His great mansion and all of his possessions were then of no comfort to him.

When this lifetime is leaving you like quicksilver, will you reach out to carry your mansion of possessions with you? Surely, you cannot. But the laughter you shared in a moment with a friend does contain dimensions of the eternal within it. That you can bring with you.

Thus, the riches of this world are experiences and not tangible items. And where those experiences are shared with others in good spirits, in benevolent spirits, those experiences are riches beyond the spoils of a thousand kingdoms.

To look into the eyes of another and see the innocent child there, and to wish them well from the deepest aspect of your being, that is a gold that ten thousand of Solomon's mines could not reckon with.

We are seeking to create a world within this imaginary game experience with foundations built on these precepts. We don't have to be in fear of whether we will accomplish it or not. The very fact that we are collectively intending it is already of inestimable value. We should also know that we have God's good will backing us in this sacred quest. However, God is not going to come into the game and do it all for us. What would be the value in that? There would be no true experience, no great movie story worth telling, if a Deus ex Machina drove the entire production.

Do you think God is afraid of what Joe Biden or Kamala Harris, or their Luciferian puppet masters are going to do next? That is a cosmic joke to consider for even a moment it could be the case. If God isn't worried in the slightest about the outcome of this political story, why should you be?

Our task within the game (and we are at a superlative level of this game, one where we can leap from one format to another-- from Pac-Man to an interactive virtual reality game) is to, on a personal level, bring unity-game dynamics into our own lived experience, so that this new version of the game can then flourish at large. We have all of the zeros and ones we need to create this. No material, conceptual or otherwise, are we lacking.

The blueprints and templates are already here. Other civilizations, both on Earth in the pre-historical ancient civilizations which make up our myths, as well as out in the cosmos at large, have already experienced this transition point. This zero point, if you will. There is nothing 'impossible' about it at all. There are precedents for it already.

We can start by not being afraid that it won't happen. Remember, we don't take the furniture of this game with us when we leave, we only take the experiences. And we also return again and again within many different contexts and personalities.

All that we are really looking to do is collectively rearrange the furniture of this world. To make it something we enjoy living in right now. The old set-up is far too uncomfortable, for many reasons. The Feng Shui is off and the lay-out resembles too much a prison for who we have become, when it could look like, and more importantly feel like, a beautiful loving home.

Home is where the heart is.

Do not ever forget that you are a beautiful free spirit. Nothing can ever bind you for any substantial period of time. There was and is only one material out of which to create beings such as yourself-- and that is the Being of the One Living God. If you were created out of this God's very Being, this God without fear and without beginning or end, do you really think that there is anything that could ever truly go wrong?

Are you actually afraid of some comic book "president" in a metaphoric rubber mask and his cackling witchy sidekick? Do you think they are going to tie you down and inject you with some vaccine that is going to turn you into a robot-slave and there's nothing at all you can do about it?

The test here is not about what the world is going to do to you which you have no power over, but rather how much power over your reality you believe (be and live) you actually truly have.

In this game it is a very real truth that you create your own reality. There is also a larger collective game reality also going on, and you chose that particular one yourself, just like the Arnold character chose that he wanted go on a trip to Mars.

You chose to be here in this particular epoch-shifting time when humanity awakens to its own divinity within a version of the game, and then creates an entirely new world construct. This is a special time and one which other beings in the cosmos have gathered around to see just how we play it all out. Many of them have experienced the same transition, but each time it is different. They want to see what we do and how we do it. It's the best movie imaginable, and to the extent they can help without interfering with our free will, they will. The popcorn and jujubes are being passed around. The theme music is swelling. What will our intrepid incarnated gaming heroes do now?

As far as the Luciferians go, they play an important role in the journey of the Hero with a Thousand Faces. We contend with these gatekeeper forces as we cross thresholds. What indeed will challenge us to the core to embrace our own indestructible divinity, if not these principalities with the fearsome masks?

These are the steps of the Hero's Journey:

Step 1: The Ordinary World
Step 2: The Call to Adventure
Step 3: Cross the First Threshold
Step 4: Trials, Friends, and Foes
Step 5: Magical Mentor (or the Mentor with Supernatural Aid)
Step 6: Dragon's Lair
Step 7: Moment of Despair
Step 8: Ultimate Treasure
Step 9: Homeward Bound
Step 10: Rebirth & The Champion's Return

You can best answer for yourself what stage you find yourself in. As a collective, making the journey from the old world to the new, I would suggest that we are transiting Step 7. When you remember that we all carry the One within us, you can put that in front of this number 7, and you will get our trusty number 17, which is a guide for this time.

Step 7: Moment of Despair

"No worthwhile adventure is easy. There are many perils on the path to growth, discovery, and self-realization. A major obstacle confronts the hero, and the future begins to look dim: a trap, a mental imprisonment, or imminent defeat on the battlefield. It seems like the adventure will come to a sad conclusion, as all hope appears lost. But hope remains and it is in these moments of despair when the hero must access a hidden part of himself—one more micron of energy, strength, faith, or creativity to find his way out of the belly of the beast. The hero must call on an inner power he doesn't know he possesses."

The other guide beyond #17 is the teaching of Jesus Christ in the Bible. While we know that the Bible has been edited throughout the ages, we should also bear in mind that the words of Christ had such power that they transcended the meddling hands of the controllers within the matrix. When the Bible relays the words and teachings of Christ, they are not merely ordinary words on paper, they are Living Words. The energy of the message is alive within the text and transcends time and space. It is no accident the Bible is the most available book on Earth. You have not been abandoned within this game or during this great transition moment.

You must cultivate the understanding that you have everything you need for the extravagant journey that is your life.

Truly you want for nothing. You do not need to go chasing after your fellow man or woman like beggars for what they might give you. The value in this world is not what we can take from it and from another, but what we can give from the generosity of our own hearts.

We draw from eternal wells that never run dry, so be not stingy with the treasures of your heart.

What you give to others you give to both God and yourself.

God already "has" the Unity of its own Eternal Source. If God "wants" for anything, it is that the individuals He has created and the game world of the temporal universe they inhabit, know themselves, as they are in turn known by Him.

"For now we see through a mirror, darkly; but then face to face: now I know in part; but then shall I know even as also I am known."

So, wake up you sleepyhead, rub your eyes, get out of bed. You have nothing to fear about the world you are in. No one has power over you beyond what you give them.

But what about President Trump? Will he come back? If so, when? I want an exact date, so that I can say: see, it didn't happen on that date. Nothing is happening.

The issue at hand is not about a particular president, but about your fearful and questioning mind, which believes an imaginary world has more power over you than your own imagination.

Are you still the Pac-Man munching up dots, fleeing blinking robot monsters, or are you the hand on the joystick with a pocketful of quarters?

President Trump will indeed return. In fact, he has never left, to the extent that God in His/Her infinite wisdom has already given the Donald a Winter White House that is far better than the one he left in January.

The Spring of a new age will soon be with us.

Are your eyes bright and shining about the beauty and creativity YOU bring to this game, no matter the circumstance?

"Awake.

Shake dreams from your hair
My pretty child, my sweet one.
Choose the day
And choose the sign of your day,
The day's divinity.
First thing you see."

An American Prayer - James Douglas Morrison

We are all awakening within the game. Some sooner than others. Help your slumbering neighbor clear the cobwebs where you can, but don't get hung up on their interpretations of events. You alone decide how to interpret these things.

You create your own path.

In moments of doubt, remember that Christ walked before you and you can do all things through Christ, who strengthens you.

You have nothing to fear. Nothing of eternal significance can ever be taken from you. Give what little you have in this world and more will return to you, by and by.

But how do we get to there from here, to this new world we seek to inhabit? How do we bring the future world into our present one?

Future Proves Past.

You were given a quantum digital map brought to you by the number 17. And you also have the original route, written in parchment two millennia ago for a time such as this.

"Then I saw a new heaven and a new earth, for the first heaven and the first earth had passed away, and the sea was no more. And I saw the holy city, new Jerusalem, coming down out of heaven from God, prepared as a bride adorned for her husband. And I heard a loud voice from the throne saying, 'Behold, the dwelling place of God is with man. He will dwell with them, and they will be his people, and God himself will be with them as their God. He will wipe away every tear from their eyes, and death shall be no more, neither shall there be mourning, nor crying, nor pain anymore, for the former things have passed away.'

And he who was seated on the throne said, 'Behold, I am making all things new.' Also he said, 'Write this down, for these words are trustworthy and true.' And he said to me, 'It is done! I am the Alpha and the Omega, the beginning and the end. To the thirsty I will give from the spring of the water of life without payment. The one who conquers will have this heritage, and I will be his God and he will be my son. But as for the cowardly, the faithless, the detestable, as for murderers, the sexually immoral, sorcerers, idolaters, and all liars, their portion will be in the lake that burns with fire and sulfur, which is the second death.'

And I saw no temple in the city, for its temple is the Lord God the Almighty and the Lamb. And the city has no need of sun or moon to shine on it, for the glory of God gives it light, and its lamp is the Lamb. By its light will the nations walk, and the kings of the earth will bring their glory into it, and its gates will never be shut by day—and there will be no night there. They will bring into it the glory and the honor of the nations. But nothing unclean will ever enter it, nor anyone who does what is detestable or false, but only those who are written in the Lamb's book of life."

As far as the details of how we will construct this new world within the scaffolding of the old, do not worry yourself about the details, but rather embrace the sheer creativity and adventure of it. If we knew exactly how, we would not be in the game, enjoying each brush stroke as it swirls onto the canvas in living color.

An Artist does not love the experience of creating his or her artwork because he or she knows exactly what the finished piece will be beforehand. True, there's an idea and conception initially, a mental blueprint if you will, but the real enjoyment is in the wonder how the masterpiece will unfold. What will it be? The best art is better than the artist himself first conceived it. And with great works of art, the materials themselves communicate directly with the artist herself. The materials have their own ideas about what they would most like to be. You can awaken these materials, these paints, by validating their existence and their experience. And they in turn will tell you what they wish to become.

The materials are everywhere before us in our world. They are planted like Easter Eggs from God. Within these materials are the blueprint of the best version of this civilization. In a very real way, it is already here if you have the wherewithal to follow through with the painting in front of you.

The Trump Alliance, your fellow Patriots and Truthers, they are all here with you and part of the process. But if someone simply handed you a finished framed painting, even if it was an absolute masterpiece, they would be depriving you of something essential, something intrinsic to why you are here in the first place.

Paint boldly on the canvas of your life. When we put all of the paintings together, then we will have this new age. The Luciferians are dark colors within the palette, necessary in their own way, but by no means the dominant shade.

As far as the little children go, their freedom to create without one of these dark hands steering their brush, is the primary concern of those angels who are here to aid in the liberation of humanity within this game. But also know that everyone at a higher level chooses their own role within each lifetime for their own purposes of both learning and teaching. Do not lower yourself to a belief in victimhood ideologies. God has not victimized Himself in His own creation.

No game lasts forever.

The game you are in now happens to be a very special one. One where quantum changes can be made. The current template is designed for that.

Embrace the gift of this time and know that the Universe supports you in your Hero's Journey and all of your endeavors, especially when they are in service to others. To the best of your ability give to others this magical world that you desire for yourself and you will have it as well. It will start small, on the individual painting level, and it will grow from there to an unimaginable masterpiece.

We take this journey together. One step at a time.

Nothing Can Stop What is Coming.

Not for you, or for anyone.

Thy kingdom come, thy will be done. On Earth as it is in Heaven.

For thine is the kingdom, and the power, and the glory, for ever and ever.

Amen.

19. SHIP OF THESEUS

"The ship wherein Theseus and the youth of Athens returned from Crete had thirty oars, and was preserved by the Athenians down even to the time of Demetrius Phalereus, for they took away the old planks as they decayed, putting in new and stronger timber in their places, insomuch that this ship became a standing example among the philosophers, for the logical question of things that grow; one side holding that the ship remained the same, and the other contending that it was not the same."

— Plutarch, *Theseus*

The Ship of Theseus (also known as the Theseus' paradox) is a thought experiment that raises the question of whether an object that's had all of its components replaced remains the same object. Plutarch asked whether a ship that had been restored by replacing every single wooden part remained the same ship.

The Ship of Theseus was rebuilt over the centuries as its wood rotted. At what point did it stop being the original ship and when did it become something else? Its change was gradual enough that the ship maintained an outward appearance of continuity the entire time. Thus, did the spirit of the ship remain all the while it was in a state of constant transformation?

In many respects, we are all Ships of Theseus, in that every seven years every cell of our bodies has been regenerated and replaced by new cells. In a purely physical sense, you are not the same person you were seven years ago, quite literally.

The changes taking place in the governments of the world and in the systems we have known all of our lives are happening in a Ship of Theseus manner. The new Ship of State is being rebuilt before our eyes, yet we may not notice it because all the changes are occurring while we are still at sea, and in a storm, no less.

Juan O Savin addressed the new quantum financial system, with regard to some of the magical thinking that takes place around this topic, and his response was that we are on an ocean liner steaming ahead in one direction and you do not simply turn a ship this size on a dime. First of all, is not technically possible, and second, if attempted without taking the hard realities of the ship and passengers into account, it could result in a metric mega-ton of damage to all involved.

The cure cannot be worse than the disease.

It is true that the central bank financial system will be replaced, as it is absolutely one of the key chess pieces being fought over, perhaps the main chess piece. You could say the banking cartel and the right to issue money is the King, and the Media, with its hypnotic control over the dissemination of information, is the Queen of the Dark Side's board.

The everyday people of the world are the pawns, but you might also note that it is only the pawn that can transform into another chess piece. Only the pawn, by crossing the entire board, can undergo the alchemy from the weakest piece to the most powerful one, the Queen.

We have seen this play out since the election of 2016, when patriot citizen journalists became the counterpoint to the mainstream media. With that in mind, we must also be aware that these selfsame citizen journalists are also subject to the same pitfalls in their journey across the board as is the Fool on his Journey through the Major Arcana, or an actor who moves to Hollywood to pursue a noble career in the arts. Is it fame and fortune that secretly motivates the Fool or is it the essence of creativity and truth itself? Can this dream be co-opted for a high enough price? Indeed, there can be a fine line between messaging and merchandising, nowadays.

We are all together on this journey, as the world gradually transforms from one era to another. That is the meaning behind Nothing Can Stop What is Coming. The world is energetically changing. It is in the cards, so to speak.

Whether this is characterized as the Earth entering/traversing the Photon Belt, which will bring about inevitable changes regardless of the details of the political battle on the ground, or that we are shifting into the 5th dimension, Ship of Theseus style, or some other metaphor of your choosing, it does not particularly matter. What does matter, is that at the end of this journey, it will be a new ship that docks on another shore. And yet, it will also be the same one, as far as spiritual continuity goes.

It would not do the world or us any good to simply wake up on the other shore of this great change, with no idea of how the ship went from being steered by dark hands, to being steered by enlightened hands. The world needs to learn not only about ship navigation, but how ships themselves are built from the ground up, because We the People are going to need to maintain this Ship of State for subsequent generations. We need to learn the real history of the world, warts and all. Confronting this darkness will not be easy for some, yet that's what this lesson is for.

Infiltration instead of Invasion, is what President John Fitzgerald Kennedy warned us about. By that point (the early 60's) the infiltration was already well advanced. And by some years later (the mid 80's), as detailed by the brilliant KGB defector Yuri Bezmenov, the ideological subversion of America was already in point of fact over-fulfilled.

With this in mind, and understanding the direct links between JFK and President Trump, it should be acknowledged that the election of Donald Trump in 2016 played out as a miracle at the last possible second, with the Ship of United States and its passengers about to go over the waterfall and crash onto the sharpened rocks below-- where it not for what transpired.

However, the Ship of State does not turn on a dime. President Trump and the Alliance had to go into a captured vessel, whose able bodied seamen had been almost universally compromised, and manage to steer that Ship onto an entirely different course, one that doesn't go over the waterfall, but shifts course to another tributary, one that had been dug out by human hands to divert the waterway, not overnight but over many years, knowing in advance that one day the Ship would pass by this very spot and there would be one last (seemingly miraculous) chance to get it onto another, far safer course.

The 2016 election, like many before it, was also rigged by the system in a certain candidate's favor. The Dominion technology is nothing new. If Team Trump was able to overcome that rigging, why some might ask did the same team get defeated by it after Trump was already installed as Commander-in-Chief? Clearly, President Trump and military intelligence saw the election fraud coming a million miles away. With the Covid plan a sloppy kissing cousin to the election fraud.

Was the Trump Alliance, which won a miracle election just a few years prior, outplayed somehow by the Cabal in 2020? Or worse, is there really no Trump Alliance to speak of?

Take a deep breath.

You can rest assured there is indeed an Alliance, working steadily on our collective Ship of Theseus, and Trump is an important part of this work. However, just like our aforementioned citizen journalists, there are many carpenters at work, and at an individual level each one, whether it is a military figure or a media personality or a judge, or anyone with their hand on a hammer-- that individual can always be compromised (or not compromised) based on the strength of their personal integrity.

The Supreme Court is a good example. The Founding Fathers did not make a mistake when they created 3 separate and counterbalancing branches of governance, with Congress, the Executive Office, and the Judicial system.

The last line of defense in the election fraud (beyond whatever the military might do) would be the Supreme Court. And yet, we're talking about only 9 fallible human beings, of which only a handful of need to be compromised by either death threats (to them and their families) or the age old 30 pieces of silver of the careerist's fame and fortune, which has waylaid many a Fool on their Journey through the Major Arcana.

After all, when push comes to shove, how many individuals in the monopoly game system of this world (each one of us included) have the guts of a Christ when presented with the ultimate choice themselves? Many people, in the public eye and otherwise, pay lip service to the Way of Christ. They might even wear the cross medallion (like jewelry) and quote often from scripture. But when confronted with a challenge that may cost them their lives (or careers) the sacred vows they made to defend the

Constitution from All Enemies Foreign and Domestic become now merely the hollow words of hollow individuals. They may have started out with integrity and good intentions, but when they were confronted by the choice of choices, they became all too human, indeed.

Christ was promised his own kingdom by Lucifer. All the fame and fortune of the temporal world could have been His, had He chosen to escape the cross which awaited Him.

"Again, the devil took Him up on an exceedingly high mountain, and showed Him all the kingdoms of the world and their splendor. And he said to Him: All these things I will give You if You will fall down and worship me. Then Jesus said to him: Away with you, Satan! For it is written: You shall worship the Lord your God, and Him only you shall serve."

Of all the nations of this world, only the United States of America has been consecrated by its founding fathers to the Living God, with the Rights of the People as given by the Creator instilled in its cornerstone documents as a sacred trust between God and Mankind. Thus, anyone occupying a key station on this Ship of State, so to speak, has entered into a covenant agreement that is either holy, if they uphold it, or unholy if they betray or reject it. It comes down to the individual and the choice they make.

"Have you made your decision for Christ?"

Alec Baldwin the entertainer has made his decision, along with many other entertainers. They took the thirty pieces, the pirate's pieces of eight, and they received the splendor Lucifer promised, for the time being at least.

Elsewhere in the system, from the media to the military to the courts, individual chess pieces make their moves across the dark and light squares, making their choices within the game. Some players appear more powerful than others, with a greater range of motion and higher win-or-lose stakes, however, remember it is only the seemingly lowly pawn that can make the transformation from one piece to another, from the weakest piece, the expendable piece, to the most powerful piece. And once the enough pawns reach the opposite end of the dark to light board, the game is soon over and checkmate all but inevitable.

From one perspective, it may appear that our world has already been conquered from within. There are compromised and blackmailed agents throughout the entire governmental system, by design. The medical world and big pharma promote disease and stifle the healing technologies which would put an end to their illness-for-profit racket. The financial system creates usury fiat money out of thin air by private interests more powerful than the governments they lend to. And the corporate media is so entrenched in the psyche of the modern individual that they are like unto a hypnotist with a hopelessly brainwashed patient. How can we possibly change this system from within when it is so systematically compromised at every level? Surely, our Ship of Theseus is going over the waterfall into the rocks below. What could possibly stop it now?

Recall once more when Belshazzar and his thousand princes and aides were celebrating their conquest of Babylon by desecrating the sacred relics of the temple; it was then that the legendary writing appeared on the wall, which said, in effect: "Your kingdom is no longer. You have been weighed and found wanting." However, when that occurred, the protective moats of Babylon had been drained by diverting the river, and the soldiers of Cyrus the Great had already surrounded the captured temple operation from within. Of course, no one at the party knew this at the time. Even after the prophet Daniel made the translation of the writing on the wall, even after the revelers had witnessed a miracle before their eyes, they still could have denied that it was all actually happening.

Like Yuri Bezmenov stated, some individuals will never get the message until a military boot is kicking them in their fat bottoms. Only then will they understand the reality of what has occurred.

"Exposure to true information does not matter any more. A person who is demoralized is unable to assess true information. The facts tell nothing to him. Even if I shower him with information, with authentic proof, with documents, with pictures. Even if I take him, by force, to the Soviet Union and show him a concentration camp, he will refuse to believe it until he is going to receive a kick in his fat bottom. When the military boot crashes his balls, then he will understand. But not before that. That is the tragedy of this situation of demoralization."

While I most certainly believe there is an inevitability to the proceedings regarding our political situation and the Destiny of the United States, and that God is involved in the outcome of this story, I do not believe that a

Deus ex Machina moment is going to swoop in and force through the change irrespective of the dynamics of individual choice and freewill. That said, I also feel we are on the precipice of a revival moment that is hinted at, or presaged by the Hebrides Revival on the Isle of Lewis in Scotland some 70 years ago.

This revival was seeded by two old women. One of them was blind and the other bent double by arthritis. Yet, together they had the faith to move mountains. You might say they were two pawns who became Queens. This revival was an occurrence wherein God's presence was felt and witnessed energetically by the people of an area at the same time. It was an undeniable and timeless moment, when the previously hollow words (to many) of the Bible took on a powerful new reality, because the living presence of the Creator was felt directly by everyone-- like a current flowing through an outlet that was formerly unplugged.

One of the most noted prayer-warriors of the Hebrides revival was a 15 year old boy named Donald. Our current (legitimate) President of the United States was named after that very boy by his mother Mary Anne MacLeod Trump-- who was married to the son of Elizabeth Christ Trump. Mary Anne gave her son a Bible that was gifted to her by her aunts, the same two women who were the seeds of this Scottish revival. Donald J. Trump was sworn in on this revival Bible on January 20th, 2017, when he was 70 years, 7 months and 7 days old, in the Hebrew year 5-777.

Do you understand why we say: It's Gonna Be Biblical?

Scotland has its own place in this story. The song 'Scotland the Brave' is similar in spirit to the 'Battle Hymn of the Republic.' Many are aware of the historic import of the Battle of Trenton, where Washington and his troops crossed the Delaware for the first great victory in the American Revolution, however fewer are aware of one of the most important victories, which came many years later when all appeared lost. This was the Battle of King's Mountain. This battle was resoundingly won by the Scotch-Irish Overmountain Men, who declared themselves free men in their own documents 4 years before the Declaration of Independence had been written. The Battle of King's Mountain was the key turning point in the Revolution, won by men who wrote their own freedom documents.

In another respect, this battle for the Soul of a Nation is like the movie

Highlander, where a Scottish immortal named MacLeod (hint hint) arrives in New York City to do battle with another immortal, with the fate of humanity at stake.

The swordsman Ramírez in this movie was played by Sean Connery, whose own real life mother, like Trump, was from the MacLeod clan. Ramirez trains MacLeod to battle for the ultimate prize, on the holy ground of a faraway land, which would end up being New York City.

Donald Trump's name (meaning world ruler) was inspired by a revival prayer-warrior, given to him by a mother surnamed MacLeod, who was given a revival Bible from the two Queens who ushered in the revival. And then he was born in Queens, New York. Donald Trump was sworn in on this revival Bible, following a miraculous election victory in which the entire rigged establishment went all-in against him, and yet he won in the end anyway. Are you enjoying the Story yet?

It is the Greatest Political Story Ever Told.

Let us return to the Highlander. The Connery character, recently from Spain but originally from Egypt, finds MacLeod after tracking his old foe, the Kurgan, to Scotland. He explains that MacLeod, the Kurgan, and others like them, were born immortals and destined to battle each other on holy ground. When only a few are left, they will be drawn to a faraway land for the Gathering and then battle for the ultimate Prize: the power of all the immortals through time. MacLeod only wants a quiet family life, however, Ramírez tells him that immortals must ensure evil people like the Kurgan do not win the Prize, or else humanity will suffer an eternity of darkness. Ramirez then explains the belief of all immortals:

"In the end, there can be only One."

Donald Trump, before he was President, bought land in Scotland which was once in his distant family. The regent of this area was noted for attempting to give power back to the people and was subsequently killed for it. When Donald was in the process of acquiring this land, he enlisted the aid of a fellow MacLeod to help push it through: Sean Connery. Today, it is one of the many properties in key places that Donald Trump the builder owns, such as the magnificent hotel near the old White House.

Cyrus the Great was also a builder. And known for capturing cities by utilizing genius strategies which his enemies did not see coming until it was too late. And so we find ourselves today in this Story, an epic battle for the fate of humanity. The Dark Team has their players, their pawns, knights, bishops, rooks, queens and kings, and the Light Team has theirs. Sometimes, it's hard to tell which team is which, as the pieces can switch allegiances by the choices they make while still on the board.

This battle has been on-going, like the battle of the immortals, for thousands of years, and even longer. However, with the arrival of Christ some two thousand years ago, the game took on a heightened dynamic.

Christ demonstrated something on the black and white chessboard of the world: the alchemy of the human spirit. He demonstrated how a pawn could transform into a Queen, the most powerful piece in play, and the main protector of the King's kingdom.

Christ did not achieve this in order to be worshipped as a famous historical individual, but rather to show the way to redemption in this world, conquering death and mortality by aligning His eternal self with the Will of God. Thy kingdom come, Thy Will be done, on Earth as it is in Heaven.

We are entering a revival moment for the world that will change everything, however the choice to align with it must be made by each individual on their own. The choice cannot be made for them or forced upon them in any way. Even in the Hebrides revival, the town of Stornoway, the very capital of the Isle of Lewis, was completely bypassed. The revival came only to small towns and villages in the Hebrides. The reason for this was that the ministers of the capital opposed the revival.

Sound familiar? The 'ministers' of our nation's capital are opposed to the revival, as well. That should come as no surprise, since many of them work for the other team, as they do in the other places they have staked their occult obelisk-- the City of London and the Vatican City.

There is a reason why demons can be cast out of a body by invoking the name and words of Christ. There is a reason why Christianity, despite the captured operation of the Roman Catholic Church, is despised by the ideological Marxist revolutionaries referred to by Yuri Bezmenov. Any other religion will be protected by the social justice warriors of the culture, but not Christianity.

The reason is that the Way of Christ has ultimate power. And every individual can claim this power. It is inherent in their being. All human rights, like our founding fathers stated, come from the Creator, who made us in His/Her Image. Jesus Christ walked the Earth not only to teach, but to demonstrate the most incredible courage imaginable, when faced with the greatest possible test.

Jesus could have ruled the world of his time and had unimaginable riches and comforts had he accepted the path of Lucifer. Instead, he accepted a torturous death. And it was a death wherein even His faith and connection to the eternal Source momentarily left Him.

"And about the ninth hour Jesus cried with a loud voice, saying, Eli, Eli, lama sabachthani? That is to say, My God, my God, why hast thou forsaken me?"

Of course, we know the end of the Story. The Greatest Story Ever Told. Christ conquered death and hell and was resurrected. He planted a seed that would grow into the Tree of Life.

We all have the same seed in us. We can grow into one of two trees. Sometimes, we grow in one direction, then change our minds and grow in another. And it's never too late to change-- until it is finally too late. In this life, at least.

"No good tree bears bad fruit, nor does a bad tree bear good fruit. Each tree is recognized by its own fruit. People do not pick figs from thornbushes, or grapes from briers. A good man brings good things out of the good stored up in his heart, and an evil man brings evil things out of the evil stored up in his heart. For the mouth speaks what the heart is full of.

Why do you call me, 'Lord, Lord,' and do not do what I say? As for everyone who comes to me and hears my words and puts them into practice, I will show you what they are like. They are like a man building a house, who dug down deep and laid the foundation on rock. When a flood came, the torrent struck that house but could not shake it, because it was well built. But the one who hears my words and does not put them into practice is like a man who built a house on the ground without a foundation. The moment the torrent struck that house, it collapsed and its destruction was complete."

You might ask yourself: Are you simply Waiting for Godot? Waiting for Youtubers and the like, however well meaning, to give you the 'intel' they received from secret 'inside sources' regarding the moves being made behind the scenes. Waiting for the US Military to announce over the Emergency Broadcast System that Donald Trump won the election and is President again? Waiting for the Supreme Court to actually uphold the Justice they took a sacred oath to protect?

We all have our own choice to make. We may be pawns at sea on this Ship of Theseus, but we also have the latent alchemy of the transformed chess piece within us.

The Military has a chain of command, yet it is also as weak as its weakest link, when it comes to the higher ups in this chain of command. Who in charge has the courage of Christ when the fate of the world is on the line? Can and would you do the right thing even if it meant the end of your temporal life? Or the end of the career you worked so hard for?

We can't pawn these decisions off on other people without also reckoning with them within our own hearts and minds. To be a warrior for the Christ Within is our only way out of the labyrinth of history the Cabal has constructed for us. Are we brave enough to do it?

What do you have to lose, as Trump himself once said?

"A warrior is never under siege. To be under siege implies that one has personal possessions that could be blockaded. A warrior has nothing in the world except his or her impeccability, and impeccability cannot be threatened. The worst that could happen to us is that we have to die, and since that is already our unalterable fate, we are free. Those who have lost everything no longer have anything to fear. Warriors don't venture into the unknown out of greed. Greed works only in the world of ordinary affairs. To venture into that terrifying loneliness of the unknown, one must have something greater than greed: love. One needs love for life, for intrigue, for mystery. One needs unquenchable curiosity and guts galore."

- Carlos Castenada

If you have gone down the rabbit hole and found yourself in the bilge pump of this Ship of Theseus, wondering just who the hell you can trust and what in the hell (if anything) is actually happening, know this:

You can trust in God.

That is our national motto: In God We Trust. We even put in on our money as an acknowledgement of our true Source. Even if you can't trust the provenance of the money itself, you can always trust in God, without whom you do not even exist, and within whom you exist forever.

This is not to say that money in itself is evil, because it is not. But in this high stakes battle, this Casino Royale for the planet, it helps to know that worldly possessions last for but a moment, so that if and when you are required to go all-in on a bet, you can do so out of love and not fear.

Our trust in Donald Trump is not mistaken, yet he is only one man, fighting the good fight. It would be unfair to ask him to do something we ourselves were not also willing to do in our own way. We may have lost all faith in our system of governance after the blatant in-your-face election steal, which was the equivalent of assassinating President Kennedy in broad daylight and then blaming it all on a 'lone gunman' with magic bullets.

Yet remember, there may be corrupted Justices who can be bought off, blackmailed and threatened, Justices who do not possess the 'guts galore' of a warrior who walks with Christ, however, there is also a Justice named Clarence Thomas.

"Your quest stands upon the edge of a knife. Stray but a little and it will fail, to the ruin of all. Yet hope remains while the Company is true."

- Galadriel, Lord of the Rings

"I knew that until I was ready to tell the truth as I saw it, I was no better than a politician-- but I didn't know whether I would ever be brave enough to break ranks and speak my mind... I could feel the golden handcuffs of a comfortable but unfulfilling life snapping shut on my wrists... I could only choose between being an outcast and being dishonest. I had sworn to administer justice 'faithfully and impartially.' To do otherwise would be to violate my oath. That meant I had no business of imposing my personal views on the country. Thanks to God's direct intervention, I had risen phoenix-like from the ashes of self-pity and despair, and though my wounds were still raw, I trusted that in time they, too, would heal."

- Justice Clarence Thomas

If one Justice (and others that follow) can make the right choice when everything is on the line, and stand up to the dark forces within the system that deign to destroy any individual who opposes them, then hope yet remains for the Republic.

Hope remains while the Company is true.

Where We Go One, We Go All.

One day we will ask ourselves the philosophical question whether the United States of America is an entirely new Country now or whether it is the same Country the Founding Fathers intended to create when they first put quill to parchment on the Declaration of Independence and mutually pledged their Lives, their Fortunes and their sacred Honor.

"With a firm reliance on Divine Providence."

We are on this Ship of Theseus together. We can ask ourselves later when we get to the other shore, just how the ship managed to change all around us while never wrecking or running adrift.

You might say it happens the same way the central bankers lose their kingdoms. Like bankruptcy, it happens gradually and then all at once.

It is still true that the Best is Yet to Come.

Yet how do we get There From Here? I will close with a simple map of sorts, internal directions from a certain Once and Future Queen, with distinctly Pleiadian features, I might add.

"Be Best." - First Lady Melania Trump

Because in the end, 'what happens' is also up to you.

Did you start out in this game as a pawn?

Will you cross the dark to light board and make the ultimate transformation?

Will you take the helm on your own Ship of Theseus and steer it in the direction Life itself wants you to go?

The choice as ever is yours.

Vaya con Dios.

20. BACK TO THE FUTURE

An important aspect of moving into multidimensionality is moving beyond a linear view of world history. If you go far enough into the past, you end up in the future.

What that means is that history has not been a simple linear progression from, let us say, Sumerian times until today, with humanity gradually progressing from a period of low technology to what we have now with our current day digital computer tech.

Advanced civilizations have been seeded into our historical continuum and some of their architecture, such as cathedrals, were not religious centers like our modern day churches, which our history books tell us, but energy centers, wherein they utilized antennas which captured electromagnetic energy from the aether and transmitted it throughout their realm via channels of water.

Watch the Water has many meanings.

These civilizations understood (and overstood) the interplay between sacred geometry, acoustic resonance, the fifth element known as aether and how it connects with and enlivens water through electromagnetic energy harvesting, which in turn creates 'livings waters' which could both provide their energetic networks, as well as heal all manner of diseases. As we well know, we are 80% water ourselves, and water has shown that its molecular structure responds to frequency, vibration and sound. So, it stands to reason that as beings composed primarily of water, we would as well.

"If you want to find the secrets of the universe, think in terms of energy, frequency and vibration." - Nikola Tesla

When we look with new eyes upon structures throughout our known world, such as cathedrals, triumphal arches (in truth horseshoe magnets) and certain majestically styled government buildings with domes, we find that these buildings have actually been repurposed by our recent generations of humanity, yet they were not built by them.

"You didn't build that." - Barack Hussein Obama

In photographs of the early 19th century, we find horse-and-cart era people traversing their land on crude mud roads. How could these same people, who apparently had access only to basic tools, as power tools were not introduced until 1895, and who moved about by simple horse and buggy, build such mind bogglingly magnificent structures of gigantic size and geometric perfection that we cannot, and also I might add, do not make today even with our so called modern machine tools? And why would they not bother fixing their mud and dirt roads, an infinitely simpler task than creating these unbelievable structures, if they had to move and place the huge stone pieces which go into these vast constructions? Were they really content with clomping through the mud to do this?

The truth is that these structures and civilizations were seeded into our historical timeline from what you might call the futurepast, in multidimensional terms, by beings that understood building techniques which we, as supposedly modern people, could only describe as magic.

We can designate these creators as Game Masters, who operate outside of time as we know it, and can create entire civilizations with thought and sound. In the beginning was the Word, was it not? And the word was a tone, a tone that brought into resonant frequency the thought creations that preceded it.

We have been lied to so much about our true history, that we are akin to beings with amnesia, that have been traumatized at some point in our journey and have forgotten where we came from and who we are, as well as what all happened here on earth. And yet the clues are planted like Easter Eggs across our world, with the clues about what the structures mentioned above point to, vis-a-vis free energy and the actual map, not only of our geographic world and our map through history, but a map of our very beings.

As above, so below, micro and macrocosm, and the notion that every cell within our bodies contains a holographic design of the whole, are important legends on this multidimensional map, which will lead us from 3D to 5D.

The Enemy is an expert in mind control and deception. The Enemy has lied to us about our history and the nature of our being and our world, but it has not been able to erase the Word of God from this realm.

A great battle was fought at some point in the indeterminate past, one side appeared to win, and the earth was subsequently strip mined for its materials, such as the giant silicon (not carbon) based trees, its gold, its crystal, and also, of course, the spiritual energy inherent in its people, as the children of God.

Recall in the movie The Matrix, people were used as human batteries for the Enemy, while they were kept alive via cannibalism machines, all the while their consciousness existed inside a virtual reality game world of sorts, put in place by the Great Deceivers.

Lucifer was the original Great Deceiver and he wanted his own kingdom to rule over, presumably by artificial intelligence technology, however Lucifer cannot create in the same way that God does, he can only co-opt what has already been created and try to steer it into his own manipulated designs. Lucifer and those that worship him also sacrifice and cannibalize people. Just like the Baal worshipers did in Biblical times. Not all that different from what the Matrix is suggesting, just in a different context.

In the Matrix, the hero Neo (which rearranges as One) is tasked with fundamentally changing the nature of his consciousness and his understanding of reality in real time. In a sense, he must go from a 3D to a 5D state of being, or from a linear to a multidimensional perspective. A very significant part of what gets him there is not simply an intellectual understanding of the Unity Consciousness Christ taught and demonstrated, but a perceiving and living of that very consciousness.

Young Monk: "Do not try and bend the spoon—that's impossible. Instead, only try to realize the truth. There is no spoon."

In the Matrix, the spoon doesn't exist—it's just a code or a program that tells Neo's brain that he's looking at a spoon.

Even our scientists of today have detailed that matter is mostly empty space, and that matter includes the most solid of objects imaginable, such as the great cathedrals mentioned above. These scientists have also brought to light the wave/particle concept of quantum mechanics. It is only when we observe it that the wave becomes a particle. Our consciousness and our attention is a key component in the creation of matter as a tangible thing which can be experienced. Note that only when science gets into quantum dynamics does it get close to the truth of our reality.

And what are we talking about bringing into our world today? A Quantum Financial System. A Quantum Voting System. It is time for us to become quantum ourselves, as a certain letter that utilizes a quantum computer might suggest.

When the quantum of technology and science merges with the Law of One and the Unity Consciousness of Christ, we will return to where we have been this entire time: to the place our consciousness created in Unity with the Source, to the Garden of Earthly Delight, wherein our being oscillates between a living understanding of itself as both individuated and the Whole, as the droplet of water and the entire ocean. At that point, arbitrary divisions between beings cease to exist. Do you think racism will be a problem for anyone then?

This living understanding has been what our seemingly historical progression has led us to, from the sands of Jerusalem and the message of Christ, to this important quantum shift in our civilization, where the wool that was pulled over our eyes is removed and we know again, as also we are known. No more through a mirror darkly. Now we will be the light itself.

Forget about the Enemy's deceptive co-opting of Christ through the Catholic Church and the Vatican, as well as certain other religions. Their ceremonies are Luciferian and their altars are sacrificial altars. When they eat the body and drink the blood metaphorically in their masses, they are hinting about what they do literally in their black masses.

The real meaning of Christ's Eucharist is thus: You Christ.

That is what Christ was foretelling, that we would walk the same path as Him, in Unity with the same Source.

"You will do all these things and more," Christ told us.

Now we find ourselves at a historical crossroads. The increasing light on the planet has caused the Enemy to come out of hiding. Where formerly it could rule by secrecy and through secret societies, now it is being unmasked for all to see, whether they like it or not. And they don't like it one bit. They would vaccinate you straight out of this consciousness if they could, however, they can not.

The advanced (by our current conceptions) civilizations that were seeded by Game Masters into our multidimensional reality suggest a world that utilizes energy, frequency and vibration to both create, power and sustain its world.

"Music is liquid architecture. Architecture is frozen music." - Goethe

Interesting that quote was from Goethe, as his name hints that it is sound and vibration (creating geometric patterns) which puts The Go in E(nergy).

The Word (frequency vibration) calls into being the manifest worlds.

If these seeded civilizations that created power station architecture which worked with the ionosphere (composed of ions and 'free' electrons), tapping into the fifth element aether by way of electromagnetic spires and receivers, then transferring it by way of 'living water' channels and canals, then naturally we can as well, when we throw off the chains of the cartel of criminals who have kept us in the amnesiac chains of their low energy technology and an entirely false view of history.

"You're low energy, Jeb." - Donald Trump

Indeed, the control mechanisms of this occult central banking cartel are low energy and designed to keep us sleepwalking through this same low energy. It has been effective throughout our recent history in setting us on a hamster wheel in their little monopoly game. I will admit, there has been a genius to their methods of control and trickery. It is not easy to keep beings such as ourselves asleep, treading our paths like automatons, and they do understand the function of entertainment as a form of containment in their clever world of mind control.

"Here we are now. Entertain us." - Kurt Cobain

With linear thinking, the idea that advanced civilizations could have existed in our past seems crazy. It goes against the Darwinian concept of history and the notion of an evolving species by natural selection along a unidirectional straight line path. The truth is, at the highest levels, the occultists who promote this origin of species don't believe it either. In fact, they laugh at it and at those who accept such simple explanations. Just like they laugh at the concept of the Big Bang Explosion of Nothingness, which 'randomly evolved' into the manifest universe and Us Fine People.

They know that it is absurd to suggest that the complexity of creation could have occurred without an intelligent design at its roots, just like it would be impossible for a something like a cell phone to be created without an intelligent design preceding it. You couldn't toss random computer parts up in the air and ever expect, even on an infinite timeline, that they would randomly assemble into a functioning cell phone. And a cellphone is nothing in comparison to the operational complexity of the human body, let alone the planet.

Unfortunately, the systems of control of the Enemy also involve the medical establishment. Do you think they are going to stop at simply using their based-on-nothing fiat currency and their corporate media mind control to keep us contained in the Luciferian kingdom of their creation? No, they must also attack our health, too, via their pharmacology, via the water, via the air, via their gmo foods, and via their designer diseases. In a way, it is incredible that we have survived as well as we have, though the death tolls at large have been truly criminal, when you consider that the healing technology has been right under our noses the entire time.

Watch the water.

President Donald Trump and President Kennedy are two sides of the same coin, in terms of what they were and are working to accomplish:

1. Ending the private central banking system put in place by the European bankers who usurped control of the United States by "infiltration instead of invasion" - just like our founding fathers warned they would.
2. Releasing free energy by means of technology which is both quantum and, in a sense, spiritual in the manner in which it utilizes the way our world really works in its true design.
3. Releasing the healing technologies which work hand in glove with the aforementioned energy tech.

Ask yourself, do you really doubt that such things exist and are possible? Do you really believe that our current understanding and utilization of the world's possibilities are at their peak in terms of their potential?

Obviously not. And the reason is that, in the simplest possible terms, Evil instead of Good has been in charge of our recent history. How long that history has really been going on is hard to reckon with, since we mostly only understand time from a linear perspective. And our history books are rife with lies and misdirection.

It's great that people can become 'good students' - but what does that really mean nowadays? That someone memorizes specific factoids and regurgitates them shortly thereafter in a test? That is really only a memory exercise, and while there is nothing wrong with a good memory, what happens when false interpretations are palmed off as truths? We become the amnesiacs who repeat this false history on command like parrots, and then believe ourselves that it is the absolute truth.

"History is written by the victors." - Origins unknown

Just like us, our origin is partially unknown. If there was a battle some time in the indeterminate past, and false cover-up histories were written by the victors, then how does a being, such as ourselves, whose own birth literally delivers them into a state of amnesia as to their prior whereabouts, come to a reasonable understanding about the world and what brought us to this place?

We must go within. That is the only way.

"The kingdom of God is within you." - Christ

The records of all histories never disappear, they are only obscured for those without eyes to see. We are, all of us, wiping the sleep of history from our eyes. We need to be fully conscious in order to shake off the shackles of a world order which is rapidly passing away.

It is a world order built on tyranny, disease, limited energy and bad banking practices. While it is all we have known in our present incarnation, and many of us have Stockholm Syndrome for our captors, it is not nearly as stable as it has been in recent years. It is a House of Cards, built on rapidly liquifying dirt. On mud, as it were.

The reason that the horse-and-cart people were clomping around in the mud of their roads while unbelievable structures of magnificent architecture towered above them, is that they didn't build these things, they inherited them. They repurposed them, into cathedrals and government buildings. Eventually, they got around to building some roads, too, and cleaned the mud off their shoes.

Majestic, awe-inspiring buildings, complete with sculptures and art which take your breath away in the genius of skill required to create it, existing alongside muddy roads and people with primitive tools does not compute. It is very likely that the muddy roads came from some sort of cataclysm which liquified the dirt beneath the roads and even caused many of the buildings to sink somewhat, which you can see in the architecture around the world where the original first floor is underground and windows appear cut off halfway at street level.

There's a lot to unpack, including how mercury (a liquid metal) and its alchemical reaction with gold (as the eagle and the lion merge) were key components to harnessing the aether, and it cannot all be addressed here, however, it is instructive to note that one cannot comprehend a multidimensional history through a simple linear lens.

Perhaps, we were once multidimensional beings ourselves and will be again. There was a battle at a certain point for this realm and we are currently in another one again, though it is primarily a hidden battle for those who only follow the narrative of the corporate mainstream media, which is a chess piece for one of the teams in the battle. It is, in essence, the propaganda arm of the central banks.

That said, there is still true communication that takes place, even on these networks, but you must dig deeper to get to the actual truth. You must be an archeologist who isn't afraid to get your hands into the mud and clean off those secret artifactual clues hiding beneath the surface.

An election was stolen by a criminal cabal that utilized a manufactured flu virus variant and merged it with their assets in the corporate media and their blackmailed agents in the government & legal system, as well as the medical establishment, to enact a coup on the American People, and by extension the world, because right now, where America goes, the rest of the world will follow.

It would seem with all of these ultra-powerful chess pieces at the Enemy's disposal (banking, media, industry, energy, medicine) that there's no way that Donald Trump and the Alliance which he is the George Washington frontman of, could possibly defeat such an entrenched Force.

Well, there was no logical way that the Continental Army could have defeated the British Army in the American Revolution. The British sent an armada of 400 warships to the New York harbor to commence the battle. The nascent USA had exactly zero warships. They were a rag-tag group of farmers and tradesmen, with no military background. Yet, they had a covenant by way of their founding documents with the Creator itself. Not simply by their own doings, but by Divine Providence were they victorious.

'Tor' is an important part of the word Creator, and all other words containing tor. Our world is energetically a Torus. The flow of energy is electromagnetic and it moves in a toroidal current. The torus is similar to an apple in shape.

In the end, it is our energy which will prevail in this battle. We are all creators in our own way of this world. We create it by thought and energy. We have his'tor'ically been steered into the creations of others, who have used occult means to capture our attention. They still do with their media, however, the giant that is us, unified, is now waking up. Gulliver is throwing off the ropes of the Lilliputians and rising to his feet.

It is said that our realm was once the home of giants. If so, who were they and what was our relationship to them?

"There were giants in the earth in those days; and also after that, when the sons of God came in unto the daughters of men, and they bare children to them, the same became mighty men which were of old, men of renown."

David defeated the giant Goliath to take back control of his realm. When David challenged Goliath, who laughed at his seemingly pathetic attempt to challenge him, with no armor and a mere sling and stone, David said this:

"You come to me with sword, spear, and javelin, but I come to you in the name of the LORD of Heaven's Armies—the God of the armies of Israel, whom you have defied."

We know what happened next. We also know what happened in the American Revolution. Now we are in the Second American Revolution. And this one is a Quantum Revolution.

Where we go ONE... we go all.

Down the rabbit hole and through the electromagnetic torus.

Like we said... It's Gonna Be Biblical. Have you seen any floods lately?

Watch the water.

We also said: Nothing Can Stop What is Coming.

Future Proves Past.

And finally...

God Wins.

Shall We Play a Game?

"When you open your heart to patriotism, there is no room for prejudice. The Bible tells us how good and pleasant it is when God's people live together in unity. We must speak our minds openly, debate our disagreements, but always pursue solidarity.

When America is united, America is totally unstoppable. There should be no fear. We are protected, and we will always be protected. We will be protected by the great men and women of our military and law enforcement. And most importantly, we will be protected by God.

The time for empty talk is over. Now arrives the hour of action. Do not allow anyone to tell you that it cannot be done. No challenge can match the heart and fight and spirit of America. We will not fail...

We stand at the birth of a new millennium, ready to unlock the mysteries of space, to free the Earth from the miseries of disease and to harness the industries and technologies of tomorrow."

- Inaugural address of Donald J. Trump - age 70 years, 7 months and 7 days in the Hebrew year 5-777, on Jan. 20, 2017.

Dump all stock in 666, because it is going to fall like Goliath with a stone to the head.

USA is right in the middle of Jerusalem. It is the third temple.
And we will build it together, not with our former crude tools, but with the living tools of our own conceptions, married to sound, energy and vibration.

That may sound fantastical and futuristic, but in truth it has been done before and the clues are all around us, right this very day.

"If you want to find the secrets of the universe, think in terms of energy, frequency and vibration." - Nikola Tesla

Tesla was a close friend of John Trump, the uncle of Donald Trump, and John Trump inherited Tesla's notes upon his death.

You're going to love how this story ends.

As it was in the beginning, so shall it be in the end.

Back to the Future.

Godspeed, Patriots.

EPILOGUE:
CAPTAIN'S LOG -
CHRONICLES OF THE 2016 ELECTION

SEPTEMBER 18, 2016 – Post:

It is truly unbelievable the free pass the Clintons get in Hollywood and on the mainstream media. Obviously, it's because the 6 companies that own 90% of the MSM are major Clinton campaign supporters. Time Warner is a giant backer of Clinton. Time Warner owns CNN.

That means Anderson Cooper works for Time Warner and is paid to promote Clinton. HBO is owned by Time Warner. So Bill Maher works for Time Warner. These media personalities are not independent agents, they are paid propagandists for one candidate. That's why Hillary Clinton can get away with having a former KKK Grand Cyclops like Robert Byrd as her political mentor.

That's why the Clintons can pocket over 90% of the money meant to go to the Haiti earthquake and the media looks the other way. That's why when Congress indicts the FBI for covering up Clinton's destruction of her emails, hiding her war profiteering, and let's face it, treason, it's not a story at all. She has one foot in jail and one in the White House.

Her first case as a lawyer was plea bargaining for a child rapist and she laughed about the fact that she knew he was guilty.

She has Parkinson's disease and can barely make a public appearance without coughing or collapsing or looking drugged out of her mind, but it is passed off as pneumonia and she's lauded for her immense effort on the campaign trail, which is basically phoned in interviews on CNN or sound bites from her plane and the occasional poorly attended speech. She went almost 300 days without giving a press conference.

To all my otherwise very rational and intelligent friends, you can be 'against' any candidate for any reason, but to be 'for' such a corrupt and scandalous duo as the Clintons is beyond the pale. Everyone from the Left knew what the Bushes were about. The Clintons and the Bushes represent the EXACT same thing. They are about selling out humanity to profit personally.

Clinton's poetic collapse on 9-11 pretty much says it all. Karma is coming back to collect. Too bad it wasn't one of the Bushes that collapsed because then I think more people would get it.

ANON: In my opinion, that's disingenuous to keep that label on Robert Byrd - even the NAACP thought so.

CAPTAIN: If you are in the KKK for one day, for any reason under the sun, your credibility as an ethical human being is done forever. Let alone if you rise to the position of Grand Cyclops. That makes you a leader of that hate cult. Pardons after the fact by any organization don't cut it.

ANON: Some people earn redemption.

CAPTAIN: One can only wonder how much blood was on those hands.

SEPTEMBER 22, 2016 – Post: Video of a Black Female Trump Employee who delivers a heartfelt testimony of his integrity.

Trump promotes black women to high executive office in his company. Clinton sings the praises of former KKK recruiter Robert Byrd. Wait, who is the racist again? #bizarroworld

ANON: You're delusional. Are you at all familiar with the alt right base?

CAPTAIN: The delusion is not looking clearly at the candidate you promote. All of the black and hispanic individuals that work for or have worked for Trump say that he is absolutely and positively not a racist. And yet the media is on an infinite loop that he is literally Hitler. Meanwhile, Clinton gets a total pass for advocating a former KKK recruiter.

ANON: Cites please - you're claiming that they exist means bubkis. Please provide more than the one - and doesn't she work for Don Jr?

CAPTAIN: Tell me again how it's okay that Clinton's mentor was a KKK Grand Cyclops because he felt bad about it afterward. But it must be a hard fact that Trump is a racist because the Clinton News Network says so. The only campaign point of Clinton is that Trump is a racist. If he isn't, she literally doesn't have a leg to stand on. Or a stool to lean against.

ANON: Let's go point by point, please. Answer me this - who do the racists support?

CAPTAIN cites article about KKK donating $20K to Clinton campaign.

ANON: Please provide any racist behavior by HRC, not by someone that she worked with 40 years ago.

CAPTAIN: Klan leaders say they support Clinton. Others say they support Trump. Only one candidate had a KKK leader as a mentor.

ANON: Smh.

CAPTAIN: Robert Byrd was part of the filibuster that almost ended the Civil Rights act.

ANON: Byrd voted *for* the civil rights act. Please read the Mother Jones article. Stop being a brick wall.

CAPTAIN: When it became politically expedient he changed his tune and was 'reformed.' He put his noose away and was magically a good man. Hillary & Bill say so.

ANON: I'm done here.

CAPTAIN: Is Mother Jones somehow the be-all-end-all of research? Ciao. Enjoy your day. All healthy debate here.

ANON: Are you really in need of more cites for Trump's support from racists? A different point, but is it true that Trump supports circumcision and Hillary doesn't?

CAPTAIN: If you were running for office and a racist group said they support you, even though you have disavowed them and don't want their support, would that make you a racist? And on the circumcision tip (pun)

Trump is definitely in the dark there. He needs to get informed. A lot of clueless people like Bono and Bill Gates are pro-circumcision. Or should I say, pro-cutting off a healthy part of a child's genitalia and selling it on the open market. When it becomes an issue people can rationally look at instead of going with tradition, everyone will agree that it should be banned. I haven't decided who to cast a vote for yet, but the constant narrative of 'Trump's a Racist' has prevented any true rational discourse.

ANON: He *is* a racist.

CAPTAIN: It has been decreed from on high. Trump is a racist. Now let's get the most corrupt candidate in the modern era into the White House tout suite.

ANON: Who are the racists supporting?

CAPTAIN: Show me the video right now where Trump advocates and praises any member of the KKK. I just showed you one of Clinton.

ANON: Clinton didn't meet Byrd until after he had begun working *for* civil rights. He apologized on the senate floor for his past. If you won't acknowledge that his civil rights record after 1964 means anything, than there is no point in debating with you. Care to address my point of who do the racists support? By the way, you use the word "women" to describe a single person, and she works for Don Jr, not the father. Your disinformation is showing. Anon2 and Anon3 - I'm really interested in your take here.

ANON2: There's no point. Who was the last person to change their mind in a political argument on here?

CAPTAIN: If you don't believe Trump is a racist, you must be an idiot because it has been proven. Nobody said anything about it for the 40 years he has been in the news and media. It became a fact the day he ran against the Clinton/Bush empire. Maybe Trump is just another politician who will say anything to get elected, that is entirely possible. But Clinton's scandals are right in everyone's face and the only answer is: Trump is a racist. The kool-aid is a bit much.

ANON: Um, Department of Justice said that he was racist in 1974 - look it up.

CAPTAIN: Anon2, you are probably right about that, haha.

ANON3: Anon, I feel your frustration on this. I haven't been able to chime in because I've been working with my producer. I will say this first, I've always respected Captain's intelligence since the days we both correctly predicted the death of film which was replaced by digital video. With that in mind, I know Captain sometimes purposely takes the less favorable side of an argument on purpose in order to prove his ability to argue points that often have very little proof or logic behind them. In other words, he's a master debater. Still, I can't in good conscience ignore the issue, despite Anon2's probably much smarter response. It feels too much like being the Germans who let Hitler rise by doing nothing. There is plenty of evidence that Trump is a racist long before he went up against the so-called "Clinton War Machine."

CAPTAIN: Clinton supports destabilizing middle eastern countries and profiteers off of trading state secrets. She destroyed all of her cell phones and emails to hide her activities. Congress just subpoenaed the FBI about her criminal activity. Does this sound like a president to you? She is our generation's Nixon. Maybe Trump is a business tycoon and a reality TV star. Comparing him to Hitler is ludicrous, but it is in the "Our Business is Crisis/Wag the Dog" playbook. Thank God it's not Clinton vs. Bush, though. At least this is good political theatre. Let's see the first debate.

ANON3: The above article refers to testimony in court where Trump bashed Native Americans in 1993. There's also the case of the Criminal Justice department investigating Trump for discriminatory housing practicing as far back as 1973. His father engaged in similar practices back in the '60's. I know Captain doesn't always have access to a television, so he may not have seen Trump's speeches where he accused Mexico of purposely sending us their rapists and drug dealers, told a reporter he would seriously consider entering Muslims into a database, a modern-day version of the Jude label put on Jews in Nazi Germany, and managed to even offend Republicans with his "total ban on Muslims entering the U.S." Then there's running an ad with Hilary Clinton's face right next to a Jewish

Star accusing her of financial greed. The statement he made years before ever running for office that his accounting office is made up of blacks and he really needs some guys with Yarmulkes in there. All these statements are on video, or documented in court cases, so I trust this information more than Captain's source, which had Trump/Pence in a big banner at the top. I'd also argue that the concept that Hilary runs the media is not only ludicrous, but something I've never heard before, even though I read Breitbart and numerous troll-type comments from Trump supporters just to see what the pro-Trump argument could possibly be. If the media were really owned by the Clintons, we'd see a lot more publicity for facts like how Hilary worked for churches and with children in her early career. Was an early supporter of Jimmy Carter, who may not be the strongest President we've ever had, but has certainly gone on to be known as one of the world's greatest humanitarians. (He supports Hilary completely, by the way) Although several trusted news sources have reported that the Clinton Foundation has actually been falsely accused and implied of wrong doing, the investigative reporting that has shown this has been buried. It's never been a lead story, there's been no apologies for raising "questions" that turned out to have no merit whatsoever... The story of the horrific Clinton Foundation just kind of drifted away when there turned out to be no actual sexy evil involved. And of course, without those facts trumpeted as loudly and constantly as the false innuendo, people choose to believe what they want rather than do any investigative research on their own. Also not reported with any sense of gusto: the fact that Hilary wrote a letter long before Benghazi happened complaining about the lack of funding (as enacted by Republican bills) for security at foreign embassies. The truth is, Captain makes an interesting point, just for the wrong person. Hilary Clinton was not seen as "evil" or "the devil" until it became clear that she was going to be going head-to-head with Donald Trump. The guy who has over 3,500 lawsuits against him, and a Foundation that has recently been outed as using charity contributions for his own benefit, has the nerve to call Hillary "crooked." I find it interesting that people who know Trump personally have nothing good to say about him. The ghost-writer for "Art of the Deal" has nothing but bad things to say. Penn Jilette, who worked with him on Celebrity Apprentice and is no fan of the Clintons, said "whatever bad you think of Trump, he's worse than you think." Yet, people who have worked with Hillary Clinton personally, seem to have mostly good things to say about her, including a number of world leaders. The choice is obvious, even if Hillary isn't squeaky clean, she's a drop in the bucket compared to Trump. And yes, I'd compare him directly to Hitler, without bating an eyelash. By the way, just for fun, here's a 17-minute list of everything disgusting about Trump, and it's mostly about since he started running for office. There's so much worse in his history. (posts list link)

CAPTAIN: So, if Clinton goes to jail for treason, a demonic messiah will be President? We live in interesting times.

ANON3: Oh yeah, I forgot to mention that long before Trump announced any political aspirations, he was the public face of the "birther" movement, in which he questioned Barack Obama's legitimacy as President. Despite the fact that he had to have been vetted by the U.S. government and eventually released two forms of his birth certificate, Trump doubted the birth certificate, continued to accuse the President of lying and not being legitimately born in the States. Then recently blatantly lied and said it was Hillary who started all that nonsense. Why would Clinton go to jail for treason? The overworked E-mail scandal is a case of bad judgement to be sure, but not intentional espionage. Will Trump go to jail for asking Russia, on television to hack government E-mails? And yes, no matter what, we live in interesting times.

CAPTAIN: Clinton's campaign staff started the birth certificate rumor. Trump ran with it. In the scope of the discussion, it's a red herring. Destroying state department emails is against the law. The Clinton Foundation is basically on trial for trading state secrets and government influence for money. Wikileaks is letting their game out of the bag. Will see if they can hang on until she's in the White House, but there's no way they can keep all the scandals quiet forever. It's a wrap on the Clintons. What Trump is or will be remains to be seen. Someone like Biden could still be a factor if Clinton is pulled.

ANON3: Yes Wikileaks, run by a rapist who is hiding out so as not to face any charges, has a hard-on for Hilary, that's true. I haven't heard that the Clinton Foundation is on trial, just that accusations have been made that some actual reporters looked into and found to be untrue. Meanwhile, the Trump foundation has been reported to continually use money earmarked for charity to pay off Trump's legal expenses from the many suits he's lost and fines he's had to pay. As a matter of public record, Trump is guilty of Perjury, Money Laundering, Discriminatory Housing practices, literally thousands of cases of breach of contract and is under investigation for Fraud and Racketeering in regards to Trump University. Also, I'm willing to believe the multiple media sources that can't find any evidence that the Clinton campaign started the birther controversy, but I am willing to believe my own eyes and ears when I see clip after clip of Trump trying to discredit the President of the United States, based on no evidence whatsoever (Republicans who defended George Bush for far less would call this Treason) for years. Then walk it back last week and blame his political opponent. It should be a "wrap" on Trump, but amazingly, it isn't.

CAPTAIN: Clinton's campaign started the birther controversy when she was running against Obama. I am all for both candidates having everything revealed about their business activities. In this day and age, everything is going to come out in the wash. The list is too long to put here on how the Clinton's used the State Dept to fill the coffers of the Clinton Foundation. Congress just subpoenaed the FBI on the cover up. I'd list links but I don't believe they will get read. But 'perjury, money laundering and racketeering' is exactly what they are being called out for. It could be that Trump and Clinton are two sides of the same coin. They are in fact distant cousins. Not a lot of people know that. Clinton did her racketeering in office, that we do know. I look forward to the rug being lifted up and all of the bugs being revealed on both candidates. The system needs a major spring cleaning.

ANON3: Somehow "the list is too long" seems like another way of saying "I don't have actual evidence, but trust me..." Yes, both candidates are flawed, Clinton is far from squeaky clean. I get articles sent to me every day by a site that is clearly propaganda for the Left, and I call it as such and never use their articles as evidence. I always research elsewhere. Our political system is royally messed-up, absolutely, and our electoral process is poor, at best. Still, comparing Trump to Clinton is, as many smarter people than I have said "a false equivalency." Trump is a train wreck, a morally corrupt person, a pathological liar whose only merit is that he's so bad at it, it's easy to see the many lies he's uttered, just in the past year. He has absolutely no experience in politics, and no business running for president.

No knowledge of foreign policy, a history of admiring dictators such as Saddam Hussein, Vladimir Putin, and Benito Mussolini. If there's any truth to the Newsweek article I posted earlier, he's also a horrible businessman who's been bailed out of ruin numerous times, and his economic policies are likely to cause another Recession that make's Bush's pale in comparison. (Both Bushes, by the way. A good reason not to vote for any Republican). You can find all the improprieties you want on Hillary Clinton, and I won't argue that there are some, but they simply don't equal up to the disaster it would be to have Donald Trump running the country. And that affects us all. You can win an argument on social media, by picking articles that serve your point, and there are plenty to support either side, but making the wrong choice will affect your own life. I have no desire to tell people "I told you so" because the country is bankrupt.

CAPTAIN: The dollar is in for a rough ride, given the trillions printed out of thin air to cover the credit/default Wall Street nightmare from 2008. Whoever ends up as president will preside over an incredibly unstable financial situation, that much is sure. I have never voted for any politician, because they can promise anything in the world on the campaign trail and then not deliver. However, I've never seen a narrative pushed so hard as Trump is a racist. Despite this narrative, he has record support (for a Republican) in the black community. What if he isn't a racist? Does the sky fall on the Clinton war machine?

ANON4: Trump saying clearly racist things (you try to say those things in a corporate environment and you would be fired in a second)...plus anything he says is non factual, lies, half-truths or insults...and no understanding of anything in politics or policies...it's endless...plus did you ever check his business ethics. On top he is the definition of a jerk on any level I could think.

ANON5: Trump represents what's wrong in the hearts of ugly America.

CAPTAIN: Wrong. Trump is revealing the corruption in the empire. You have a candidate smashing her state department phones with a hammer. Destroying 30K emails with "bleach" technology to hide the pay-to-play between Clinton as Secretary of State and the Clinton Foundation. Clinton and her cohorts stand for endless regime changes in the middle east and war-for-profit. Trump is the first candidate to come from outside the political system and call them on their corruption, which is so in-the-face of the American public it has reached epic levels of absurdity. He has spoken out about 9-11 being an inside job. He has brought the issues about vaccines to light. He has stood up against war profiteering. He is getting more support from the black community then any Republican in modern history. Black churches are literally blessing this man, because they see what he is taking a stand against. They are rejecting the media-forced kool-aid that Trump is a racist, which is simply not true. How do you think the powers that be are going to react when someone challenges their power and exposes their corruption? They are going to do a full court press on character assassination with every tool at their disposal. The Clinton/Bush tag team represents the ugly heart of, not America-- but the co-opting of America by criminals who deal in drugs and weapons while selling out what is left of America's freedom. Wake up, Anon5! You are supporting the most blatantly corrupt politician in our lifetime. One who is literally collapsing before our eyes as we watch what she symbolically represents collapse as well. You have been indoctrinated to believe that Trump is a racist. You have believed the big lie, along with many others. Trump doesn't need to run for president. He has already won in American life. But he is risking his life to take a stand against a system of darkness and manipulation that has stood for too long. I applaud his courage, given the length and breadth of the Clinton dead pool. He is drawing record numbers to his rallies, 40K, while Clinton has to bus in high school students when she deigns to speak somewhere in public. The American People are speaking. The old order must go. I have never voted in my life, because I didn't trust whoever was in charge of counting the votes. But in this election, I have registered, and even if it is only a symbolic vote, I hereby declare my vote for Donald Trump. He's not perfect, but he is the one that has stood up to challenge the corrupt anti-freedom, anti-humanity globalist agenda. I'm not drinking the bullshit racist hater-aide forced on us by the media, owned by companies that support the Clinton campaign. The Truth will out. #Trump16

ANON6: I'm with you.

ANON4: So I watched those pro Trump videos.....but I like real facts and this article below is not a lie, plus I watched the debates before and he just completely lies about almost anything...how do you ignore that?

CAPTAIN: CNN is owned by TimeWarner, which is one of the Clinton campaign's biggest supporters. If you are getting your information only from main steam media outlets, you are woefully misinformed.

ANON4: I don't... but who are in your opinion media outlets that tell the truth? Look I have seen the debates and appearances of Trump and those are actual facts... He lies constantly, it's mind boggling.

CAPTAIN: Trump is up against the most deceptive candidate in political history, Nixon on steroids destroying all of her secretary of state communications to hide her activity. To get a full scope of the story one must explore independent media on-line that don't answer to mega-corporations, but want to support the truth as it comes out. There will always be a bias. But the new media is a game changer in this election. So is Wikileaks and Anonymous. The people are actually faster at reporting than anything the mam can do. The only reason we know that Hillary had a seizure and collapsed on 9-11 is because a kid had a cellphone at the ready when in happened.

ANON4: You seem to forget to use the same rules from Trump and question him. And how does the "seizure" story (a seizure is something much more serious by the way) matter at all... that is just so not important and just shows what this has become... substance goodbye.

CAPTAIN: I do question Trump and can't say for sure what he represents. Clinton is a proven bad egg. If there's a chance he can be better than the corruption she is neck deep in, I think it's worth a shot. Her health is a real issue, especially if she's going to be president. I've known about the dark dealings of the Bush/Clintons for years but never thought anyone could challenge them. Maybe Trump can't. But I like that these things are at last coming into public discourse. Either way, man, I respect your views and I really enjoyed working with you and hope we can again. Same team ultimately, my man-- the people on a quest for truth.

ANON4: Look I really don't think it is possible for "normal" citizens anymore to have really enough knowledge about all the (incredibly complicated) issues and on top of that know and check who tells the truth. That is why I go mostly by what I see/hear myself and/or various different news organizations like NPR and similar foreign news organizations reports (knowing that there are always people involved and they have their own views of things). Even if Trump would become president, most things would just stay the way they are... at least that is what history tells us. Most mechanisms cannot be changed by a President and in the end Congress has a lot more power.

CAPTAIN: Those that try to/or might possibly reveal the Clinton corruption often end up in the Clinton Dead Pool. The water is murky and there are no life guards, because they've all been whacked.

ANON7: Captain, I will debate Clinton over Trump with you any day of the week.

ANON8: Write it up and put it out there. Let Everyone see it... I'd like to read it. I don't care much for Killer, however, I'll read it...

CAPTAIN: Robert Kennedy's speechwriter and JFK staff member just endorsed Trump, the only time in his life he has not backed a democrat. The reason he stated is that Clinton is a warmonger that wants to destabilize the middle east with constant regime changes. On the same day George Bush senior endorsed Clinton. Why did Bush do this? Because they are in the same game ever since they ran drugs out of Arkansas while incarcerating a record number of "super predator" blacks.

ANON7: Trump has said he would nuke Europe. If that's not a war monger then I don't what is.

CAPTAIN: That is patently untrue. Trump does not support unnecessary military campaigning for any reason. He wants strong borders because Europe has been intentionally destabilized by regime overthrows in the middle east, followed by the import of the same refugees into cultures they struggle to assimilate into. Hillary's main supporter George Soros is a master of this. They want to destabilize sovereign countries to create a need for a one world government they can control and profit from. I don't believe in this approach. I would like to see Ireland remain Ireland. And America remain the bastion of freedom and possibility that it was founded to be.

ANON7: And you really think that will happen with Trump? This man is a self proclaimed Demi God! Are you f**king serious, Captain? Trump stands for nothing, he lies through his teeth about everything & he makes a thing about being rich, when he wont even release his taxes. The guy is a joke!

CAPTAIN: Trump is someone who has come from outside politics to challenge the corrupt system. He already has the American Dream. He doesn't want to compromise the very things that made him what he is. He is a businessman and a fully behind-the-curtain media person. If anyone could run this gauntlet and stand up as a patriot it would have to be someone like him. Any lesser figures would be destroyed instantly, given what he is up against. He is a legend. Trump hasn't put out his tax return and Clinton is smashing phones with hammers and bleaching emails after being subpoenaed. Wonder which one is hiding the more important elements and for what reason?

ANON7: Trump hasn't put out a tax return because he owes foreign banks billions. He is the one guilty of treason! I'm going to bed. I'll pick this up tomorrow. Sigh. F**king insanity.

CAPTAIN: Owing money vs selling out the state department are two very different things. Let's catch a drink soon, Anon7. #Eire

ANON8: Wait. Run that by me again... Anon7? Trump is guilty of... what? Treason? While's he's been a totally free citizen, able to enjoy his life as he sees fit (and hire thousands while he did that)... That's a pretty large statement - considering he's never been an elected official of state (nor really ever wanted to be, as far as I can tell). May I suggest you turn off msnbc for a few weeks.

ANON5: I miss Bernie.

CAPTAIN: Bernie won but had the nomination stolen from him. He knows it, too, but Clinton scared him, so he endorsed her. After saying she was unfit to be president.

ANON9: There is something for everyone here on both sides of the argument. And from a credible news source. (Cites John Oliver clip from Huffington Post.)

CAPTAIN: John Oliver works for HBO, which is owned by TimeWarner, which is one of Clinton's biggest campaign supporters. He has to go easy on Hillary and hard on Trump or he'd lose his gig. He is a funny guy, though. But he will never takes the gloves off for Clinton while the election is going. Neither will Bill Maher, another TimeWarner employee.

ANON8: Let's Not Forget ClearChannel, amigo. If a 4th grader 'took the gloves off' w/ Hillary, it'd be over.

ANON7: Suggest to me anything you want. I know what I see. (posts photo of a girl in a Trump/Putin tee-shirt.)

ANON5: Captain... I'm not by your side, and I should be. Bernie is scared by Trump, not Hillary.

CAPTAIN: Behind the scenes Bernie was given a deal. Endorse Clinton or else. His legacy could have been different, but you can't really blame him.

SEPTEMBER 26, 2016 – Post: Trump photo on campaign stump.

Donald J. Trump. Putting his life on the line for the American Dream. #Trump2016

ANON10: (posts memes about recent US Presidents that don't support Trump and the other world leaders that do: Putin and Kim Jong Un. Also a UK article about Trump's plan to sign anti-LGBT laws).

CAPTAIN: Wrong. Trump has pledged to defend LGBTQ rights, the first Republican in history to do so. Don't drink the kool-aid. The Advocate interviewed him in 2000 and he has defended gay rights.

ANON10: Look man, I'm not saying Hillary is a great choice. But Trump? Really? You gotta be kidding me. Listen to any of his debates, he's a giant child. His wife plagiarized her speech, he's endorsed by the KKK, ISIS supports him... His solution to terrorism is to kill women and children, he makes fun of disabled people, he thinks Muslims (a group of people in a religion, not a race) should be put into a registry?? Who was the last guy to want to do something like that? Oh right... Hitler.

CAPTAIN: Hillary's political mentor is Robert Byrd, a former Grand Cyclops and recruiter for the KKK. Trump has nothing to do with the KKK. He hires black women and makes them executives in his company.

ANON10: As I said, she's not a great choice either. But I'd rather support no one than support Trump. Not supporting Trump =/= supporting Hillary.

CAPTAIN: You have bought the big lie about Hillary. She is a puppet for the globalists like George Soros who fund her. Trump is a citizen who is risking his life by standing up to them. Of course, they will lie and smear him in any way they can. They own the mainstream media. Trump has nothing to do with the KKK and has repeatedly denounced them. Meanwhile, Hillary is in bed with you know who. (posts picture of George Soros.)

ANON10: (Cites Time Magazine article about ISIS supporting Trump.) Again, I'm not saying to support Hillary. (Cites Daily Beast article comparing Trump to Hitler.) I'm simply showing you how terrifying Trump really is.

CAPTAIN: ISIS was created by criminal elements within US intelligence. They fund them to create a destabilized world ripe for a one world government. Trump is the one guy who took a stand to stop it. They will probably kill him for it, but he is officially an American hero for doing so. He could have sailed off into the sunset, as he was already a great success. If you want to go Hitler, get to know the Bushes and the Clintons. They are in bed together and George Prescott Bush was a major profiteer from the Holocaust. Then, he imported top ranking Nazis into the CIA in Operation Paperclip. Learn your history. This in no joke. There are some real Nazi sympathizers here and they are not Donald Trump. That is what he is doing battle with. The mainstream media is owned by Clinton campaign funders and they will never tell you this.

ANON10: Dude, what crazy conspiracy theory articles are you reading?? Seriously, read the things I linked and look at the sources. ISIS is a group of religious extremists that originated in the middle east and is using Trump's hatred campaign to gather more ground. Every time some idiot acts out against Muslims, more people join ISIS because they too use fear mongering as a recruitment tactic.

CAPTAIN: Your article is from the Daily Beast, a publication with Chelsea Clinton on its board. Enjoy your propaganda.

ANON10: Seriously, give me a single source, any legit article proving your point and I'll read it and take it into consideration. But everything you're saying comes from the bullshit that Trump spews. I've posted 6 different sources.

CAPTAIN: Do your own research. The info coming out from Wikileaks is almost infinite. Hillary is a criminal. Trump is not about hatred, simply a strong border and no more war profiteering in the middle east.

ANON10: For the 3rd time, I never said to support Hillary. I've done my research and this is what I have come up with. Trump is about fear mongering, about teaching his followers to hate Muslims (except that's a religion and not a race, so instead they just hate people with brown skin), making fun of disabled people, suggesting we murder women and children as a solution to the war (actually caught on live TV during an interview), and saying things that make no sense, such as we're going to build a multi billion dollar wall to keep the Mexicans out but Mexico is going to pay for it, to which the President of Mexico said, and I quote, "F*** you." His foreign policy is nonexistent, his companies have almost all gone bankrupt or failed, he lusts after his own daughter, and has shown himself repeatedly to be incapable of having what it takes to run this country - unless you count running it straight into the ground and destroying it on the way. (Cites various videos including one of Trump supposedly mocking a disabled reporter.) This isn't some media campaign. This is out of his own mouth. This is Trump talking. This is direct quotes, video evidence, of him saying and doing these things.

CAPTAIN: I don't think Trump is some perfect candidate. In a way, anyone running for president is going to be a bit of a mess. Clinton has already stated she wants war in Syria and Iran and wants to challenge Russian and China. She also might end up in jail for her destroyed emails hiding her using the state department as an ATM. A lot of politicos are jumping ship because of her war mongering and ill health. Yes, Trump can be an egomaniac at times and say stupid things. But I don't put him in the category of the Clintons by any stretch.

ANON10: Most of what you're saying about Clinton is a smear campaign and media propaganda, BTW. Lol. She fainted because she had a cold and was wearing all black in the sun on a 90 degree day while dehydrated, that was debunked already. The whole "Clinton/Bush" empire is conspiracy theory bullshit. The Bushes are right wing and the Clinton's are left. They are civil to each other and that's about it. Please link me to where she says those things, I'd really like to know. (Posts video about Muslims marching against ISIS and extremism in general, calling for unity.)

CAPTAIN: I like that video. Thanks for sharing it. This is about finding a way to make unity work.

ANON10: Trump is extremely anti-Muslim. I don't see how you can like that video and support him.

CAPTAIN: Research George Soros. He is Clinton's biggest financial supporter. They use the countries they bomb to create destabilization in other countries after the fact. Trump has nothing against Muslims. Anyone can come to the US legally.

ANON10: He literally said he wants to stop all Muslims from coming to the US and put American Muslims, American Citizens, in a registry.

CAPTAIN: He has changed his position on this. "When I'm elected I will suspend immigration from areas of the world where there's a proven history of terrorism against the United States, Europe or our allies until we fully understand how to end these threats," Mr. Trump said in his foreign policy speech last week. It's not related to Muslims as a whole. Trump, like any presidential candidate has people around him bring him back to reality when his ideas need fine tuning, like this one.

ANON10: Ah yes, let's put the country into lock down and prevent other people from entering. Hmm, why does that sound familiar? (Posts encyclopedia article about Hitler.) "Beyond Marxism he believed the greatest enemy of all to be the Jew, who was for Hitler the incarnation of evil. There is debate among historians as to when anti-Semitism became Hitler's deepest and strongest conviction. As early as 1919 he wrote, "Rational anti-Semitism must lead to systematic legal opposition. Its final objective must be the removal of the Jews altogether." In Mein Kampf, he described the Jew as the "destroyer of culture," "a parasite within the nation," and "a menace."

CAPTAIN: Prescott Bush funded Hitler's rise to power and profited from the Holocaust. His son just endorsed Clinton. Make the ties to the real Hitler and don't get misdirected, which is the name of the game for the Clinton's. (Cites Washington Times article on Bush bank ties to Nazi funding.)

ANON10: "The alliance also enabled him to seek support from many of the magnates of business and industry who controlled political funds and were anxious to use them to establish a strong right-wing, anti socialist government. The subsidies Hitler received from the industrialists placed his party on a secure financial footing and enabled him to make effective his emotional appeal to the lower middle class and the unemployed, based on the proclamation of his faith that Germany would awaken from its sufferings to reassert its natural greatness." "The Reichstag fire, on the night of February 27, 1933 (apparently the work of a Dutch Communist, Marinus van der Lubbe), provided an excuse for a decree overriding all guarantees of freedom and for an intensified campaign of violence."

CAPTAIN: The Bushes funded Hitler and are in bed with the Clintons. How much more direct a tie do you need? People want Trump to be evil so badly, then go deaf, dumb and blind when it comes time to look at the Clintons.

ANON10: "From 1933 to 1939 and in some instances even during the first years of the war, Hitler's purpose was to expel the Jews from the Greater German Reich. In 1941 this policy changed from expulsion to extermination. Hitler's success was due to the susceptibility of postwar

Germany to his unique talents as a national leader. His rise to power was not inevitable; yet there was no one who equalled his ability to exploit and shape events to his own ends."

CAPTAIN: Anon10, I am down to stop the individuals connected to the real rise of Hitler, who was funded by banks after WWI, when Germany's currency was nearly worthless. These people are still in political power. (Reposts Bush funding Hitler article.)

ANON10: Ah yes, Bill Clinton, born several years after the rise of Hitler, funded Hitler's campaign. That's not a wild conspiracy theory at all. I really think you have it backwards, man. People go deaf dumb and blind when trying to accuse the Clintons of being evil, while also blindly supporting Trump. Do the actions of your grandfather concern you? Did his actions have anything to do with you besides assisting your existence? If you or I cannot be held responsible for the actions of our grandparents, why then would you hold another responsible for the actions of their grandparents? That doesn't make any sense. That's just conspiracy theorist propaganda and really reaching for reasons to dislike someone. That would be like saying since my grandparents are Italian, and Italy supported Hitler's rise, that I had something to do with it and I support Hitler.

CAPTAIN: Prescott Bush helped FUND Hitler. And then his son and grandson went on to be presidents of the US. If that doesn't disturb you then I can't say much more. And it's well established that the Bushes and Clintons have deep ties. They support each other. I think we have established here that it is nearly impossible to change someone's mind on social media. We disagree and history will have to give us the truth. I respect your putting your ideas forth and I thank you for the discussion, Anon10. As for the Clintons and Bushes they go way back to when Bill was in Arkansas. Drug running and then incarcerating blacks in record numbers in the "super predator" era. You can be against Trump. You might even be right. History will tell. But the Clintons are as corrupt as can be. It's all coming out. And they are not on the side of humanity. They are done. If Trump turns out to be a bad egg, I will admit it. As far as the Clintons and Bushes, it's a cold fact.

ANON10: I'd love to see some sources on that, send me some links so I can read up on it.

CAPTAIN: (posts various links)

ANON10: Okay, this article cites a sketchy YouTube video and Wikipedia. Not to mention it has almost nothing to do with Hillary. This is all the actions of her husband's employees and some other people. It's very likely she had no knowledge or part in this, if it is even true. Do you have a credible article?

CAPTAIN: Anon10, spend a week researching everything you can find online related to the Bush & Clinton crime families. Any one article or source can be discredited. So if you have the interest, the material is almost infinite. I can't do it for you. You have to want to know the truth about these people. For most of the general public it is too dark to face, so they run in the other direction.

ANON10: I'd just like to know what you read that convinced you it was truth.

ANON14: Go get 'em, Captain.

ANON3: This is one of the more entertaining encapsulations of this election. I have a lot of respect for John Oliver's team of researchers on other topics. If nothing else, this is an entertaining look at the situation, but this does back up everything I said to you the last time you railed on Clinton. (Posts John Oliver video)

CAPTAIN: Yes, I have been getting this sent to me. John Oliver is hilarious. Clinton has the better professional comedians promoting her, to be sure. However, HBO is owned by TimeWarner, one of Clinton biggest campaign supporters. It's Oliver's job to bash Trump and go light on Clinton. If he went hard on Clinton, or even let a little hard truth come out, he would be fired like Dr. Drew when he mentioned concern about Clinton's health.

ANON3: That's an interesting conspiracy theory. And the Washington Post, The New York Times, The Los Angeles Times, CNN, Politifact, FactCheckOrg, and Newsweek, are all on Clinton's payroll too? I guess the Clinton Foundation had better have scammed all that money that no one can actually prove they did to pay all these people off. Also, great to know that Trump has softened his stance from tactics directly comparable to Hitler because he has people that will reign him in. Sounds like they will be busy during his tenure as President. I hope they don't quit on him like all the Latinos on his staff did after his fiasco in Mexico.

CAPTAIN: It's more the other way around, Anon3. 6 companies own 90% of the mainstream media. These companies fund Clinton's campaign. So they have very direct interests in each other. They are not on her payroll, she is on theirs. And of course, the cuddly and lovable George Soros.

ANON3: It seems rather convenient that all these news sources who are supposed to be objective and have a history of being trusted news sources are all going to blatantly lie just to get Hillary elected. In essence, your defense is that any news forum that doesn't agree with your point of view has a vested interest in completely shirking their stated purpose to make sure Hillary gets elected. It begs the question, if you don't trust any news source, how can you trust any source that you've read that favors Trump? What if they have a vested interest in him? You seem to have your mind made up, but this is one case where I certainly wouldn't enjoy saying "I told you so."

CAPTAIN: I didn't say I don't trust any news source. I check the mainstream and I research other streams outside of that because I like a full view. I may be accused of being a conspiracy theorist, but I think there is a certain darkness out there that needs to be revealed. We will see how things shake out. But ultimately we are on the same team, citizens seeking the truth.

ANON3: Fair enough. I try to check a variety of sources myself. The debates should be interesting.

CAPTAIN: I agree, Anon3. And I have always respected your opinion, knowing you as well as I do. Let the political theatre begin...

ANON11: If he'd like to put his life on the line perhaps he should put on a uniform and head for Iraq. Barring that I think his kids could enlist. I mean, cut bone with bone if you're serious.

CAPTAIN: I don't think anyone should go to war, let alone in the middle east. If someone wanted to draft me for one of those engineered conflicts I wouldn't get anywhere near it. Trump is against military campaigning in the Middle East. Hillary already has Syria and Iran in her sights, as well as Russia. She's the warmonger of the two. Trump is far from a perfect candidate, but he isn't a war-for-profiteer.

ANON11: Like he profited off the 9/11 funds?

CAPTAIN: Or the Haitian relief funds that went into the Clinton Foundation? We may have a corruption fest on our hands in this one.

ANON11: Which went through the foundation and into AIDS medication for Haiti. Holding on to their 92% record of where the money went... no paintings.

CAPTAIN: Not what the Haitians say. They've been protesting, along with their President. Phones don't get smashed with hammers because there is anything good on them. Nor emails bleached, after being subpoenaed.

ANON11: And leave the world to the kindly and beneficent care of Putin.

ANON12: Oh god no.

ANON11: You'd think with all that money Donald would be able to afford some quality Peruvian flake.

ANON13: (Posts Guardian article about Prescott Bushes ties with Hitler.) Is this the article, Captain?

CAPTAIN: Yes, Anon13. The Clintons and the Bushes really mean well. They have experience running things, don't you know.

SEPTEMBER 26, 2016. - Post:

Some of you may find it odd that I'm supporting Trump. What he turns out to be or represent remains for history to tell. He has been outrageously smeared as some kind of new Hitler. Meanwhile, the money ties to funding the REAL HITLER connect to Prescott Bush. George Bush senior has endorsed Clinton and those two families have long been in bed together.

Put 2 and 2 together and figure out what that means. I am for Trump because of who he is taking on. The further we get into history, the less you can hide from your past. (Links Washington Times article on Bush family funding Hitler.)

ANON14: 100% You are a very few of the brave. Those that are opposed to Trump will ravage anyone that truly believes in him.

ANON15: And here I was thinking of going to visit you and Anon5 in Abiquiu. <sigh>

CAPTAIN: It's simply politics, Anon15. It's my belief that Clinton is getting a free pass with all the Trump hate. Some balance is needed.

ANON15: To a degree, I can agree with that.

ANON16: He's the one getting the pass-- the bar is set so low for him that all he has to do is put his name on the test and he gets an A. He is unprepared, unfit, and incapable of running this country.

CAPTAIN: If you play the Trump lottery, Anon16, you get to smash him with a hammer and bleach him. It's hard to win, tho. Hope you're doing well, miss you. Wine night to discuss politics.

ANON16: Miss you, too! Prob best to just stick to wine and reminiscing - just found you again and would hate for The Donald to come between us.

CAPTAIN: Would it build a wall?

ANON16: No wall cuz no way Mexico would pay for it!

CAPTAIN: Get a bottle of Trump wine.

ANON16: Too bad that was one of many of his business failures.

CAPTAIN: He got the licensing money up front.

ANON16: As long as he got paid... I actually would like to hear your views- even with all my fancy degrees, I don't understand how rational, intelligent people can support him. Gonna need more than a couple of bottles- may require entire Solvang wine tour worth of wine!

ANON: Ah, the Washington Times, owned by Sun Myung Moon's Unification Church, and a funder of the American Legislative Exchange Council (ALEC), whose agenda extends into almost all areas of law. Its bills undermine environmental regulations and deny climate change; support school privatization; undercut health care reform; defund unions and limit their political influence; restrain legislatures' abilities to raise revenue through taxes; mandate strict election laws that disenfranchise voters; increase incarceration to benefit the private prison industry, among many other issues.

ANON17: I don't find it odd at all and I agree with you, Captain.

ANON12: You've lost your marbles.

ANON18: Ahhhh politics... it's tricky. (Posts campaign sign meme that says: Everyone Sucks.)

CAPTAIN: Here we are now. Entertain us.

ANON18: Haha... Captain, you are the one with the gift to entertain us... I just think we are in for a ride regardless... Religion, money and politics and sometimes relationships... not good subjects... ever.

ANON8: Anyone can search: BUSH CLINTON MENA ARKANSAS - and should... but will they?

CAPTAIN: They have to want to know, Anon8. Many are comfortable simply hating on Trump and going full 3 monkeys on Clinton. But the curtain is being pulled back.

ANON4: I did and why would one believe all this when u see who is behind it and how it was done? If you really do, then someone should really make a "real" documentary about it and dig... or it does not mean a thing.

ANON8: Are you saying that you doubt what happened in Mena, Arkansas? Wow. PS. There won't be a "real" doc, by anyone who wants to "live." Take it from a doc filmmaker (me). Look up the term "arkancided" (term used to describe those murdered in Arkansas while Bubba was governor) - then later ruled to be "suicide." There are too many to count; many of the murders were gruesome; some involved kids. PS. A deep reader, or researcher could ask "where's the doc" on So Many Things, often just too dangerous to document. People have tried, many have died. *Conversely, the fact that you're seeing something on a screen doesn't always make it real these days, either. Good luck, Captain.

SEPTEMBER 29, 2016 – Post:

Clinton will probably make the White house. They stole the democratic nomination from Sanders and can likely do the same in the presidential.

Remember when Bernie's massive popular support got no mainstream media coverage? When mega-corporations want a candidate in there, they get them in there. They control the narrative and largely the voting process. It would take a miracle to stop them. Half the population think getting the most corrupt candidate in history elected is a good thing because they find the hate Trump kool-aid delicious, projecting everything they despise onto him. Trump will go back to making buildings. Many will miss being able to demonize him. They may even admit he was an interesting candidate, got good ratings. And then you will get your Clintons. There's no way to keep the scandal at bay for 4 full years in the White House. The Nixon helicopter is warming up in the background. (Posts Straight Outta Crooksville meme of Hillary and Nixon.)

ANON3: You mean Trump will go back to committing perjury, money laundering, being involved in thousands of lawsuits, strong-arming small businessmen out of their livelihoods, not paying any taxes and bragging about it, foolishly denying climate change, doing business with countries we have sanctions on, fat-shaming women, denying African Americans housing (but not admitting guilt when settling with the Justice Department, so it's all good), and threatening to punch people that are "mean" to him after presiding over a convention where a near lynch mob shouted "lock her up!" over and over again? Captain, I respect your intelligence as well, but I think the Kool Aid may be on the wrong foot, to mix a metaphor or two.

CAPTAIN: Clinton will continuing selling uranium to Russia via the Clinton Foundation, selling ambassadorships, etc. The Clinton's crimes are real and getting more and more documented. There's too much to keep a lid on. When Trump is gone they won't be able to project attention away from themselves onto him. She will get impeached like her husband, but this one will stick. And people will have to answer for voting for her.

ANON3: Trump's crimes are documented as well and new scandals get unearthed almost every single day. If we were to call it a wash in regards to how hard it is to say who's more corrupt and unethical, I give Clinton points on her experience, relationships with foreign leaders and/or their representatives, intelligence (isn't she supposed to be a member of the Illuminati?), temperament (yes, I said it. Just look at him in any debate and his twitter feed), established relationships with existing members of our government, tax plans that actually might benefit people like you and me, and the fact that Bernie Sanders, whom you feel was robbed and would have been the best candidate, is likely to be in her corner, possibly as part of her administration and has informed a lot of her current policy. While we were doing our back-and-forth, a friend posted this. Speaks to her good qualities better than I could. (Posts pro-Hillary Huffington Post article.)

CAPTAIN: I'm not saying Bernie was the best candidate, but just that he was robbed. The head of the DNC had to retire because of it. Then she was hired by Hillary. Thanks, Deb! haha. What Sanders and Trump signify in this election cycle are populist candidates calling out the inherent corruption of mega-corporations controlling democracy. I don't mind that people dislike Sanders or Trump because at least the message is getting out there. Trump is the first political figure since JFK to bring up the dark dealings of the Federal Reserve. That got JFK killed, so I respect Trump greatly for it.

ANON3: Don't get me wrong. I agree that today's generation of voters are making a clear statement with both Sanders and Trump that we as a people don't want to accept the status quo of politics with a shrug and a "what can you do?" Politicians shouldn't have to be only crooks and liars, and the people are saying we don't want to accept that, and I am all for that. The thing is: baby steps. The statement is made. Bernie had a lot of pie-in-the-sky ideas that were never going to happen. Trump is a liar on an epic scale among other things, so he's not really as big a change from "politics-as-usual" as people would like to believe. Hillary may be mega-flawed, but she represents all that is good with the concept of being an experienced politician if only in the sense that she knows what she's doing enough to not fuck up the economy, or the world beyond repair.

CAPTAIN: The economy may already be f**ked up beyond repair since the trillions of dollars printed out of thin air to patch up the credit/default swap of 2008 could wreck our currency.

ANON3: I'm not sure where you're getting that from. Even Republicans say we are in a recovery, they just like the buzz-phrase "it's the slowest recovery since the Great Depression" as a way to downplay that it is a recovery, and that it's a recovery from failed Republican policies that have put us in a Recession twice in our lifetimes. The stock market is at record highs, Unemployment is down more than even Mitt Romney promised he would get it to if he were elected... I'm not exactly rolling in dough myself but I'm a damn sight better off than I was in early-2009. It's interesting just how many Billionaires support Hillary and are actively campaigning against Trump.

CAPTAIN: It's basic math. You can't print trillions out of thin air without it devaluing the dollar. Fiat currencies are very susceptible to this and ever have been. Will see how it comes out in the wash. It may take a little while. They may propose a new currency. There are a lot of possibilities. Hillary does have more experience. But like Trump said, it's bad experience. But I do enjoy the tete-a-tete with you, Anon3... The final answers will end up in the book of history. Trump may turn out to be a blip on the radar, like Bernie. But the Clintons can't hide. Nor can the Bushes.

ANON19: Can't believe you equate HRC's sometimes blurry actions to the life-long career of thieving, deception, cheating and flim-flammery of the promoter of "Trump University," phonied up steaks, undelivered condos for retirees, a fraudster who systematically defrauds small business owners (of a class with the naive but racist and hateful rubes erecting "Trump/Pence" banners up and down R. 29 through Virginia!). If she pressured unsavory oil despots to pitch in to the Foundation, or they chose to because they assumed it gave them points, so much the better for the help it provides poor third-world kids! The Foundation has been very thoroughly vetted and gets high marks, unlike the Donald's phony "charity" front, where he just takes other's money, and PAYS HIMSELF! How can you compare those things? The uranium deal was blessed by 9 other unrelated federal agencies, see John Oliver 9/25/16. Read the comments of Trump's biographer about how he can't hold a thought for two minutes, doesn't read (except Hitler's speeches!) and knows nothing. And you denigrate HRC, a past master on policy and world events with 8 years in the Senate and a full tour as Sec State? I know, she has sold out to Goldman and Walmart, but at least, unlike Trump's patrons, they're American! Her worst things are befriending Kissinger and appointing Salazar, both unforgivable but I'm gonna go get a drink and try to forget about that stuff.

CAPTAIN: I think history will be kinder to Nixon than the Clintons. But you do have a point about that drink, Anon19.

ANON3: I still think you like your conspiracy theories so as to make life more sexy and intriguing than it really is. Hillary has a lot of history of pushing bills and working with the poor and children and churches and the like that I don't buy that she's pure evil. Read the article I just sent you and see the history of Bills and Acts that she was behind. A lot of them are undeniably good causes.

CAPTAIN: There are many examples that represent Trump as a good person, as well, but he is painted as pure evil. The Orange Hitler. Just a few years ago he was on Oprah and she was encouraging him to run for president and the audience cheered. That same audience might boo him today, because the media narrative shifted on a dime once he went up against Hillary. The powers that back Clinton are very powerful. They can make Trump seem like whatever they want him to seem like. Some people actually believe he's some kind of Nazi, which is insane. Either way, the odds of him winning are roughly akin to Luke Skywalker blowing up the Death Star with one shot, so I don't think you have anything to worry about if you actually want the Clintons in the White House.

ANON20: I'm calling BS right now on this whole thing. I don't think you believe one thing you have said.... this is a practical joke to see how far you can go with Trump rhetoric. Either that or you've been hacked.

CAPTAIN: Anon20, I think the truth will come out on the Clintons much more fully once they are back in the White House. It's the information age and you can only keep these things secret for so long. Wikileaks is just the start. My vote for Trump is largely symbolic as the odds of defeating a candidate with such corporate titans behind her is nearly impossible. And she does know the insider game much better than Trump, having been in political power for many, many years.

ANON20: Nope. You're smarter than this. You know Trump is a lying, womanizing, racist crook who is unfit to lead anything and only has interest in the presidency for himself. Fun hoax you're pulling!

CAPTAIN: Trump has been portrayed as the root of all evil by the campaign running against him. But the campaign will soon be over and unless something unbelievable happens, Clinton will be in the White House and have to face her own record without Trump there to deflect attention to. There will be a celebratory few months... and then the shadow of Nixon will gradually appear on the horizon. Nobody destroys 13 cell phones with a hammer and bleaches 33K emails after being subpoenaed by Congress because there is anything good on them. That's basic Nixon math. And no amount of Trump hate can change it. He will soon be gone and those action will still be there.

ANON3: I agree with Anon20, Captain. I know you're a smart guy, and I know you like to take the less popular side of an argument because it's more challenging, and the popular side seems more like what all the "sheep" are doing. There are times, though, when the popular side just happens to be right. I don't think Trump became "suddenly evil" due to Hillary somehow controlling the media and getting every trusted source of news to risk it's reputation by blatantly lying. I think Trump, as a private citizen, had no reason for the media to delve into his character, until he ran for President. Not "against Hillary" but "at all." The People have a right to know who they're voting (or not voting) for. I again point to the Newsweek article that documents Trump's history of failure in business, being bailed out by his rich Dad, prejudiced actions against Blacks, Hispanics, and Native Americans long before he was ever involved in politics, with most of their source material being from court records. That isn't a "biased media," that's viewable court documents from cases that actually happened. Trump's not being "painted" as Orange Hitler, he's being "revealed" as Orange Hitler. Up until he entered the race, we knew a few bad things about him already, like his tendency to cheat on his wives just as an example, but nobody cared, because he didn't matter. As a reality TV star, he was executive producer on the show and had control over how his image was presented, and he still looked like an asshole. Now that he has put himself in the spotlight, and demanded to be taken seriously as a candidate for the highest office in the country, people are shining a deep, detailed spotlight on him and his history, as they should. That he can't handle people "saying mean things about him" is another case for him not being suited for politics in general. Oprah, I'm sure, has changed her mind. The President gets criticized often and by almost everybody. If he wins, he should get used to people "not being nice." You never know when some jackass of a private citizen, with no understanding of politics, might come out of the woodwork and jump on a bandwagon to question his birth certificate. Wasn't his Mother born in Ireland? Was she a naturalized citizen when she gave birth to him? I don't know...

CAPTAIN: I disagree with the official assessment of Trump, Anon3. You are parroting the campaign attack against him to me and I'm already very familiar with it. There are many other sources out there that reveal him in a completely different light. But people at this point are going to believe the narrative they want to believe. I've researched both of them exhaustively. However, my real point is this: Trump is not going to win unless something unprecedented happens. Then there will be nothing to deflect attention to and you'll be left with the fact that no one smashes 13 cell phones with a hammer and bleaches 33K emails after being subpoenaed because there is something good on them. I stand by my Nixon comparison. The helicopter will come...

ANON3: I don't enjoy arguing with you in the sense that I'd rather we just agree. I don't doubt that Hillary covered up something she knew was a foolish mistake and hoped wouldn't see the light in time to ruin her bid for the Presidency. I don't doubt that she's made some huge errors in judgement, and has ties to some shady things, as most politicians do. I'm not promoting any attack. I'm using my eyes and ears and observing a guy who's a hot head, a crybaby, a liar, not very smart, and completely unprepared for the position that he's aiming for. As you said, people believe what they want to believe, but I'm just calling it how I see it, often on live television. If you have to dig deep into conspiracy theories that involve the entire media working in concert to slam a poor innocent businessman, I think it shows that you're stretching a bit to make a point you want desperately to believe despite mountains of evidence to the contrary. I'm not sure why you want to believe it. As I've said before, the last thing either of us should ever want to say in this case is "I told you so."

CAPTAIN: It's not a argument, but a healthy debate. Which we both enjoy. If you don't want Trump in the White House and view him as a danger, you might be better served viewing him as intelligent, which he is (156 IQ, Ivy league graduate Wharton School of Business, owner of a billion dollar business, media manipulator, etc) and perhaps more of an actual threat because of that. If he was a rank and file dummy he never could have gotten to where he is, whether you love, him, hate him or are indifferent. If there's one thing I don't think Clinton is, it's a moron. They are both very calculating, very intelligent people. For better or worse.

ANON3: Sure, it's healthy debate. I just hate being so opposed to you that I feel I have to counter everything you say. I would agree that Trump has shown cleverness and the ability to manipulate people... And then there's times where he announces he's smart and has "the best words" and then says "My plan is going to cut taxes Big League and yours will raise them Big League" and you just gotta wonder. The smartest guy in the room is never the guy who tells you he's the smartest guy in the room.

ANON11: I'd rather have someone inside the tent that's pissing out that outside the tent that's pissing in.

ANON2: Not supporting a side in this argument but quick question, if Hillary controlled the media that much, wouldn't she have beaten Obama? Ok, I'm back out of this conversation. Good night everyone. I'm voting for the hologram of Lincoln!

CAPTAIN: Hillary doesn't personally control the media. And as an individual agent she doesn't have that much power, or at least not power that couldn't easily be transferred to someone else. But she is the candidate of certain very powerful interests that want her in the White House. Candidates don't always represent different factions in this respect, but this is an unusual election. Back when Bush ran "against" Kerry they might as well have been the same person with two heads.

ANON3: Sorry, I don't agree with that either.

CAPTAIN: What aspect of it, the Bush vs Kerry?

ANON3: Probably all of it, but the Bush vs. Kerry thing in particular. The difference in economic polices was vast and definitely affected me personally. I doubt I would have had a full-on panic attack in 2009 that I was going to lose my house under Kerry. Anon2, Not taking a side is really taking a side Switzerland.

ANON2: no hablo ingles.

ANON21: Captain, Andy Kaufman wants his shtick back.

CAPTAIN: I wish Tony Clifton was running, Anon21. The debates could have a lounge singing segment.

ANON11: If it's one thing I've learned is this: the people who think they're in control, aren't. The people who want to be in control, shouldn't be. And the people who think they're being controlled, are being controlled by themselves to absolve themselves of responsibility.

CAPTAIN: Well said, Anon11.

ANON3: I agree.

ANON22: With all due respect, Clinton is no Nixon. Nixon was a paranoid personality just short of a psychopath, who lied as a strategy for daily living. It was only when his lies, which included extending the Vietnam War and costing tens of thousands of American soldiers their lives, caught up with him publicly that he was forced to resign. Hillary is not that dark. She's drifted a bit, but she's never claimed to be Snow White. Nixon was a truly dark figure, and one who did not recognize the extent of his own darkness to the end of his days. The comparison, just factually, does not hold water. We have not yet seen Hillary in the presidency. People are making premature judgments about her, for many reasons. Some of it may prove true, but it is still premature. Nixon we can judge as a whole, and except for his support of the Clean Air Act and his overture to China, he does not come out well in history's judgment.

CAPTAIN: I predict Hillary will top Nixon when all is said and done, provided she gets the throne. As secretary of state, she's in a class with Kissinger, though he's a tough one to beat. Would be great if you did the astrology charts of Trump & Clinton, Anon22.

ANON22: These are well known, Captain, but I might do one for those who do not already know the charts.

CAPTAIN: An article on both of their charts and what it might mean for our current cycle would be a fantastic post, Anon22. Count me in.

ANON11: Nixon got a favorite cousin of mine killed in Vietnam by his useless invasion into the Parrots Beak. So any reference to him boils my blood. Might be one reason I've never voted for a Republican in 40 years.

CAPTAIN: Virtually the entirety of my cause, Anon11, is to bring down the war-for-profiteers. Clinton is a proven warmonger. It's really less about her then the interests that back her like Soros and the corrupt aspects of the word banking empire that engages in these activities, financing both sides of every war, etc. It's the old guard that needs to fall. Undoubtedly, we both agree on this as we are artists. Does Trump represent a change from this? It's impossible to say because he hasn't held office. He could be almost anything. He could even be helping Clinton get elected. I hope that's not the case, but it is in the realm of possibility. He has stated he wants to end unnecessary wars in the middle east. He has spoken out against the Fed. He may only be a sign of the times, a bellwether, like Bernie Sanders, of a populace fed up with the violence and the propaganda being force fed to us. I appreciate your intelligence and your viewpoints and we truly are both on the same side here, as we look through the funhouse mirror of the strangest political cycle of our lifetime.

OCTOBER 1, 2016. - Post: Ben Garrison illustration of "The Crooked House of Clinton."

ANON23: We should hold career politicians and the entire ruling political class to a far higher standard than any non-politician who runs against them. This country was established on the idea of "No taxation without representation." We need representation, or we overthrow the government. We did it before, we can do it again.

CAPTAIN: A reformation is better than a revolt. Has to be someone from outside the establishment order. A Cyrus or a Trump card.

ANON23: However we establish representation for our taxation works for me. It was enough to give us what we have enjoyed for 250 years. We should be willing to defend it. As Thomas Jefferson said: "The price of freedom is eternal vigilance." As Ben Franklin said: "We need a revolution every 200 years."

ANON11: And what an amazing President she'll be. I look forward to eight years of her saving America from Itself. Replacing four SCOTUS judges and the waning of the Alt right to a few toothless enclaves in the mountains of Kantucki and Orange country. All of them living on some form of 'guvmint' subsistence whilst all the while railing against 'big guvmint.' Internationally, she'll tell Putin to fuck off, tell China to keep their little boats in harbor and send ten C-130's to drop relief into Aleppo under heavy AWACS and fighter cover and dare anyone to fuck with us. And don't forget rebuilding this country, which is already great.

CAPTAIN: She'll be a brain in a jar by the end of the first term at the rate her health is collapsing.

ANON23: Anon11, That's just more American Imperialism. You took the hook, line and sinker... you should definitely vote for Hillary.

ANON11: Considering the alternatives, I will. Captain, I know she's not good enough for your exacting standards, but I'll settle on her nonetheless.

ANON23: Vote your conscious, on principles, not the lesser of two evils or out of fear. Otherwise, the truth will not prevail.

CAPTAIN: Most important election in US history, we can all agree on that...

ANON15: I think Bush v. Gore might have been the most important, sadly. And Gore won.

CAPTAIN: Ah... the hanging chads... There is something unusual about this election, tho.

ANON11: I like her, she's a tough bitch that's handled mountains of shit from all sides being thrown at her and does so with class. Putin and the Republicorp© pigf**kers are afraid of her and that's good for me. She's not the lesser of two evils but the best qualified to run the country. Call me what you will (and you will) but I'm good with her. Compared to your favored Baboon and/or the pothead.

CAPTAIN: Trump is closer to an independent candidate. But he wisely realized that he had to be in one of the two major parties to have any chance at the presidency. Even the Republican establishment tried to block him every step of the way. And yet here he is. Tied with Clinton in October. In an existential battle for the soul of America. Conceived in Liberty... The story ain't over yet, Anon23. It's always darkest before the Don.

ANON39: If we finally get the FEMA camps we keep getting promised all will be forgiven.

CAPTAIN: Trump will covert the FEMA camps into Sharper Image stores.

ANON16: Time to change the congress! They failed us the most!

CAPTAIN: Who has been in charge? That's what needs to change. Spring cleaning time. Starting with a new president from outside the current political system.

ANON8: You def. have some work cut out for you, Captain. Tho not certain "critical thinking" will be in everyone's toolkit. Good Luck!

OCTOBER 2, 2016. - Post: Meme of Trump and Eagle in front of sparkling American flag.

The Eagle knows and has chosen.

ANON25: Seriously, Captain. I can't take it anymore. Say what you want about Hillary but please don't promote this poor excuse for a human being.

CAPTAIN: He's the beginning of the end of a corrupt and dark system. Many lies and untruths have been promoted about him in the campaign to bring him down. He's not perfect, nobody is, but he is the right person at the right time to take these forces on. You will see. Many peoples opinion of him will change and change dramatically.

ANON25: I have no interest in social media political discussions and My mind is made up listening to all of HIS own words, alone. I guess I'm just shocked by all the pro Trump posts.

CAPTAIN: Something is going on that is not so obvious on the surface. I've never voted in my life and I'm voting in this election. I love you always no matter who you vote for. I've made my choice, after a great deal of research. Me and the Eagle.

ANON25: Captain, obviously ditto, just wish this enthusiasm was for someone else! Like Bernie or Jill Stein.

CAPTAIN: In order for it to matter and for the change to be real it has to be someone who can win. Bernie actually did win the democratic nomination, but Clinton stole it from him. It will be much harder to do that to Trump-- though they will most certainly try.

ANON11: Ok, Captain, you want to bring the entire corrupt system down and smash the world because it isn't living up to your standards. Good luck with that... you do know that includes the entire film industry along with it.

ANON26: He went to my hometown and embarrassed himself there. And that's no conspiracy theory. It's one of those things like that song "I'm not crazy, everybody ELSE is crazy." As my dad would say, he's a bad actor. And you know, Ben Franklin wanted the wild turkey to be our national bird. With Trump, he gets his wish. But, love you anyway!

CAPTAIN: A reformation of the system, not a smashing. We've come too far to destroy. And love you guys, as well. Hollywood is not going anywhere when Trump is president. Make Movies Great Again!

ANON17: And even if Hollyweird was affected, it would not affect the independent film industry.

ANON12: (Posts photo of Eagle making Trump flinch.)

ANON27: Haha, classic.

CAPTAIN: Trump faced the judgement of the Great Bird. It is not a creature to take lightly. The Clintons would not even be in the same room with the Eagle as it would whisk them away to kingdom come. Was going to delete image but will leave it because it illustrates something: the Eagle is real. Not CGI. Trump weathered the storm and got the shot. The Eagle has chosen.

ANON27: Ha!

ANON5: (Posts article from writer who claims Trump is making him a hypocrite).

CAPTAIN: When you have billions at your service and the complicity of most of the mainstream media, you can destroy the reputation of anyone alive. They are going all-out to ruin Trump now because they know he can win on votes and he equals the end of their rule. Files have been leaked from their campaign. They have already filed three fake Jane Doe lawsuits with women that don't exist so that they can frame Trump for rape of minors right before the election. Do you think they will give up their power without pulling out every sick and dark trick in the book? It is going to get very dramatic in the next weeks. People will be calling for Trump to drop out or even be arrested. And yet here we are and the story is not over yet. I'm proud not to be one of the sheeple easily hypnotized by the media. I do my own research and the real information on both candidates is out there for any patriotic American who desires the truth and isn't lazy about finding it. One day, maybe in a month, maybe in 10 years, what I have said will be common truth. Until then, I stand for Justice. The Clinton's time in power will not last long.

CAPTAIN deletes some derogatory anti-Trump posts from Anon12.

ANON12: Captain! Stop deleting my comments! You react like an upset child.

CAPTAIN: You know where your own page is. That is where you go to show how much you believe in your own candidate.

ANON12: Truth hurts, honey. "The Eagle" doesn't like your boy. Sorry bout'cha.

CAPTAIN: We will see on Nov. 8th.

ANON12: This is real life, Captain. Not LOTR. Birds don't come from the sky and choose our leaders. Get a grip, kid. Jesus.

CAPTAIN: All part of the fun. Trump made politics fun again. It was gonna be Clinton vs Bush. And no bird could save us from that.

ANON12: I suppose the white guy who fails recognize gender inequality would consider misogyny and racism "fun." You're a real winner.

ANON6: Clinton voted against gay marriage. Remember...

CAPTAIN: The guy who hired the first female campaign manager in GOP history. The guy who's getting the most African American support in modern GOP politics. Not everyone is buying the racist sexist BS.

ANON12: The only people not "buying into it" are those too ignorant to look anywhere beyond their own privilege.

ANON6: That's america-the-ignorant-masses speak.

ANON12: Aka: You.

CAPTAIN: The deplorables, haha. And maybe some of the super predators. And probably more than a few of the women Mr. Clinton raped.

ANON16: Am all about ending corrupt and dark system, as you call it, but would rather 1,000 years of our government as is than to support the next Hitlerian dictator. There is no conspiracy to knock him down-- he does that all by himself. He is constitutionally incapable of putting the needs of others ahead of himself. You very eloquently herald the rights of boys to not have their bodies altered thru circumcision-- what of the rights of women to choose, the rights of the LGBT community to marry who they love, the rights of workers to form unions, the rights of Muslims to worship freely, the rights of young men of color to walk the streets without being profiled? These are just a few of the rights at stake if Trump were to appoint justices to SCOTUS.

CAPTAIN: Trump is pro LGBT, always has been. See his interview with The Advocate in 2000. He was the first Republican candidate to state he will defend their rights and he got a cheer from the crowd. And he said thank you for cheering that. Another first.

ANON16: He also used to be pro-choice.

CAPTAIN: There is no such thing as a perfect candidate. But this is the one who has come forth to right the system. The Eagle has two claws. One for each of the Clintons.

ANON16: At least her appointments to SCOTUS won't send us back to the dark ages. His will.

ANON11: Eagles are scavengers.

ANON6: lol.

ANON23: Good luck with your choice. (Posts George Bernard Shaw meme: "All great truths begin as blasphemies.")

ANON28: As the father of two daughters, any man who sticks up for another man who says such things about women has lost all respect. Period.

CAPTAIN: Would you leave your daughters with the Clintons? Bill rapes them and Hillary destroys the women who come forward about it. Get real. This is about deeds. Not political correctness. The Clinton's dead skeletons are getting up to dance.

ANON28: Captain, this really requires a stronger b.s. detector: (posts link to "Blinded by the Right" wikipage.) Turns out that whole vast, right wing conspiracy thing was true.

CAPTAIN: The writing is on the wall. The Clinton/Bushes have been weighed and they have been found wanting.

ANON28: American foreign and domestic policy has always been wanting... thinking of this as a referendum on the "system" is a red herring. As if a real estate investor/developer who inherited all his wealth is an outsider to the American power elite. C'mon...

CAPTAIN: Trump is not a shill for mega-corporations and globalists like Hillary is. Neither was Bernie, who took that system on, but folded like a weak tent. Trump will not fold.

ANON23: Anon28, the late Christoper Hitchens critique? "The whole book is an exercise in self-love."

ANON28: Anon23, the same self-critique could be said of Hitchens--though he varies between self-love and self-hate... Trump is a vacuous shill for himself. To think Trump is ever going to represent anyone other than himself is an exercise in self-deception.

CAPTAIN: People all over the world. Join hands. Start a Trump train.

ANON23: This election is not about Trump v Hillary. It's about rattling the cages of the ruling political class, Republican or Democratic. And whoa are they angry... since they control the press, evidently. So are we supposed to be angry? On the contrary, we should be celebrating the opportunity for breaking their hegemony, without a revolution. Trump is a small price to pay for that. He is the ultimate parody of their hold on power.

ANON29: You have brass balls, Captain... and I for one admire that. Best to you, sir.

ANON28: More Andy Kaufman! (Posts meme of Kaufman pulling off Trump mask.)

CAPTAIN: Andy votes Trump.

ANON23: I'd put 90% of the responses to your posts, Captain, in the Anger/Bitterness column. This is why artists are important to society. (Posts meme about how information bell curves from denial to anger to exploration to acceptance.)

OCTOBER 3, 2016. - Post: Braco illustration of Hillary being propped up by the Networks, while standing on a carpet that hides all of her scandals.

ANON23: Cattle Futures?... That's news to me.

ANON11: Captain, Captain, Captain.

ANON23: Weekend at Hillary's.

ANON11: I notice that Fox isn't one of the networks shown. Is that because they're honest in being the Duck's bum boys?

CAPTAIN: If one major station doesn't present a somewhat Pro-Trump POV it would be too obvious even for Hillary supporters. But for every clear Trump fan on Fox like Hannity, they will balance it with a Megyn Kelly. Clinton will not get hit with any gotcha questions at the debates, or on CNN, least of all by CIA "intern" and TimeWarner employee Anderson Cooper. The debates will be controlled to give Clinton the usual edge (moderator in the pocket, 40 interruptions of Trump vs. 2 for Clinton, 15 specific questions directed to Trump vs 2 to Clinton. Addressing all of his 'scandals' like tax returns and none of hers, like email destruction, etc). Even still, Trump will match or best her in the debates. Clinton cannot beat him with hard votes. They already know that. Trump is breaking stadium records for attendance and Hillary has to bus in high school students to her small closed & staged rallies. The race is not tied now as the polls suggest. Trump is well ahead. They have to steal the election. It is the only way they can win and of course they will do everything in their power to steal it. They will probably get caught stealing it. The question comes down to whether they can power through getting caught (like with Bernie) and still make it into office. Clinton's supporters need to ask themselves: would I be okay with Clinton cheating the election process in order to beat Trump? If you are okay with that because you hate Trump, then you have given up on even the pretense of a free and just election, and it will mark the end of the USA as we know it. And it won't feel fine...

ANON30: I don't follow it anymore. I just try to not get any of it on the bottoms of my boots...

ANON8: 4 months old... Even truer now!? - yeesh.

ANON31: Great picture! Nails it!

OCTOBER 5, 2016. - Post: Photo of Trump in the Oval Office already.

"Some people want it to happen, some wish it would happen, others make it happen." – Michael Jordan

ANON11: He's reading the NY Post.

ANON32: If you know anything about Jordan, then you know he'd never endorse any candidate.

CAPTAIN: My endorsement. Jordan's work ethic.

ANON15: What is the "it"? Bankruptcies? Lawsuits? Sexual assault charges? Cascades of false claims, hurtful statements, and impoverished workers? You are so talented and so visionary, Captain, this is just hard to understand.

CAPTAIN: Probably the only person in the US who can stand up to the globalists and stand a chance. I see through the lies put forth to bring him down. The Bush/Clinton empire is over.

ANON15: All righty then!

CAPTAIN: Forget about Trump for a week, Anon15, and do some serious research into the Clintons outside the mainstream media.

ANON15: I don't follow Trump at all. Nor do I unreservedly support Clinton. I've pretty much been following Clinton all my adult life, as she was the friend of a close friend who went to law school with her... I'm aware of her lies (less outrageous and racist than Trump's, but still disconcerting), but equally aware of her strengths, and what is at stake. But I don't think we will persuade each other, so I'll look forward to your next film. That is to say, I have more important things to do with my time than follow Trump's every foible! I've considered him ridiculous since his reality show, and haven't wholly supported Clinton since she voted to send troops into Iraq. So there we are, and Clinton is my choice between the two.

CAPTAIN: I respect your choice. And I never let politics come between friends. See you in Taos.

ANON15: (smiley emoji)

ANON28: What makes you think this guy is anti-Bush/Clinton or anti empire?

CAPTAIN: He's the first candidate with a real shot that is not owned by mega-corporate donors. Bernie wasn't owned, but he was a career politician and he buckled when it counted. Trump may be a Hail Mary pass, but at least there is a chance. A chance to have a chance. As a student of history (that often repeats itself) he is reminiscent of Cyrus, who was a very, very unlikely personage to assume the mantel of leadership. Something very unusual is happening in this election, the likes of which I have never seen. I've never voted before or even taken the process seriously, but this is a historic moment.

ANON28: And how do we know he's not owned by mega-donors without seeing his taxes? Because he says so? I find it bizarre that people who are reasonably skeptical of career politicians seem to completely suspend their skepticism of someone who so clearly uses lying as a strategy.

CAPTAIN: Many people are skeptical of the mainstream media. It has, in fact, never had less credibility. And they wonder why it is almost entirely arrayed against Trump, when the most blatantly corrupt politician (plus husband) is also running for office. A good deal of the world is hoping & some are praying that Trump actually wins, because they instinctively get that Clinton equals war and with Trump there is at least a chance that he's someone who wants to promote prosperity and not permanent war-for-profit end game.

ANON28: People are right to be suspicious of media, particularly as it is so dominated by corporate interests. But arrayed against Trump? The mainstream media gave him 5 months of free press covering his every move. As the head of CBS said "Trump may be bad for America, but he's great for us." The mainstream media has given Trump a free pass with wall-to-wall coverage because they have made millions off of him. Outside of the US, who is hoping and praying that Trump wins? I'd be particularly interested in an analysis of Netanyahu as a Trump supporter who is someone opposed to a state of permanent war.

CAPTAIN: The media couldn't resist the ratings Trump brought, so they promoted him at the same time they demonized him, which was a strange tactic, but brought us to where we are now. You do however make an interesting point with Netanyahu. Israel might be the most complex piece of the entire world puzzle.

ANON16: He may not be owned by mega-corporations, because he IS the corporation! The conflicts of interest that will exist if he is elected are beyond anything we've seen. He would literally have to sell his entire company and all their holdings and the money placed in a blind trust-- he clearly isn't going to do that. He and his kids don't even know what a blind trust is. How can you trust he would put anyone else's interests ahead of own?

CAPTAIN: Years of deep research (initially for a writing job) into the Clintons & Bushes revealed to me that you cannot get any worse or dark than their record in office or out. You make good points, Anon16, about the complications of having a giant business and then transitioning into presidential office. Personally, I'd rather cross that bridge than the other one. But that's what this comes down to. Making a choice between these two options or not making a choice at all and rejecting the entire electoral process because you think it's a charade. My entire life I have gone with the third option. This time I'm voting.

ANON16: I may not agree with your beliefs, but I do believe in getting involved and voting! I'm not gonna stop giving my opinion or challenging you on yours. I also will keep trying to see things from your perspective.

CAPTAIN: Thanks, Anon16. And I'm right there with you on that. Love ya, darling.

ANON16: Time to share that love over a few goblets of wine!

ANON33: (Posts article from Everyday Feminism regarding Trump's 'emotional abuse' of Clinton in the first Presidential Debate, a Trump cheated workers story, and a Pro-Bernie meme)

CAPTAIN: What they did to Bernie was shameful. They stole the nomination from him in cold blood, right in the face of the American Public and the MSM contributed to the robbery. H. Clinton can't be emotionally abused at this point, least of all in a debate. She's the destroyer of the women who came forward about her husband's sexual assaults and rape.

ANON33: You know I'm the biggest Bernie supporter... I canvassed for him, opened my home for a Venice canvass for a month. Yes, the DNC mistreated him... but Drumpf is very very dangerous. He is a liar. He is a fraud. He scams people. He is a racist. He is a misogynist. He is in bed with the Russians. He thinks we should use nuclear weapons. He thinks that women who get abortions should be punished. He is unpredictable. He acts like a child. He's defensive. He is very very dangerous. I shutter at the thought of him as President, responsible for appointing one, two or three supreme court justices; responsible for running our foreign policy without offending anyone. Moreover, the greatest threat to our nation right now is climate change. We have passed 400 ppm of CO_2... we have more CO_2 in our atmosphere than at any time in the last 2 million years. We are headed to global disaster. And Drumpf thinks climate change is a plot created by the Chinese. We need thoughtful leadership. Yes... Hilary is manipulative and played unethical games to beat Bernie... but she does stand up against climate change, she does believe in a woman's right to choose, she is not childish and reactive, she will get along with other nations. Voting for Drumpf is suicidal for our nation.

CAPTAIN: Clinton didn't merely play unethical games. The democratic process itself was potentially revealed as a joke and a scam. I don't know how much research you've done into the Clintons and the Bushes, but their history is very, very dark and they have been in office and in power for many, many years. The campaign against Trump is immense, backed by some of the most powerful agents in the world. There's a reason they don't want him in there and it's not because he is childish. Clinton will most assuredly not get along with other nations. She has plans for war in Syria & Iran and possibly Russia & China. Trump has expressed no interest in war beyond defeating Isis and maintaining strong borders.

ANON33: Did you watch the video above about how he cheated the architect? There's a few more with glass maker and a piano dealer telling their story of Drumpf refusing to pay them... and how it destroyed them, and their small business went bankrupt. Then there is Trump University and all the students he cheated. And the undocumented immigrants he refused to pay $8/hour. Captain, you've hired people to work on your films. Tell me, what kind of person does this? What kind of person hires people, agrees to a price, then refuses to pay them? And not because he can't... he's a billionaire worth $10 billion he claims... but because he's greedy and mean. What kind of person doesn't care about the suffering they cause by cheating people? He is a bully. He's a sick bully. He's dangerous and immoral. As awful as the Bushes and Clintons have been... and I have read about it... they have never not paid their workers. You know there is a biblical injunction that was just read in synagogue for the Jewish New Year about paying your laborers within a day. Paying the people who work for you is fundamental, ancient, the basic behavior of a moral person. Drumpf is an arrogant immoral hypocritical lying bully who doesn't even have the human decency to pay his workers... not one incident but tens, maybe hundreds of examples when he didn't have the human decency to pay his workers. What the Clintons and Bushes did was driven by political ambition. I'm not excusing them... but Drumpf's horrific behavior is at a whole other level in hell. He's a selfish narcissist who doesn't care about people and who would be a horrible dangerous president.

CAPTAIN: Um, Papa Bush financing Hitler's rise can't be written off as mere political ambition. I know the msm narrative is that Trump is some evil businessman. But when you research the 1,000's of people that have worked for him, they paint a very different picture, and they are voting for him. He's promoted more female executives to high office then any major businessman. He became public enemy #1 when he went up against the Clintons. Before that virtually everyone in American life knew him to be what he was, a builder and a TV personality who employed a lot of people. The Clintons meanwhile have a dead pool of 114 people, all of whom had dirt on them politically. Unfortunately for them, but fortunately for us, their time on stage is over. I think you're a great women, Anon33, and this whole process is about uncovering the truth behind power. Let's see what is revealed in the end. I wouldn't vote for a Bush or Clinton if there was a gun to my head. Trump, like Bernie, is a sign of the times. Populist candidates getting record support challenging a corrupt system. I know you don't believe in Trump, so I won't try to change your mind. But the Clintons are not going to be granted anymore power. Their time is up.

ANON16: If promoting women to executive offices is a trait you admire, how about promoting a woman to the HIGHEST office!

CAPTAIN: The first woman president is going to happen but to have it be Hillary Clinton would be tragic. It would be like having Richard Nixon as the first US president. I'm sure George Washington was no saint, but history preserves a reverence for him. In the information age, there's almost no chance Clinton could get through office without being subsumed by scandal and possible impeachment. It would be more of a setback than a step forward. But I understand the great interest in seeing it happen, regardless of who it is. It's just too bad that it's Hillary Clinton.

ANON33: I so wish Bernie were running. But I think Drumpf is pure evil. I don't see how Papa Bush's war profiteering in the 1930s is relevant to this election. Its not the msm narrative that Drumpf is an evil businessman... the horrible way he treated his workers and his investors has slowly leaked out in spite of the msm obsession with Drumpf. I don't know who these 1,000s of people are who have worked for him and love him. Why don't you post a link? From what I have read and heard first hand, he's a greedy, selfish human. Read the article I posted on my page about his taxes... He stuck it to his employees, the banks that loaned him money and the investors in his company. He's a selfish bully. I would say to you... be careful what you wish for... but I'm confident Drumpf will never win.

CAPTAIN: (Posts video about a Black Female employee of Trump who gives her testimony of his good-heartedness)

ANON33: Nice video about one employee that they treated well. Great. But meaningless in terms of all the harm Trump has done. I'm glad he treats some of his friends and close employees well. Also, I would add... In terms of the Trump charity... it has been revealed that Trump talked a lot about charity but never contributed. And that his charity was illegally taking donations. And that he was using his charity illegally for personal benefit. I can provide links to his charity fraud if you are care.

OCTOBER 7, 2016 - Post: Newspaper memes declaring Trump has already won the Presidency in a landslide.

The 45th President of the United States of America. Donald J. Trump.

NOTE: Shortly thereafter, on this same day, the infamous Access Hollywood tape emerged...

ANON3: What newspaper is that? I have a friend who tells me not to trust anything I see in the media.

CAPTAIN: When it can no longer be denied, it will finally be embraced.

ANON3: Uhhh, right.

CAPTAIN: (posts Trump Triumph meme)

ANON34: Not in my lifetime...

CAPTAIN: Love you, Anon34! And we both love a good story– so let's see where this goes.

ACCESS HOLYWOOOD TAPE NOW RELEASED...

ANON28: Your guy killed it today...

CAPTAIN: Town hall on Sunday.

ANON35: Disgusting. (Cites Washington Post article about the tape and how establishment Republicans are now distancing themselves from Trump)

CAPTAIN: The October surprise. A big factor, that I will concur with. Not a remotely good look at all. However, it will bring the Bill Clinton

Rape-a-palooza into full effect this Sunday, with Hillary's destruction of the women who came forward. They will both take the gloves off at the town hall. But I agree that this sets back Trump and advances Clinton on the chessboard. Andy Kaufman is making more popcorn...

ANON35: Andy might be enjoying this. (Posts Kaufman/Trump mask meme)

CAPTAIN: I think you get why I enjoy this election so much, Anon35.

ANON35: Captain, I think I might.

CAPTAIN: "It never got weird enough for me." - Hunter S. Thompson

ANON4: At the end the GOP deserves all this... he is so completely unfit for a position like president, it makes one speechless... and they know it too... and on a human level, he is just such a gigantic asshole... I really don't know how else to describe a person like that. There is no way any of us would accept people like that in our social circles. At the core he is an entertainer and people believe that is the qualification one needs... that tells us something.

CAPTAIN: I respect that you stand strong for your viewpoint, Anon4. You are voting for Clinton, yes?

ANON4: It is not about who I vote for or about my viewpoint. There are certain things in life that should be viewed the same way by all. This is one.

CAPTAIN: Don't play it safe. You want one of the two candidates to win. Everyone who turns up in these discussions has a strong preference between the two. If Clinton wins, then we go through one door, if Trump wins, we go through the other. If the Clinton presidency is terrible, the Trump-bashers have to answer for it, and if the Trump presidency is terrible, the Trump-supporters have to answer for it.

ANON4: I am for progress and the GOP is conservative at the core and that is my main problem with most anything. That said, Trump is impossible for an amazing amount of reasons. Hillary has a lot of experience and nothing would lead you to think that the US and therefore the world is going is going to be worse off. Just to give you an example, there is basically nobody in Europe that wants Trump and most of them fear him since almost all agree the world economy would take a huge dump.

I am not for war in any shape or form, but we all don't know enough to even come close to even have a educated opinion... plus the US has been terrible at solving conflicts for forever so we will see. That carpet bombing bull-crap has of course never worked.

CAPTAIN: Trump supporters view him as the peace candidate and Clinton as the war candidate. There's a great deal of important policy differences between the two, but they don't seem to shift sentiment on either side of the fence. It's kind of devolved into... do you want bad Mommy or bad Daddy in the public consciousness. However, Clinton is a globalist and Trump is a nationalist, and those two agendas are radically different. That's the real issue.

ANON4: I never thought of him as a peace candidate at all... and for sure not his core supporters. But I do think he would not be like Cruz at all. And what makes you think she is a war candidate... Europe for sure sees things differently in that Trump would destabilize everything to a degree we have never seen. Let's take the Middle East... I just talked to my wife about it yesterday and it seemed before, the thought was that if you took out the "bad guys" (sounds almost like Trump) that then the main/basic problem is solved and the good guys take over with the US helping with transition and then there will be a new functioning society... but that ain't so at all. Those countries are maybe off worse then before and I think that is something that has to be acknowledged. The world is so complicated and each country very unique... and Hillary knows more than anybody about those important "world issues" and hopefully could learn from previous mistakes, or what we now see as likely mistakes.

CAPTAIN: Clinton has been in the game for a long time now. There's a long history there of regime changes in the middle east. She has said Syria and Iran are up next and there has been agitation against Russia and China. We will see, my friend. Right now, because of the personality issues with Trump, particularly as they relate to women, we may indeed find out what a Clinton presidency is all about.

ANON4: Did she ever say that? I don't think anybody knows how to handle Syria... I follow some journalists that lived in the Middle East for decades and Syria is almost "unsolvable." Russia for sure is a major player there since that is one of the last places they have some real influence. And of course Clinton is not the one who started the major mess (like invading the wrong country!)... she might be in it for a long time, but not as Secretary of State, which she was "only" from 2009-2013... Of course the other side likes to act it is all her fault.

ANON16: This disqualifies Trump-- period. Please do not equate his predatory behavior with anything Hillary may have said about women upon learning of her husband's infidelity. I know you to be a better man than that.

CAPTAIN: Hillary destroys women and it is definitely a factor. Her first law case was plea bargaining a rapist of a 12 year old girl and she laughed about it. And of course Bill's vast history of rape and sexual assault will be brought into focus. Get ready folks, it just got turned up to 11.

ANON16: When you are sexually assaulted by a man who feels entitled to take what he wants, I believe your views will change.

CAPTAIN: Then call for the immediate arrest of rapist Bill Clinton.

ANON16: This is not about Bill Clinton - stop deflecting.

CAPTAIN: It is absolutely about both of the Clintons and Trump. Those are the players in the game.

ANON15: Bill Clinton has never been accused of, or convicted of, sexual assault or rape.

CAPTAIN: You must be joking, Anon15.

ANON15: No. Did he cheat on Hillary? Undoubtedly. But what does this have to do with Hillary Clinton running for President, and Trump's statements about women?

CAPTAIN: Janet people are jumping in front of news cameras with the Bill Clinton rape shirt. It's not because he's innocent.

ANON15: Show me the article/s that say he was tried and convicted. Or even accused. Then I will believe it.

ANON23: (posts Juanita Broaddrick tweet and article about $850K payout to Paula Jones.)

ANON15: Yes, I saw this. I'm not sure how I escaped this information before-- perhaps it occurred prior to my discovery of the internet, and it is now irrelevant to me, as Hillary is the candidate running. As far as the payment goes, again, Paula Jones agreed to the settlement, apparently, and again, Hillary was not the rapist. So paying almost a million dollars for your husband's misbehavior-- I don't like it, nor am I excited about Hillary as a candidate, but it pales besides Trump's *policy* atrocities.

ANON23: Actually, if you read the Guardian story closely, Bill made the payment, not Hillary.

CAPTAIN: Anon15, you haven't heard much because a legion of women came forward about the assaults and rape and Hillary destroyed them.

ANON15: Right.

CAPTAIN: Anon15, something called the internet exists. Please catch up.

ANON15: I did see some accusations, and I had never seen them before. All of this atmosphere is revolting. I'm voting for Clinton, but I must agree this situation is bad.

CAPTAIN: You owe it to yourself to follow the full story. This is pure epic Greek drama.

ANON15: I don't care to. I'm holding my nose and voting for Clinton.

CAPTAIN: Don't be lazy.

ANON15: I beg your pardon. I don't know you that well.

CAPTAIN: Research is imperative in this one. See you in Taos. Post election.

ANON11: Captain, Not only will he win by a landslide but in the next election he'll have done away with that two party system and Donald will receive 98% of the vote. And when he retirees after his forth term at the age of 88 he'll turn the reigns of power over to Eric, Ivanka and the other one to rule America as a troika for thirty years. Oh happy days, until they don't get along and there's a civil war that leads to a true peoples revolution and the upshot will culminate with three fat old people being hung by their heels like Mussolini so the crowd can spit on them and beat them to a pulp with sticks and stones in the middle of Times Square. You know, that traffic island just in front of the Flatiron building. Then their bodies will be dumped in the middle of the square so tens of thousands will drive over them until they're no more that a wide stain for tourists to take pictures of themselves in from of. And Captain, you will be there (like Leni) to document it all.

CAPTAIN: Wow, Anon11, the poetry is really coming out now. Can you believe we still have a month left?

ANON11: $E=MC_2$

CAPTAIN: Figures, the day I say landslide, Trump goes full JFK. Where is Hunter Thompson when we need him?

ANON11: Because Hillary with cancel all his debts with Russia if he loses.

CAPTAIN: And Billy Bush gets in there, too. Epic. And the nuclear button goes to...

ANON11: Albert Einstein was once asked how we would fight WW3. He replied. "I don't know. But I can tell that we'll fight WW4 with sticks and stones."

ANON36: How you could support this misogynistic, racist, narcissist is beyond me. Do you really want this person speaking on behalf of our country?

ANON12: Captain is so blinded by his fortunate privilege of being a straight white man that he obviously couldn't care less. I mean, it's not like it will affect him anyway, right?

ANON7: Nice! I can't wake Captain up. I've given up.

CAPTAIN: Anon7, JFK is your hero. He'd never survive a week of our news cycle. No excuses for Trump, though. How he handles this on Sunday could decide the election.

ANON12: I know your pain, Anon7. Apparently we both severely underestimated the intelligence of the poor fool and he's going to make us reap the consequences for him.

ANON7: JFK was an extraordinary man. A true leader that brought people together. Trump isn't fit to shine his shoes.

CAPTAIN: Are you putting the fate of the free world in my hands, Anon12? I'll take that. I haven't insulted you, but I also don't think you care about anything beyond some vague concept of 'privilege' you're in love with.

ANON12: Quite the contrary, my compassion for others below and above me is the sole reason I could never support a vile human like him.

CAPTAIN: Fair enough. Who are you voting for?

ANON12: Anyone but him.

CAPTAIN: Well, there's three other people.

ANON12: You act like I'm not aware of that.

ANON7: JFK was a playboy but he had class and more importantly intelligence.

CAPTAIN: You don't want to put your name behind Clinton, I gather.

ANON12: Nope. But if that's what it takes to keep him out of office, I'll submit. I favor Jill Stein, out of everyone.

CAPTAIN: Anon7, if only Bobby Kennedy could re-animate, we wouldn't be having this discussion...

ANON7: I take it you're speaking to Anon12? Clinton is far from perfect but I'd take her any day over Trump. The Kennedy's as a political dynasty are gone. The Irish Americans will rise again tho... Martin O'Malley 2020!

CAPTAIN: Unfortunately, Martin O'Malley has the charisma of a tube sock. You know we are in Hunger Games America now. No ratings, no spotlight.

ANON12: Anon7, I'm seriously considering moving my ass to Ireland if this clown is elected. Where would you recommend??

ANON7: (referring to O'Malley) He has time.

CAPTAIN: With some help from the right fellow Irishman, perhaps...

ANON7: He won't get elected, Anon12, but if he does I'll take care of you. I'll make sure you're sorted. Galway would suit you.

ANON12: Been there, done that. I'm always seeking out somewhere new

ANON7: (to Captain) Perhaps... Anon12, Waterford then, or maybe Wexford. Either way, I got you.

CAPTAIN: This is the October surprise, as far as Trump is concerned. Video tape is everything, just like when Hillary collapsed on 9-11 and it was caught on tape. This is a game changer and it will majorly effect the debate this Sunday and probably the whole narrative leading up to the election.

ANON11: Been reading a lot of Breitbart have you?

CAPTAIN: No, I don't go to Breitbart. What are the acceptable propaganda sources? I'll stick to those.

ANON11: You might want to try RTV or Xinhua, CCTV, and People's Daily.

CAPTAIN: Anon11, Anon11, Anon11, haha.

ANON23: (posts articles regarding rape accusations against Bill Clinton.)

OCTOBER 7, 2016 – Post:

As a writer, I am almost beside myself with how good the political theatre has gotten. Been waiting for the October Surprise and now we got it. The 'War on Women' will now decide this election. Put the mud tires on because the arena is thick with wet dirt. This makes Greek dramas look dull by comparison.

ANON37: Interesting.

CAPTAIN: The Clintons have a serious back story, so all dirty laundry comes out now. Invest in Tide.

ANON38: It's honestly worse than a Paddy Chayefsky farce.

CAPTAIN: Paddy would love this. And I wish Hunter S Thompson was alive to weigh in. He is truly missed. Although he may very well have supported the Clintons.

ANON38: It's amazing too since she was the runner up 8 years ago. By far, too. And she represents yet another dynasty. Like Great Britain's monarchs dynasty. You know... why we split from England in the first place.

ANON29: Hunter Thompson. Unique, hysterical, and of course all the rest. Thanks again, Anon8, for the book.

CAPTAIN: The next Clinton chess move: when you have billions at your service and the complicity of most of the mainstream media, you can destroy the reputation of anyone alive. They are going all out to ruin Trump now because they know he can win on votes and he equates to the end of their rule. Files have been leaked from their campaign. They have already filed three fake Jane Doe lawsuits with women that don't exist so that they can frame Trump for rape of minors right before the election (with billionaire pedophile and co-founder of the Clinton Foundation, Jeffrey Epstein, who got immunity.) Do you think they will give up their power without pulling out every sick and dark trick in the book? It's going to get insanely dramatic in the next weeks. People will be calling for Trump to drop out or be arrested or killed. And yet here we are and the story is not over yet. I do my own research and the real information on both candidates is out there for any patriotic American who desires the truth and isn't lazy about finding it. One day, maybe in a month, maybe in 10 years, what I have said will be common truth. Until then, I stand for Justice. The Clinton's time in power will not last long... the clock its ticking.

ANON39: What plain fact can you assert from your research to justify you deeply felt claims? If the Clintons are as Machiavellian as has been asserted how can they also be so incompetent? I don't love them, she's not my first choice, but c'mon. I swear, I think you're just screwing with people.

CAPTAIN: They are not even remotely incompetent when it comes to what they do. There's even a dark genius to it that is impressive from a pure strategic standpoint, if it weren't so bad for humanity. In any previous era they would win this election with their tactics. It's going to be a rough stretch for Trump supporters. But their checkmate move, the rape of minors play will ultimately backfire on them and cost them the election. The reason is because that's what they are guilty of and the attempt to pin it on Trump will turn back to them. Truth prevails in this election. The soul of a nation depends on it.

ANON23: According to Noam Chomsky, here's some nefarious guiding plot points in the fight for good versus evil: 10 principles of the concentration of wealth and power:

Reduce Democracy
Shape Ideology
Redesign the Economy
Shift the Burden
Attack Solidarity
Run the Regulators
Engineer Elections
Keep the Rabble in Line
Manufacture Consent
Marginalize the Population

Who will be the hero and save us from certain destruction in the nick of time? It will be legend if it is a happy ending...

CAPTAIN: Donald J. Trump is the hero. And all who support him-- the Rebel Alliance.

ANON39: Trump the champion of Noam Chomsky? That is a crazy script. Looks like the FEMA camps will have their work cut out for them.

OCTOBER 9, 2016 - Post:

"It's just awfully good that someone with the temperament of Donald Trump is not in charge of the law in our country."

"Because you'd be in jail."

Even the controlled audience cheered. End of story.

ANON8: And How Bout This One? - (posts video link to Trump's pre-debate press conference with the four female Bill Clinton abuse victims.)

CAPTAIN: Trump is Cyrus.

ANON8: Anyone who wants to see that Known Rapist back in the White House is too dumb to cure...

CAPTAIN: They will falsely try to frame rape charges on Trump after this. It will backfire and fail and cost them the election.

ANON8: They will stop at nothing. And Truth is, he went EZ on her... didn't even mention her muslim-brotherhood Lover of 20 years! (all my DC friends have known about it for years, kids) - now, if we could only find out who is putting the ZombiePills in the water... PS - (she can sleep w/ whomever (?) lol she wants - but the fact that she lies about it... well that's another story, entirely.)

CAPTAIN: That's the least of her problems. But now they play their Ace cards and it's gonna get ugly.

ANON8: And brother... if this Ain't Been Ugly So Far, folks just ain't been watchin, eh!?

CAPTAIN: Endgame time.

ANON8: THE DEVIL'S CHESSBOARD! Who, exactly, would file that charge? a troll? would they file it anonymously, on TWITTER!? - oh wait - PUTIN will have a hand in it!?... or, maybe - Abe Lincoln!? (the Ghost of Abe)!?

CAPTAIN: They already filed 3 Jane Doe cases for women that don't even exist and have Jeffrey Epstein with immunity to back the story up. The tricks up the sleeve are significant and media is very easy to manipulate. They will try to "end" the election and get Trump out. It won't work.

ANON8: With JEFFREY EPSTEIN to back the story up!? The pedophile Billionaire - Bill Clinton's Sleazy Pal!? HA! Even I would pay to see that one!

CAPTAIN: That's what will sink them if they play that card.

ANON8: That is comical - and frightening. Saying "the media is easy to manipulate" is like saying running out of oil may be bad for ur car!

CAPTAIN: So true. The msm is on trial in this election.

ANON8: CNN has almost No Viewers any more - viewer trust is at an all-time low across the board (as it should be) - even FOX is unrecognizable after Roger Ailles "ousting." Media is showing its True Colors - and it's waking some folks up.

ANON16: We don't lock up political opponents in America. If you want to live in a Fascist nation, move. Xo

CAPTAIN: I'm not going anywhere. And proper Law and Order is coming back to this country. A Special Prosecutor will be assigned to look into her case.

ANON16: I am not trying to convince anyone to vote for her, but to challenge views on him. What do you mean by "proper law and order"?

CAPTAIN: An FBI that will answer to Congress and not play cover up games. Most of the FBI are furious that their leader was complicit in subverting justice. I told you that nothing good comes from destroying 33K emails after being subpoenaed.

ANON17: (posts "That's Funny Sh*t Spock" Star Trek meme).

OCTOBER 10, 2016 - Post: A Tombstone-themed memefest in which Wyatt Earp arrests the Clintons.

"Alright, Clintons, you called down the thunder, well now you got it. You see that? It says United States Marshal. The Clintons are finished in this town, you hear me."

There's a new sheriff in town. And the authority that backs him will be denied at your peril. Criminals will no longer run our country.

ANON11: Perhaps we should take all these 'undesirable liberal' people and put them in camps. For their own protection of course. And just to keep track of them we'll place barcodes on their arms. Personally, I think perfect place would be in Harrington Park, New Jersey. Think of the boom to the local economy with all the people employed as cooks and guards and administrative personnel.

ANON22: This works as satire but not if you really mean it.

CAPTAIN: Work on your sense of what is coming, Anon22. Isn't that your line of work?

ANON22: Captain, I'm afraid you might not like the astrology aspects that I see for November 8th. I'm not the only astrologer who sees them, either.

CAPTAIN: Make a post about it on your wall and put yourself on the line. I have already done so. Donald Trump is President.

ANON22: I've been predicting the election informally. You're right I should do it formally.

CAPTAIN: Anon11, you are so wrong it is truly sad. The reason Trump is already president is because in his America, everyone will be protected under a Just and True Law. Your Clintons are finished. Their authority is over. What you have suggested in your post is exactly what will be put to an end and what the Clintons themselves have stood for. Get used to it. Donald Trump is the next president. And the fools who thought the Clintons were good leaders will be treated just as well as everyone else. And I will toast with some 45% bourbon. For the 45 President. It's merely a chaser. For the Old World Order.

ANON40: To heck with that sippin BS. Let's roll out the barrels!

OCTOBER 11. 2016 – Posts memes of massive Trump rally and Clinton in a half empty high school gymnasium. With the meme "Love Trumps Hate."

That time you thought you could win the most important election in history by spending 18 months on petty social media snark while Trump filled stadiums every day with patriotic and informed Americans from all walks of life.

"Racist, sexist, homophobe!" is not a campaign. It is a tool used to demoralize, divide and conquer a populace. There's no truth in it, but it has effectively blinded many otherwise very bright people into failing to discern two sick career political criminals angling to get back in the White House, namely the Clintons.

This election is about whether the US remains a sovereign nation or whether we fold like a lawn chair to the globalists. This is about policies like open borders and trade agreements and the wise use of military power so as not to stumble headlong into World War III.

Fortunately, for all of us, the leader best suited for the job, the one who arrived by fate in the 11th hour will assume office. And no amount of mocking posts will change that. You have no idea how lucky you are. Everyone will have their rights protected in the Trump administration. The people have spoken and the numbers never lie.

ANON28: The picture isn't a Trump rally. It's the AIPAC conference.

CAPTAIN: Doesn't make a difference. Every rally, like yesterday, breaks stadium records, turning more people away at the door than attend Clinton's biggest rallies. (posts video of giant Pennsylvania rally).

ANON28: You're constitutionally unable to discuss issues that are troubling about your candidate. I am not here to defend Clinton. She's not my candidate. You think he's winning?

CAPTAIN: By a landslide.

ANON28: Trump has gotten free media throughout the campaign.

ANON41: This was especially true during the Republican primaries. He simply makes a cell phone call to one of the networks (most notably Fox's Hannity and O'Reilly), and he immediately receives unlimited exposure at absolutely no cost to him. At that time he was far more "media-funded" than self-funded.

CAPTAIN: When David takes on Goliath he deserves all the free press he can get.

ANON41: The Clinton/DNC/media machine definitely fits the Goliath analogy, but Trump was hardly a noble underdog during the Republican primaries. He was more of an arrogant, obnoxious, Goliath-like Dolt.

CAPTAIN: He ran the gauntlet in the way he needed to run it. Our culture is our culture and he both navigated it and manipulated it. Politics is a bloodsport. One Bush down. One Clinton to go.

ANON41: Honestly, the way he should've run that gauntlet is not at all. Without his celebrity and arrogance, and his willingness to say just about anything regardless of logic or consistency, he is very much a political empty suit. The only thing positive either of these candidates have going for him/her is the overwhelming negatives of his/her opponent.

CAPTAIN: How wrong you are.

ANON41: Persuasive argument. What, in your opinion, is Mr. Trump's strongest argument for deserving the presidency (besides HRC's lack of fitness)?

CAPTAIN: His preservation of American sovereignty vs. a globalist open border agenda. Reformed trade deals, increased US manufacturing, strict immigration vetting until we can get ISIS under control, protection of the dollar, no more regime-change destabilizing wars in the middle east, and a reformation of the relationship with Saudi Arabia, a backwards culture that treats women like cattle and kills gays. As an added bonus, good relations with Russia and China so we don't start WW3.

ANON41: That is an agreeable list of ideals. However, they are all broad generalizations and talking points Trump uses. Of course he is not as articulate as you. What makes you think Donald Trump knows how to accomplish any of these "reforms" you speak of? If you really believe Trump understands these concepts, that's fine. I don't believe that. His answer too often ends up being that he is going to "make better deals." I'm not so sure he understands what trade deficits mean and how tariffs work (see Smoot-Hawley). Do you think he is going to build the wall and make Mexico pay for it? To me, Hillary is unacceptable, but do you really think this guy knows what he's talking about, and do you think he has enough humility to listen to people who do?

CAPTAIN: Trump is a lot smarter than you think. He has a 156 IQ and is an Ivy graduate of the Wharton School of business. He has been bombastic at times, but he has also articulated his policies very well in the hundred or so speeches he has given. Trump is a once in a lifetime candidate. He's our JFK, without the complication of the mob ties JFK had through his father. Trump is a leader and he gets respect from other leaders. That's why all of the generals back him. They know he has a strategic mind and he's tough but fair.

ANON28: Trump doesn't have mob ties? What world are you living in? You don't work as a developer in NYC for 50 years without mob ties. In Trump's case the mob ties were documented long before his campaign. He can't get a gambling license in Nevada because of his mob ties.

CAPTAIN: Trump did normal legal business with the construction players in NYC. JFK's father was a bootlegger who used to his mob ties to help tilt the endgame election in his favor. The mob had expectations after that and then when the Kennedy boys went after them they could't believe it. There were other factors involved, but the rest is political assassination history. Trump is not tied to the mob like that.

ANON41: Are you sure that 156 figure is accurate? There are a lot of claims on the internet about the IQ's of different famous people, and the overwhelming majority of these claims are not based on standardized IQ tests, but instead are based on subjective "expert" evaluations, using various factors, for example number of books written, and typical admission requirements of school attended. Trump was not admitted to Wharton through normal means (big surprise). I'm not saying he's not a smart person. He can be a smart person and still not know what he's talking about concerning certain issues. I believe he doesn't know, or doesn't care.

CAPTAIN: Donald J. Trump is a very intelligent man, beyond any IQ score. It's why he's such a good financial negotiator and why he understands exactly the games China plays with currency manipulations and how to correct that. He makes Obama look like a 3rd grader. Barry is a good public speaker, slick with the politically correct tongue and a good hustler, but no genius. Trump's intelligence is very strategic, like a General, which is why he brings up Patton and MacArthur all the time. And why he has the backing and respect of almost all of the United States Generals. And believe me, he cares. He put his life on the line, and I mean that absolutely literally, to right the wrongs of this country and protect it from a corrupt takeover. He will succeed in his appointed task.

ANON28: How did Trump put his life on the line?

CAPTAIN: There have already been attempts on his life. Do you think those in power are just going to roll over for him? They despise what he represents.

ANON41: Trump mentions two famous wartime generals because his intelligence is strategic like a general? I'm sorry, but I just don't receive that vibe when I hear him speak. I get the feeling he is dropping those names in an attempt to invoke patriotic sentiment, and maybe imply some familiarity with important historical figures. And maybe my IQ is just not elevated enough to fully understand his bigly/big league strategy. He is a salesman, essentially always selling himself. And making that sale is more important than the best interest of the buyer.

CAPTAIN: Look where he is, Anon41, and stretch your mind to encompass all of the incredibly complex game play, both in front of the scenes, and especially behind the scenes. He is one of two people in line for the throne of America. Both him and Clinton are genius level tacticians.

ANON41: Hillary, though, is not an acceptable alternative. I wish I felt the level of confidence that you feel in a presidential candidate.

CAPTAIN: Any sane person would eliminate her. That leaves Donald J. Trump. I would urge you to get beyond the manufactured Trump hate and put your faith in him. He was born for this moment in history.

ANON41: I'm sorry, Captain. I just don't see them as geniuses. There is obviously something about them that has allowed them to be the two main candidates while maintaining the highest negatives of any two candidates ever. I really think name recognition, celebrity, and political power/leverage have been more important factors than either candidate's intelligence. They are both clearly smart people, but smart people don't always do everything well.

ANON28: Anon41 - great use of bigly.

CAPTAIN: Genius tacticians. Beyond that intelligence can be measured in many ways. The problem with Clinton's intelligence is that she uses it for bad works. Bad, that is, for America. Maybe good for herself in the short term. But her dark creations are returning to her now and karma, in her case, is a serious bitch.

ANON8: Just wish Mr. T would kick Giuliani and the corpulent Christie to the curb... they strike me as being "compromised." (still, that's a pretty small "gripe list.")

CAPTAIN: Giuliani has impressed me at points. Christie I couldn't say, haven't seen much from him recently. But the palace intrigues all over are epic in and of themselves. This is one of the greatest stories ever written.

ANON31: I am with you, Captain!

ANON42: It's a sleazy world, ain't it?... The whole thing is an insult to any kind of an intelligence no matter where in the universe... And along with it; you may detect a faint, yet distinct odor...

ANON11: And all these 90% white crowds plus another 55 million votes and he's president. Big rallies doth not an election make. Do the math.

ANON42: Due to our failed educational systems, 'math' may no longer be an option... Button pushing has replaced math... And a plethora of other intelligence insulting subject matter that has replaced common sense and knowledge...

CAPTAIN: Men and women of every race, color and creed will decide this election. It will be a horse race. May the best horse win.

ANON42: What is happening now will prove, or not prove to be very beneficial in the long run... Provided that we learn something from this time in our history... And what a time, eh?...

CAPTAIN: Most beneficial.

ANON11: Let's talk on November 9th.

CAPTAIN: You got it.

ANON8: How Deep does this Rabbit Hole Go? When it's the Clintons, there's No End in Sight – (posts article about Clinton's emails).

CAPTAIN: For certain agents, it goes all the way to hell, on a one way stop.

ANON39: (posts Business Insider article about Trump telling supporters to vote on Nov. 28). I know this is some sort of gag. You are like the Sauron of trolls. Come to my legion.

ANON8: Now's your chance. Get off the bench... REGISTER; SPEAK YOUR HEART, MIND and SOUL.

CAPTAIN: (posts meme of first American Flag being displayed by the Sons & Daughters of Liberty). Voted for President and Commander-in-Chief Donald J. Trump today. #13 on the ballet. As in the 13 stars on the Betsy Ross Flag.

OCTOBER 12, 2016 – Post: Memetics linking Trump to Cyrus.

ISAIAH 45

**THUS SAITH THE LORD TO HIS ANOINTED,
TO CYRUS, WHOSE RIGHT HAND I HAVE HOLDEN,
TO SUBDUE NATIONS BEFORE HIM AND TO STRIP
KINGS OF THEIR ARMOR, TO OPEN DOORS BEFORE
HIM SO THAT GATES WILL NOT BE SHUT.
I WILL GO BEFORE YOU AND WILL LEVEL THE
MOUNTAINS; I WILL BREAK DOWN GATES OF BRONZE
AND CUT THROUGH BARS OF IRON.
I WILL RAISE UP CYRUS IN MY RIGHTEOUSNESS:**

**I WILL MAKE ALL HIS WAYS STRAIGHT.
HE WILL REBUILD MY CITY AND SET MY EXILES FREE.**

ANON2: I miss the old days when you just complained about circumcisions.

CAPTAIN: Duly noted young Anon2. Are you voting in this one? Come on, join the fun and make a pick. For the record and all.

ANON11: Thus were they defiled with their own works, and went a whoring with their own inventions. - Psalm 106:39

CAPTAIN: There you go, Anon11. No reason we can't make a story of the whole shebang, add a little flavor it.

ANON43: .....you may have gone off the deep end on this one.

CAPTAIN: You may join me for a swim before this is all over. The water will reach flood levels.

OCTOBER 13, 2016 – Post: Link to Trump West Palm Beach rally speech. If you're not watching these speeches, you're missing American History being written.

ANON23: He's finally taking the gloves off and telling it like it is.

CAPTAIN: Anon23, we are witnessing and indeed part of one of the great moments in history. Congratulations on being with the rebel alliance and speaking your truths. It's going to be an incredible celebration the world over come 11/9.

ANON23: Thanks Captain for your outright enthusiasm. It is stunning to see how influential a tiny group, the .01%, can be given enough resources and how compliant are their minions. It is in human nature to trust our leaders and to follow direction. That trusting nature that was so useful to survival as small societies from eons ago can now be so easily co-opted to control entire nations. All this tiny group has to do is to control our leaders, the political class. With Citizens United, the game was finally over. The pretense of democracy can now safely be put to rest. All that remains is to either continue to go along with the pretense and descend into a form of indentured labor, or make a decision to crack thru the thin veneer of what we now call a democracy to throw out the politicians, remove the financial base that enables the .01% and reassert a full sovereign democracy with fair distribution of wealth on an even playing field. 'No taxation without representation' was the clarion call that led to the establishment of this nation 250+ years ago. What will be our call to action this time around? Perhaps it is indeed 'Make America Great Again.' It seems to fit.

OCTOBER 14, 2016 – Post: Memes of Trump in the White House and the Clintons in jail.

Tick tock...

ANON39: In due time we might get a balanced budget. Wait! Who was the only president to have a balanced budget since the last "entertainer" ran for president?

CAPTAIN: Tick tock...

ANON4: "If a guy's spent 70 years on this earth showing no regard for working people, there's no record that he's supported (the) minimum wage or supported collective bargaining, invested in poor communities, and then suddenly he's going to be the champion of working people? Come on," Obama said.

ANON20: I can't wait until your little test to see how many people will defriend you when this is over.

ANON39: Is this some sort of Andy Kaufman gag?

CAPTAIN: Tick tock...

ANON39: Straight to the FEMA camps for you. Thin vegan gruel. Giant movie screens that play Glee on a constant loop. Forces to build solar panel farms in the Mojave. It's coming.

CAPTAIN: Tick tock...

ANON11: Captain, I get it. It's a performance art piece you're doing. I think I'll title it: 'Contrarian cognitive dissonance orange series 70 (A circle with a part missing) #2.'

ANON23: Since it appears you're struggling to understand, allow me to help you by offering a less abstract and more pragmatic metaphor: "global unfair wealth concentration = bad: please fix in this country."

ANON11: So we'll hire a fox to guard the henhouse?

ANON23: The fox has been guarding the hen house... that's the problem... Trump could have run anytime in the last 20 years... my take on it is he is doing it now because no one else is willing to step up... and the timing is right... it's one hell of a daunting challenge and he's been very successful so far against tremendous odds. Anyway, it's not about the cult of personalities, it's about the issues. If you want to know where his base is coming from take a look at some of these numbers from the Federal Reserve and draw your own conclusions: (posts link).

CAPTAIN: Tick tock...

ANON39: ATF agents will soon be arriving at your house in UN helmets. Get out to Russia while you still can.

CAPTAIN: Tick tock...

OCTOBER 15, 2016 – Post:

Following this election so closely has taught me many life lessons. One of the deepest ones, we're in the midst of right now: the effects of slander and mob mentality.

Last year, while promoting one of my films, I went on a podcast where the topic was initially the movie, but then pivoted into a segment that went into a very negative take on Michael Phelps based on some tabloid story about him.

For one reason or another, the hosts of the show had a bone to pick with Phelps. To my great disgrace, I played along with this and made an off hand, but lewd and disparaging remark about Mr. Phelps. My fellow producer didn't take the bait, and he wisely remarked that he knew nothing about Phelps other than that he was a great Olympic champion and that stories like this can be faked or come from people with something financial or otherwise to gain from it.

Now, over a year later, I wish I had responded so wisely. Watching Phelps at the 2016 Olympics and cheering for him as he represented his country so well, I felt ashamed that I'd spoken even in passing negatively of him when I knew absolutely nothing of him personally, and in fact have been inspired by his courage, dedication and athletic excellence.

And even now, to this day, that brief, tossed off remark to get a laugh, still sticks in my gut. The comment meant nothing to Phelps, he will never even know about it, yet it has come back and stuck to me, because it was spoken without regard or wisdom.

Words have power. False accusations have tremendous dark power for those who speak them. By our words we will be judged.

I'd like to take this post to deeply apologize to Michael Phelps and his family, though they will never see this. He was and is a great inspirational champion of sport and an Olympic flag bearer for the United States of America. I salute him and hope to apply his great dedication to excellence in my own life.

I have indeed learned a powerful lesson about piling on with disparaging remarks when I have no true knowledge of what or whom I am speaking such slander about. The words do not land on who you speak of, they come back and stick to you.

When Michael Jordan won the 1996 NBA championship on Father's Day, after his Father died that very year, he fought back tears to express what his Father meant to him. He later stated that one of the biggest lessons his Father taught him was how to turn a negative into a positive.

To that end, I intend to take my negative comment and turn it into a positive life lesson about the dangers of slander. I'm ashamed about the flip comment I made, but I pledge to never fall into that trap again.

"But I tell you that men will give an account on the day of judgment for every careless word they have spoken. For by your words you will be acquitted, and by your words you will be condemned."

Amen.

ANON14: You are amazing.

ANON44: Yes, I remember that interview.

OCTOBER 17, 2016 – Post: Memetic display linking Ancient Babylon to the Swamp in DC, with a Winged Trump on hand to point out the falling twin towers and the corrupt US Presidents, with a Red, White and Blue Eagle there to witness it all.

The Eagle sees all and knows all.

It has begun its descent, spiraling downward in concentric circles, charting time from ancient Babylon to modern day Babylon... in Sin City, Las Vegas.

Its eyes are locked on its prey, as they scramble for escape options and secret exits. But there is nowhere to run to now and nowhere to hide. They will not escape its terrible grasp.

And now the Eagle has a partner. Lady Liberty has picked up her sword, holding it high and wielding it with a terrible swift Justice.

Their assault on American Freedom began on 9/11. But now these very numbers have conspired a great reversal of fortune for the originators of these dark plans.

Hillary Rodham Clinton collapsed on 9/11 before the eyes of the world during her campaign for Presidency of the United States of America.

The final debate is on 10/19. That is a reversal of 9/11 with a 0 included. The 0 represents the chances of the Clintons and those of their cabal being granted the authority of the White House. You can also add a .0 after that, with an infinite number of 0's extending indefinitely into the horizon.

The day after the election is 11/9. This is the final reversal.

A thread of tyranny has woven through high office since the assassination of JFK, the crown prince of America, who was killed for his attempt to spread the truth about the Federal Reserve and the small, but powerful secret society that threads the halls of government, corrupting it from within.

But a new dawn has arisen and a new flag of Liberty is being woven by the sons and daughters of the republic. Freedom is at last replacing tyranny as the thread of this glorious flag.

A new voice has also emerged, along with a new leader to herald it, beckoning in a Second American Revolution; one that does not use violence to reclaim power, but information, and an awakened, informed and empowered populace. We are installing a strong and just new President into the halls of power, to lead this nation to reformation and prosperity and to stand as a beacon of light to the world.

For virtually all of our history, the Kingdom of Darkness has held the upper hand. They had the first ten moves on the chessboard, before the Light could make one move.

They operated in secret, behind front organizations. In their dark genius, they created their own opposition, so that they could control it from within. They created banking systems that usurped the power of nations and governments.

They created wars for profit, sending innocent youths to die on both sides of the conflict, while promoting a destabilized world and a populace in the dark. They thought that their reign would last forever. They didn't believe in a Higher Power or God and in their supreme arrogance assumed that their ship was unsinkable.

They made a fatal error in their understanding of existence.

You may have thought this whole time that you were witnessing an Election. You are not. You are witnessing a Trial.

For their crimes against humanity and country, they are on Trial. For their plans to usurp the sovereign power of the United States of America, they are on Trial. And most especially, for their crimes against innocent children they are on Trial.

The United States was the last beachhead of Freedom and Liberty. Had they succeeded in overthrowing this country and installing their New World Order government, their dark plans would have been put into full effect, crushing the freedom of the remaining populace under a jack boot forever.

They have now played all of their remaining cards. They will go to any length to retain power, including starting a Third World War.

But they didn't count on One last thing... the Trump Card.

They behaved in History as if there was no one to answer to, except perhaps whatever dark principalities they held their occult rituals to.

They were very, very wrong. They have been found. They have been apprehended in Spirit. And now their kingdoms will turn to ash, as they turned the World Trade Centers to ash.

These battles are fought in realms celestial before they materialize in the physical. They have already been defeated and apprehended in Spirit.

And now they await their Trial, not from God, but from the People.

In Hillary Clinton they played their final card. Despite being the most corrupt politician in modern history, they counted on using her gender as a Trojan Horse to get her through the gates, much in the same way they did with the race card of Barack Obama. They know that the American public is essentially good and stands for Freedom and Opportunity for all, so they played on those virtues in order to use them against us.

Their open border policy, coupled with a welfare state and a demoralized and emasculated populace at war with itself, has an antecedent in history. It is called the Fall of Rome.

But there is another antecedent that Trumps this. It was the moment Cyrus arrived to redeem Babylon. Cyrus was anointed as the right hand of Spirit to discipline, reform and rebuild Babylon, ushering in an unprecedented prosperity.

Cyrus drained the moats of Babylon and his army surrounded the convention center where Belshazzar had gathered a thousand of his closest schemers and politicos, as they drank deep from golden goblets, artifacts hijacked from the Temple.

But then a hand came forth from another dimension, and writing appeared on the wall. Belshazzar soiled himself in mortal fear. Belshazzar called forth Daniel, the only man in the Kingdom who could interpret the writing, promising him half of his Kingdom if he could tell him what the writing on the wall said.

Daniel said: Your Father, he was a great King. But you, you're nothing. You keep your riches. And I'm sorry to inform you, but you don't have half a kingdom to give. But I will interpret the writing on the wall for you. It says...

"You have been weighed and you have been found wanting."

Belshazzar's reign ended that very night. Cyrus assumed the mantle of Babylon, as a strong, just and true leader of the people.

Cyrus was a builder, famous for conquering kingdoms without the need for warfare, like a corporate takeover. Cyrus was also a pagan and an extremely unlikely candidate to be the right hand of God in the civilized world. But, in his own way, he was the perfect man for the job and he arrived according to prophesy, a prophesy that named him by his exact name and predicted the very day he would arrive on the steps of Babylon 150 years before his birth.

Which brings us to the final Trump, the last Trumpet. Like Cyrus, Donald Trump is not a perfect man. He is no Messiah. He is, indeed, one of us. An ordinary man called forth for an extraordinary task. His entire life has prepared him for this very moment.

As President, he will curb violence and usher in a healing of the nations. He will rebuild our decimated cities like Detroit and many others, adjust and reform trade deals, lower taxes, protect the currency, and return jobs to an American population desperately in need of them.

He will also cease any further talk of WW3. Since we passed the marker of December 21, 2012, a graduation of sorts, the destruction of our world is no longer permitted.

There is a long road ahead. Much work, reformation and reparation needs to be done. Yet the first triumphant victory over the Kingdom of Darkness has been achieved. Their authority will only lessen from here onward.

This heralds a Golden Age for Humanity. This is cause for a true and genuine celebration. It's been a long, long time coming.

For those with young children, you can embrace the hope that a beautiful and safe world awaits them, one with new technologies and energies and one in which all citizens of the world unite in a common humanity, knowing they all originate from the same Source.

In these final days of the "Election" all masks will be removed. The endemic corruption in the system at all levels must be revealed in order that it can be addressed and corrected. But the power is truly with the People now, and we have always vastly outnumbered those that would control us with their dark and secretive machinations.

It was a race to see if humanity could awaken before the darkness could bind us in the chains of mind control and actual physical control. This battle, the Second American Revolution, was fought with information. The very technologies that they thought would control us were used to defeat them.

It is truly a great time to be alive. We can look forward to a great celebration with everyone on 11/9, the world over. No one will be left out, regardless of what side you voted for. Because now the dust will be washed from our eyes and every tear will be wiped away.

"And I heard a loud voice from the throne saying: "Behold, the dwelling place of God is with man, and He will live with them. They will be His people, and God Himself will be with them as their God. He will wipe away every tear from their eyes, and there will be no more death or mourning or crying or pain, for the former things have passed away." And the One seated on the throne said, "Behold, I make all things new."

Then He said, "Write this down, for these words are faithful and true."

Amen.

ANON45: Wow, very interesting reading of history repeated.

ANON22: Unintentionally hilarious!

ANON46: (posts meme of tinfoil hat)

ANON33: Pure unadulterated insanity.

ANON47: U write this?

CAPTAIN: Tin turns to Gold 11/9. #Alchemy

ANON20: Don't you mean 11/29?

CAPTAIN: That will be a good day, too.

ANON46: No it does not. #science

CAPTAIN: Looks like we got ourselves a showdown.

OCTOBER 24, 2016 – Post: Meme comparing Trump to Secretariat and the Belmont Stakes win.

Big horse race coming up. That hair looks familiar on ole Secretariat. #31Lengths #Landslide #TrumpCard

ANON35: I think I see a horse's ass.

CAPTAIN: That means you're in second by 31 lengths.

OCTOBER 26, 2016 – Post: Video disparaging late night comedian types for laying off Clinton and only attacking Trump.

Dance monkeys, dance.

No guts to shine your comedy light of truth on the Establishment. Bang your monkey cymbals for the Clinton's corruption. Bill Maher, John Oliver, Seth Meyers, and all you other bought and paid for shills. You aren't men, you are circus monkeys.

ANON13: Very good, Captain.

CAPTAIN: Emmys turn to dust too like everything else. Just another trophy. But what you stood for, that lasts. Integrity can't be bought.

ANON20: Can you hear my eye roll from there?

CAPTAIN: Don't go full zombie. It's not Halloween yet.

OCTOBER 28, 2016 – Post made after the FBI reopened the Clinton case following the Weiner lap-top seizure by the NYPD:

The FBI and the Department of Justice are reopening the Servergate investigation.

The Clintons are going to jail, as I have ever declared. They are two of the most transparently doomed individuals walking the face of the earth. You couldn't pay me all the loot of a thousand empires to walk the path they must now walk.

ANON3: As someone who recently told me to "do my research" I offer you an article to read down below. I would suggest you keep your dancing shoes in your closet. Let's not forget, Trump goes on trial in a few weeks for raping a minor, and then for Fraud and Racketeering, and I believe some former lawyers of his are now suing him because they got stiffed. Race to the White House? Or a room with iron bars? Who gets there first? (cites msnbc article about Comey investigation of Trump).

CAPTAIN: The Trump case is a fraud, filed to disrupt his campaign by a "Jane Doe." It will dissolve into nothing after the election. The other accusations against him will result in law suits, with full cross examination. Let's see where the Truth takes those who took the money to alter the outcome of an election. Bill Clinton has real rape on his hands, it's why he lost his license to practice law. And his trips on the Lolita Express will now come back to haunt him. A tape is in the hands of Israeli military intelligence of him raping a 13 year girl, which was made to blackmail the White House should the Clintons take office. They won't. I promise you that. Their past is coming back to swallow them whole.

ANON3: The fact that Trump's case is going to trial is proof there's no fraud. She's called "Jane Doe" to protect her identity because who wants to be known as the girl Trump raped and threatened in a sex dungeon? I can't speak for Bill Clinton. If he winds up in jail while his wife runs the country so be it. Trump is a criminal several times over, and as the Trump brand takes a huge hit, he may not be able to afford the lawyers he needs to keep him out of jail. If any will take his case, that is, since several firms have reported being stiffed by him. He's a scumbag through and through, and he lies every day to followers like you.

CAPTAIN: Nothing will come of those cases, I guarantee you that, because they are patently untrue, filed by the Clinton campaign to bring him down. Unfortunately for them, their tried and true 'Rules for Radicals' approach of projecting their own evils onto their opponent will not work this time.

ANON3: How do you know they're "patently untrue"? And how can you guarantee me anything? There are already court records of numerous crimes by Trump including perjury, money laundering, and discriminatory housing practices. He's documented as having paid fines or settling on all these cases. Your "guarantee" doesn't mean anything. Your sources spout ridiculous things. Will you "guarantee" me that Hillary and Barack are possessed by demons and smell of sulfur, and are somehow at the same time, lizard faced aliens plotting to take over the earth? You're being taken advantage of and it's painful to watch in all honesty.

CAPTAIN: You are going to watch it play out before your eyes and then we can talk. How many days left now? T-minus 10 days and counting.

ANON3: 11 days. I'm not sure what there'll be to talk about. I'm not going to do a dance and tell you "I told you so" if Hillary wins. I'll just breathe a sigh of relief and move on. I just feel bad for you that you buy into these alt news sites as real. They're ridiculous.

CAPTAIN: I'm not going to do a dance and say I told you so, either. My friends are my friends, regardless of whether they take the mainstream media as gospel. I always appreciate your point of view, Anon3, you know that.

ANON3: And I've looked up some of the articles you've posted on the Clintons and have changed my opinion on how faultless they are. The mutual respect is still in place. I think you have to be more willing to count some of the "mainstream media" as actually reporting facts. Follow the money. To report pure fiction for The New York Times, Newsweek, The Washington Post, and The New Yorker among other publications would be suicide.

CAPTAIN: Not pure fiction, but biased in favor of one candidate for what I believe are corrupt reasons. Nevertheless, I look forward to returning to a focus on movie making after 11/9, a passion we both share. Namaste, brother.

ANON3: Just know that me trying to talk what I think is some sense into you comes from the best place possible.

CAPTAIN: Ditto, brother. Let the cards fall where they fall now.

OCTOBER 29, 2016 – Post: Carlos Danger meme re: Anthony Weiner.

The Year of Living Carlos Dangerously.

ANON43: Weiner screws Clinton.

ANON13: That weiner. C'mon, Captain, you gotta laugh.

ANON23: Life is not worth living unless living dangerously. Turns out DNC's WMD was Wiener's wiener after all... There's no way u can make this stuff up.

CAPTAIN: The greatest political story ever told, and there's still a week left.

ANON13: Did u laugh??

CAPTAIN: I haven't stopped laughing since Weiner came up! Apart from the aspects of old Danger that aren't even funny, because he's one sick pup. But birds of a feather...

ANON23: However, it does expose clear connections directly or indirectly to Muslim theocracy in the history of Huma Abedin's life which have national security concerns which apparently do not appear to be HRC concerns due to, dare I say it, possible conflicts of interest in Clinton Foundation practices (which are still under FBI investigation).

CAPTAIN: 650K emails. The ship is going down and the rats won't go down with the ship, they will be about saving their own necks. Spring cleaning time for Washington, led by Trump.

ANON13: I hope one day in our lifetime we will be able to read some of these infamous emails, Captain. Maybe a movie, so the whole truth is told.

CAPTAIN: Oh, there will be a great big book about it. A best seller. Truth is so much stranger than fiction.

ANON13: If she can write that many emails a book or two should be no problem... the weiner, well he's another story altogether... he's got issues far greater than my little imagination. I wonder where he came up with that name carlos danger??? Wth

CAPTAIN: Game of Thrones has nothing on them!

ANON23: This defeats minimum reasonable expectations about how politicians should behave, no matter which side of the isle. This seems to me to be about basic ethics and how we as an electorate are so willing to sell our dreams... souls?... for convincing leadership... is there some way we can come up with a metaphor for defeating this? Perhaps 'Let's build the world we want to live in (tm)' ... a clarion call for the next generation.

CAPTAIN: It starts with "Draining the Swamp." Then we can rebuild from a foundation that is supported by ethics and justice.

ANON13: It's all about the power, Anon23. But at the same time if we don't laugh about we might drown in our own tears.

ANON23: With no science of mental health, comedy and parody are not terribly bad substitutes for a coping mechanism. I just hate to see the greatest experiment in the history of the imperfect science of Democracy/Capitalism go down the drain and be replaced by socialism (BORING!). If we could solve the greed problem we could have a very dynamic society... it's a matter of values and desire for happiness.

ANON13: And thus is life... kill them all with kindness... March on... good night.

ANON23: 'Compassionate Capitalism (TM)'... where greed is dishonorable... that may be the solution.... or we innovate our way out of it by inventing a new energy source or go to a different planet (thanks Elon!) All of this because of some stupid prick... unbelievable.

CAPTAIN: When the Rule of Gold transforms into the Golden Rule in free market Capitalism, we will make it work beautifully. Innovations in new energy will be a major factor. Killing Big Pharma off won't hurt, either.

ANON23: Artists are often co-opted to set the narrative by the ruling classes (whoever they may be). I would argue that each artist, as for each engineer, etc... has a moral obligation, beyond their employer, but rather to the society they claim to be a member of, to stand-up for certain principles, among which I imagine should be mutual respect, support, and concern, as well as fair treatment and reward for original thought.

CAPTAIN: Indeed.

ANON23: It is time that we become self aware as a society. We have the technological basis for doing so (perhaps beyond social media). We are no longer reliant on a ruling political class (and a ridiculous Electorate College) to make decisions for us, espec if they are biased by special interests (or other anachronistic ideas),,, anyway,,, I'm out too. Good night.

OCTOBER 30, 2016 – Post: Image of Trump in the debate in front of words from the Declaration of Independence.

The Writing is on the Wall. The unanimous Declaration of the thirteen United States of America:

When in the Course of human events it becomes necessary for one people to dissolve the political bands which have connected them with another and to assume among the powers of the earth, the separate and equal station to which the Laws of Nature and of Nature's God entitle them, a decent respect to the opinions of mankind requires that they should declare the causes which impel them to the separation.

We hold these truths to be self-evident, that all men are created equal, that they are endowed by their Creator with certain unalienable Rights, that among these are Life, Liberty and the pursuit of Happiness.

That to secure these rights, Governments are instituted among Men, deriving their just powers from the consent of the governed, — That whenever any Form of Government becomes destructive of these ends, it is the Right of the People to alter or to abolish it, and to institute new Government, laying its foundation on such principles and organizing its powers in such form, as to them shall seem most likely to effect their Safety and Happiness.

Prudence, indeed, will dictate that Governments long established should not be changed for light and transient causes; and accordingly all experience hath shewn that mankind are more disposed to suffer, while evils are sufferable than to right themselves by abolishing the forms to which they are accustomed.

But when a long train of abuses and usurpations, pursuing invariably the same Object evinces a design to reduce them under absolute Despotism, it is their right, it is their duty, to throw off such Government, and to provide new Guards for their future security.

CAPTAIN: (posts meme of recent US Presidents at a funeral) Ashes to ashes, dust to dust. Your kingdom is no longer.

ANON4: (posts Business Insider article about Trump's bad economic plan).

CAPTAIN: Article links won't alter what is to come.

ANON20: (post Jackie Chan meme: "DAFUQ")

ANON48: (posts meme of actress saying: "Stop Trying to Make Trump Happen. Trump is Not Going to Happen.")

CAPTAIN: It already has happened. Thank you for putting your stance on record, though. It is noted.

ANON39: Lots of drugs out in Hollyweird.

CAPTAIN: 8 days.

ANON39: I hope you're keeping all these threads for some sort of art project. Let me ask, which side of the FEMA fence do you expect I'll be on?

CAPTAIN: The side that's taking it down.

ANON39: That's heartwarming.

CAPTAIN: You can still visit the ruins if you want to fantasize about what could have been. I'll get you a day pass.

ANON39: I heard Pink Floyd is giving a free concert of The Wall in the El Paso Juarez urban Complex. VIP seating for party members.

CAPTAIN: Stay gold, Ponyboy.

ANON39: We'll need good men to run the Orange County camps, stay in touch.

CAPTAIN: The OC, that's where we're setting up the liberal tear bottling facility. The '16 vintage will be one for the ages.

ANON39: That's about all we have to fight with since we don't believe in guns.

CAPTAIN: The individuals who were paid $1,500 to incite violence at Trump rallies believed in fists it would seem.

ANON39: What can I say Clinton supporters are passionate-- wait where did hear that before? I'm really liking the FEMA camp meme, not only is it totally absurd it has dual connotation of an abusive federal govt and of feminization in all CAPS. It works on so many levels. The good thing is that most of inmates already live in trailers so all we need is a big fork lift, some barb wire, and a water tower filled with estrogen and salt peter and we are in business. In 8 days in begins.

NOVEMBER 4, 2016 – Post: Steve Pieczenik video regarding Clinton pedo-crimes and the coups & countercoups in DC.

When it is finally fully revealed what the Clintons have been up to, they will need military protection from a large contingent of the general public, including their former supporters. Prison may be the only safe place left for them.

ANON8: Pieczenik is a bad-ass.

ANON4: Besides that this is completely nut talk... why would the NYC police not have done anything about that?

CAPTAIN: The Clintons are under 24/7 surveillance. They aren't going anywhere. She may step down Monday or maybe they go through with the election. Either way, Trump wins in a landslide. There is a 0.0 chance- with an infinite number of zeros extending after it- that Clinton becomes President. Prepare accordingly.

ANON4: Good thing this is still the best country in the world....sometimes I have a moment where I doubt it.....but just a moment.

CAPTAIN: It's about to get a whole lot better. The (almost) entire world is going to be proud of the United States for pulling this off. Massive celebration worldwide on 11/9.

ANON11: They'll be celebrating in the Kremlin.

CAPTAIN: Russia will be an ally in defeating Isis. And yes, they will be very happy that WW3 will be cancelled.

ANON11: Once we destroy NATO for Putin they will help Assad complete the genocide of his people. Excellent strategy, Captain. And the good thing is you won't have to worry about all that messy democracy we have in America anymore. It'll be a single party rule from here on in. Jesus, where did you learn history?

ANON4: You do not read European publications... I have not talked to anybody who does not think Trump is crazy or a crazy asshole... There would be no celebration... only groups that make the GOP seem left.

CAPTAIN: If you think the Clintons represent democracy, Anon11, you have officially lost your mind.

ANON22: Amazing rationalization.

CAPTAIN: What is your prediction, Anon22? I have made mine in absolute terms.

ANON22: I have already published mine. Perhaps you missed it. Go to Star Presence Astrology and read the whole thing. Data is data, not opinion. And by the way, nothing is absolute.

CAPTAIN: Trump is President. The Clintons in prison or exile. That's my data. Now watch it unfold.

ANON11: So what country are you going to move to when he doesn't win? Argentina perhaps?

CAPTAIN: That's not my concern at all. Zero chance Clinton wins.

ANON22: I read all sorts of articles, from the left and the right. If you are sincerely interested in things such as I have to offer, I suggest reading my prediction and the data which I present. Thanks.

CAPTAIN: Wow, Clinton's a double Scorpio. "Political trouble and negative revelations leading up to election day" for Clinton. Got that right.

ANON22: Thank you for reading it.

NOVEMBER 6, 2016 – Post: Video from Fox News re: Brunnel Donald-Kyei bringing up the Spirit Cooking revelations from the Wikileaks drops. Only two days out from the election!

Spirit cooking, child sex trafficking, FBI investigations, closet racism, broken glass... the Democrat club has everything this year.

Brunnel as always for the win: "She's out the closet now!"

ANON5: LIE + BS = GOP

CAPTAIN: Weiner's laptop + NYPD = Prison

ANON39: OMG just looked up spirit cooking. I hope Maria Abramovic becomes our Poet Laureate. America will truly be great.

CAPTAIN: Leave your kids with them for the weekend, they'll come back covered in blood and ready for a career in showbiz. Extra credit is a week at Bohemian Grove. No funny stuff, it's just a big art project, we promise.

ANON39: Did you get invited to one of those eyes wide shut parties?

CAPTAIN: No, but Kubrick died before he got final cut. Wonder what was in the deleted 24 mins of his version...

ANON39: It showed the tiki doll from the brady bunch special. Big no no!

CAPTAIN: Do you play the piano? You can tickle the ivories for one of those Eyes Wide Shut parties.

ANON39: I never get invited to stuff like that. They barely talk to be at the franks and beans dinners down at the Shriner's Lodge. Now I want to listen to the Magic Flute, that's what got Mozart done in,,,, supposedly.

NEWS BREAKS ON COMEY ENDING INVESTIGATION

ANON39: Breaking news, Comey ain't bringing charges because he ain't got bupkiss.

CAPTAIN: No, because Comey is a chump with no balls.

ANON35: Boo.

CAPTAIN: "Nothing to See Here" Comey. The man who singlehandedly and permanently disgraced the FBI. I'll take the NYPD every time.

ANON39: J Edgar Hoover beat him on that score, but come on why say anything if you got nothing. They got nothing cause there is nothing.

CAPTAIN: Right. And I've got some swampland to sell you. Strategy-wise, the FBI monkey dance was meant to act as a countermeasure to the Wikileaks revelations. To plug the dam. 1 day left. Apres le deluge...

ANON39: I fail to see this logic. You think the spirit cooking has legs?

CAPTAIN: The hourglass has been turned over. The best is yet to come.

NOVEMBER 8, 2016 – Post: Trump will win meme with Trump under the Presidential seal of the United States. It is noon and the final day of voting is underway.

> "They don't have to like it. They can even hate it. But they will be forced to accept it."

2- Conor McGregor

Donald J. Trump is the 45th President of the United States of America. #DeusVult #9/11-11/9

ANON46: The sad part is that if the election doesn't go your way, your delusion will prevent you from believing it. #intoodeep

CAPTAIN: We will see what you say when Trump wins. The Russians did it! lol #tinfoilhats

ANON46: I understand that rigging our voting system is fairly hard and historically non existent... unlike in voter suppression, however, something your candidate and party seems to favor.

CAPTAIN: Historically nonexistent? How old are you? Rigging has happened and it happens. Old Bernie had it rigged against him this year. Then his passionate supporters jumped ship for the criminal that stole it from him because they don't feel honest elections are all that important. But you can't rig against a landslide, not this time at least.

ANON3: Captain, you understand that if you truly want Bernie's policies to be enacted, and for him to have a real power position in the coming government, there's no choice but to vote for Hillary. And landslide? If Trump wins at all, it'll be by the skin of his teeth. Get thee to a television, my man!

CAPTAIN: I don't want Bernie. I only liked his huge corporations rig the game bit. But he sold out. His wife had way more guts than him, said he shouldn't endorse Clinton. 100% Trump here. And TV is your problem. The mainstream media wanted Clinton so badly because their allegiance can be bought.

ANON3: You're ridiculous and I hope for your sake you know it. My comment about TV was to look at the poll breakdowns of states, which shows an incredible uphill battle for Trump. I suppose if all TV news are just lying liars then you'll have your treasonous, child raping, small-business destroying, misogynistic, racist, 3rd grade bully, know-nothing candidate in place, but I doubt it will do you any personal good. By the time I get to say "I told you so" we'll all be f**ked.

CAPTAIN: The Clintons are involved in child sex trafficking, not Trump. And for that they should be locked under the prison. Anyone who turned a willful blind eye to this should be deeply ashamed of themselves. Brainwashing works, but it won't get the Clintons back in office. Justice will be served.

ANON3: Wrong again. Trump goes on trial for raping a 13-year-old at one of Jefferey Epstein's parties next month. You were wrong about the emails, you were even wrong when you corrected me that it was 10 days to the election. I checked a calendar and it was indeed 11. Your sources are awful in every way. What has become of you?

CAPTAIN: The Clintons practically lived on Epstein's Pedo Island and the Trump case is a fraud filed to derail his election. I trust your judgement not one bit. Wikileaks has revealed to the world what they are up to and have been up to ever since they came into power in Arkansas. It's disappointing how many fools think these two career criminals who have been plagued by scandal their entire career are good choices to lead our country and provide safety to our children. They are the very worst among us and I reject them and their authority with every fiber of my existence.

ANON3: I'll remember that you don't trust my judgement not one bit the next time you want me to work for you for free, yet again.

CAPTAIN: On movies yes, but not on this. As it appears you do not trust mine. History will tell who was right.

ANON46: Who need facts when you have "facts"?

ANON3: Anon46, hey man, don't I know you through another Anon? How do you know Captain?

ANON46: I just friended you. I didn't want to take any space away from Captain's tinfoil hat ramblings.

CAPTAIN: Anon46, the information is all out there, as the Clinton duo has compiled a greater crime/scandal log than any other political team in history. If this means nothing to you because the mainstream media and some corrupt officials in government told you there's nothing to see here, then it's on you. Pat yourself on the back for voting for them.

ANON46: There are lots and lots of "facts" out there. Breitbart is full of it. It is when you accept the "facts" in lieu of actual facts that people start looking at you weird.

CAPTAIN: Well, glad you got to the bottom of all those Clinton scandals and have declared it a "no fact" zone. I'll check back in with you when they are arrested.

ANON46: I have done just as much disbelieving without evidence as you have done believing without evidence... so lets just call it a draw.

NOVEMBER 8, 2016 – Election results are rolling in. Trump has taken the lead. Post:

Just a heads up. Sham did not come from behind to beat Secretariat.

ANON49: Go TRUMP. Shock the world.

ANON50: Wow. What a night! Go Trump!

ANON50: We need FL & PA. Ironic eh, Captain? My states baby.

CAPTAIN: Got Florida. PA would be a beautiful closer. Swamp Draining stock is going up in record numbers.

ANON39: (posts Washington Post article about stock market tanking under Trump)

ANON51: HRC Can't pay up on her promises. LOL.

ANON39: This won't be good for regular folks.

ANON51: It will bounce rite back next week.

ANON39: You're kidding yourself.

ANON51: Same thing happened when Mr. O got elected.

ANON39: You just elected an existential threat to the white house.

ANON51: I did not vote for him. LOL. I am not worried. That nut-case can do no more harm than Mr. O and Bush wacker.

ANON39: Yeah, like a year before got elected. The stock market was at 1,600 when he got elected. Grocery store shelve were bare. Now its at 19,000 and we got 4.9 % unemployment and a shrinking deficit. See how long that lasts. We've been in 7 years of recovery, longest in a long time, if a little tepid. What happens when he cuts taxes and raises spending? Because that is what he does, he spends. He doesn't pay his bills, but he'll spend other people's money all day every day, always has always will, and they all get f**ked and we're about to get f**ked, you dumb f**ks. Happy Holidays.

CAPTAIN: A Washington Post article, hahaha!

ANON39: So, Captain, in all seriousness, is this all a gag or are you for real? I was giving you the benefit of the doubt, but be real. Are you ready for this because this will change the world for the worst?

CAPTAIN: This is a win for America and a win for good. You know what's next for your favorite criminals.

ANON39: I don't care about them, but this guy is a complete ass. I mean, do you listen to the stupid contradictory irresponsible stuff he says on a regular basis? He goes bankrupt for a living-- this what he's going to do to America.

CAPTAIN: Trump is President. Deal with it.

ANON39: So your telling me this isn't a joke, you're really down with this? You're ready to flush the world down the toilet because you read some shit on the internet? Sad. I thought it was gag.

ANON6: Kinda quite at the DNC.

ANON39: Not my president. Never will be. I will bang heads every day with this kind of ignorance. Might be time for a New England Brexit.

CAPTAIN: I hear Canada is lovely this time of year.

ANON49: Trump! Trump. Trump. Trump.

ANON39: I feel like it's 1933.

ANON49: Ridiculous. It's 2016. People woke up brother.

ANON52: Trump must offer film tax credit!

ANON50: Trump kicking butt here in Arizona - 49% to 46% - should announce it soon. That would be 11 extra electoral points. I sure am looking forward to that new wall. OH YEAH OH YEAH.

ANON39: A man who is famous for fat jokes and gold toilets is president because of fools like you. Ridiculous, but not in a funny way.

ANON49: Drain the Swamp!!!!!!! C'mon, PA. CNN can't believe it. And I f**king love it.

CAPTAIN: When the Clintons abused little children they brought on the wrath of God. No more power for them.

ANON49: Anon5 ain't happy about Iowa. Lol. Remember Austin. Smh.

ANON25: My only consolation is these rants will end, I can only hope.

CAPTAIN: You can hope that you do your research next time.

ANON49: Captain, you're one of the few that never flipped. I love that brother. Cmon Trump. Close this sh*t out! New York Times has a pic of Trump on cover at this moment with "Loser" written on it. Well. I say. WINNER. Idiot Media. F**k off. True Story. Clinton HQ quiet as a mouse. Lmao.

CAPTAIN: The mainstream media went into this with a 6% confidence vote. That just dropped to 1% - only because of sports scores and the weather.

ANON49: Trump is leading in PA, Michigan and NH. See ya Killary. Wouldn't wanna be ya.

CAPTAIN: Pennsylvania just did it, Anon49.

ANON49. Trump, baby.

NOVEMBER 9, 2016 – Donald J. Trump has won the election.

The Greatest Political Story Ever Told.

All Glory is to God.

Anon53: AMEN!

CODA:

What happened next was history. And where we go from here will now be determined by us: We the People.

God Almighty set this great Country on a course and He will not forsake us. But we must do our part. We must stand up for the Truth and speak from our hearts without fear of the repercussions of the mob or of losing our place on the corporate gravy train.

There are some things more important than money or popularity. Protecting the future of our innocent children is one of them, for we were once innocent children ourselves and will be again some day.

Where We Go One, We Go All.

The Best is Yet to Come.

Future Proves Past.

It's Gonna Be Biblical:

"My little children, I am writing you these things so that you may not sin. But if anyone does sin, we have an advocate with the Father—Jesus Christ the Righteous One. He Himself is the propitiation for our sins, and not only for ours, but also for those of the whole world.

This is how we are sure that we have come to know Him: by keeping His commands. The one who says, 'I have come to know Him,' yet doesn't keep His commands, is a liar, and the truth is not in him. But whoever keeps His word, truly in him the love of God is perfected. This is how we know we are in Him: The one who says he remains in Him should walk just as He walked.

Dear friends, I am not writing you a new command but an old command that you have had from the beginning. The old command is the message you have heard. Yet I am writing you a new command, which is true in Him and in you, because the darkness is passing away and the true light is already shining.

The one who says he is in the light but hates his brother is in the darkness until now. The one who loves his brother remains in the light, and there is no cause for stumbling in him. But the one who hates his brother is in the darkness, walks in the darkness, and doesn't know where he's going, because the darkness has blinded his eyes.

I am writing to you, little children,
because your sins have been forgiven
because of Jesus' name.
I am writing to you, mothers and fathers,
because you have come to know
the One who is from the beginning.
I am writing to you, young men and women,
because you have had victory over the evil one.
I have written to you, children,
because you have come to know the Father.
I have written to you, mothers and fathers,
because you have come to know
the One who is from the beginning.
I have written to you, young men and women,
because you are strong,
God's word remains in you,
and you have had victory over the evil one."

John 2:14

ABOUT THE AUTHOR

James O'Brien is an independent filmmaker and writer. He grew up in Harrington Park, New Jersey and following his graduation from Providence College, he moved to Los Angeles to make films. Among his recent work is the metaphysical wild west film *Western Religion* and the road movie *Wish You Were Here*. Today, he travels the country in his Jeep and spreads the word of the Great Awakening.

He currently resides in Taos, New Mexico.

For information contact: V Publishing at revjames13@protonmail

Made in United States
Orlando, FL
23 January 2024